From a Broken Web

FROM A BROKEN WEB

SEPARATION, SEXISM, AND SELF

CATHERINE KELLER

Beacon Press   Boston

BEACON PRESS
25 Beacon Street
Boston, Massachusetts 02108

Beacon Press books are published under the auspices
of the Unitarian Universalist Association
of Congregations in North America.

92 91 90 89 88 87 86   8 7 6 5 4 3 2 1

Library of Congress Cataloging in Publication Data

Keller, Catherine, 1953–
From a broken web.

Includes index.
1. Self (Philosophy)   2. Self.   3. Women—Psychology.
4. Women in literature.   I. Title.
BD450.K368   1986   126   86-47508
ISBN 0-8070-0732-6

To Jane my mother.

Contents

Contents

Anger and tenderness: the spider's genius
to spin and weave in the same action
from her own body, anywhere—
even from a broken web.
   —Adrienne Rich, "Integrity"

Acknowledgments

This book traces the texture of threads which connect selves with each other, with their worlds and their histories. Like all texts, *From a Broken Web* owes its life and form to an indefinitely extended web of selves—a few of which are my own. Of the other selves ingredient in the history of this project I can here only name the most prominent.

The book began to unfurl in Claremont, California, when a discussion group called Thiasos (Claremont Women in Religion) took it upon itself to plan a symposium which featured Mary Daly as keynote speaker. The momentum of her thought, as well as the organizing and the aftermath of the total event, rerouted my thinking and writing. At the same time Thiasos took shape as a supportively subversive community. Nelle Morton was there from the start, embodying her ideas: hearing us all to speech. I am grateful that she hears me still, through the many drafts of this book. Rita Brock, Sue Dunfee, and Lydia Cosentino, also founding collaborators, remain special friends and muses, without whom this book would not be conceivable. "Tess" Tessier soon joined Thiasos, and brought sister-vision of the Tehom, the woman-identified cosmic depths. Throughout this time, my teacher John Cobb was not only sharing his rich analysis of a world in process, but unflinchingly encouraging my feminist preoccupations. Bill Wheebee's steadfast faith in the book, not to mention his emotional and editorial munificence, was indispensable. I am grateful to Tamara Eshkenazi, whose readings of early versions lent the process a special sparkle; and to Cliff Cobb for his generous aid with manuscript and move.

After I began to teach in Cincinnati, the final draft emerged within a new configuration of sustaining influences. My friend

Acknowledgments

Mary deShazer offered uninterrupted feminist sanity and wise advice, while Lynda Hart provided solidarity and stories. I want to thank my colleagues in theology, Joseph Bracken, Christine Gudorf, and Paul Knitter for their multiple modes of encouragement. During this time Glen Mazis's brotherly and philosophical friendship facilitated writing. A burgeoning young philosopher, Pierre Keller, my brother, struggled valiantly to upgrade the logic of various arguments. And thanks to Amy Raymond, one gifted undergraduate from Arkansas, for her incisive critique of chapter 4.

Then there are all those who typed various phases of the manuscript, beginning with my mother, who handled the messy first draft, and to whom this book is dedicated for entirely non-typographical reasons. At Xavier, Eunice Staples's typing of the final versions constitutes a work of amazing grace and patience. Meanwhile my editor at Beacon Press, Caroline Birdsall, contributed seemingly endless energy, empathy and skill in sifting the wheat from the chaff. What would I have done without persistent long distance understanding (and oracular cheerleading) from Elizabeth Cunningham, who has also added her talent to the production of this index? And I am more than grateful for the collaboration of Edward Casey, who from near and far, with phenomenological (and phenomenal) finesse, kept reading, commenting, questioning and yes-saying until the book was done.

Which it seems to be, though happily this web of relations cannot be: this I sense as it stretches to include new friends at Drew. Finally, I am grateful to those of you who now, with "wild patience," enter through your reading into its life.

Madison, New Jersey
October 15, 1986

Introduction

You may add that in the hive and the anthill we see fully realized the two things that some of us most dread for our
own species—the dominance of the female and the dominance of the collective.
—C. S. Lewis, *Surprised by Joy*

Still it is the one true cord,
the umbilical line
unwinding into meaning,
transformation,
web of thought and caring and connection.
—Judy Grahn, "Helen you always were/the factory"

TO BE A SELF, must I be something separate and apart? How else
could I be myself? Myth and religion, philosophy and psychology
center our civilization on the assumption that an individual is a
discrete being: I am cleanly divided from the surrounding world of
persons and places; I remain essentially the same self from moment
to moment. Common sense identifies separateness with the freedom
we cherish in the name of "independence" and "autonomy." The
assumption that selfhood requires separation is even rooted in language. The Latin for "self," *se*, meaning "on one's own," yields with
parare ("to prepare") the verb "to separate." For our culture it is
separation which prepares the way for selfhood.

In this book I shall question this sense of separateness. Word has

I

gotten out that women do not measure up to the norms erected in a society of separate selves. As daughters, wives, mothers, sisters and friends, women have been enmeshed in relational complexities that blur the boundaries of self and other. Softening the edges of a separative world, women's traditional specialization in relationship seems to have taken the place of both strength of self and social power. Nonetheless I shall argue that the pull toward connection, when coordinated with feminist sensibility, can and does generate a new meaning of what it is to be a self. To be "on one's own" does not necessarily mean to be out of relation. Is there even such a thing as a separate self at all—or only a posture?

The thesis of this book can be summarized quite simply: separation and sexism have functioned together as the most fundamental self-shaping assumptions of our culture. That any subject, human or non-human, is what it is only in clear division from everything else; and that men, by nature and by right, exercise the primary prerogatives of civilization: these two presuppositions collaborate like two eyes to sustain a single worldview. With a worldview one just sees; one does not challenge the eyes with which one sees. In the course of the last century, however, the women's movement has disturbed habitual sexism, while in another sphere multiple developments in theory have upset the separative universe of isolated atoms. But until we learn to recognize the crucial interdependence of both assumptions, the old worldview will retain the momentum of unconsciousness.

To question the long-standing human project of becoming separate, autonomous, and on this basis socially responsible persons, is to evoke a chorus of protest from feminists as well as antifeminists. By advocating a new connectedness, am I recommending that we slide into a soft, undifferentiated slime of emotional dependencies? A host of anxious associations with nonseparateness spring to mind: a world of clans or crowds, of preoedipal narcissism or collective unconsciousness, of annihilated privacy or unrelieved sameness. Would I jeopardize the narrow margin of consciousness, freedom and justice that civilization has achieved? These are legitimate concerns. The unique integrity of a focussed individuality, traditionally linked to the independence of a clearly demarcated ego, represents an irrefutable value, indeed a touchstone for any liberating theory of interrelation. But we need not be misled by pairs of false alternatives like "self" versus "relation". Relation can either foster dependency, or test and nurture freedom.

Fear of merger and self-dispersion motivates all insistence on separate selfhood. But let me suggest that in such fear of self-loss lurks a profound fear of women. Because of this basic gynophobia, any articulation of a feminist perspective, especially one unfurling a sense of radical interconnection, will be suspected of advocating female dominance and the defeat of the differentiated individual. To relax the severity of masculine ego-boundaries threatens to unleash a tidal wave of matriarchal collectivism. But those who have absorbed the fear of "the hive and the anthill" are not limited to sexists. Most of us have grown up in intimate connection with mothers whose creative energies, trapped in domesticity, pose an overpowering emotional threat. As I shall argue, only as women and men outgrow this covert and culturally ramified matriphobia can any new consciousness begin to fashion itself in and among us.

At this moment in history women still have special reason to dread the loss of self. Women's self-definition in terms of relationship has been more or less equivalent to psychosocial bondage. So the logical escape route would seem to lie through achievement of the separate individuality heretofore expected only of men. Indeed many women would insist that the last thing they want is more relationship. Often we hear women say that first, or finally, they must get separate and develop their own autonomy: an especially pressing motive among women coming up to breathe after long immersion in marriages, families and disappointing love-affairs.

But I do not believe that such women, seeking an empowering center in themselves and often furious at the sums of selfhood drained away in futile asymmetries, are actually repudiating connectedness. I think rather that women desire *worlds*—places of inner and outer freedom in which new forms of connection can take place. Liberated from relational bondage, we range through an unlimited array of relations—not just to other persons, but to ideas and feelings, to the earth, the body, and the untold contents of the present moment. In other words, women struggling against the constraints of conventionally feminine modes of relation desire not less but more (and different) relation; not disconnection, but connection that counts. So a woman will not long find herself energized by the path of separation, requisite though it remains in any male-defined workplace. Nor will a woman who has assumed the traditionally masculine ego-patterns find her spirit rekindled by any return to classically feminine habits. Something new is needed.

And what of those still very few men who hunger after a new way of being male, who are (sometimes) willing to deconstruct sexist assumptions and so risk considerable loss of prestige? They will help neither themselves nor women by simply reacting against the independent ego of the stereotypical male, merely to succumb to patterns of passivity and dependency associated with stereotypical femininity. But only as men come to grips with their yet armor-plated defenses can the intimacy and equality they claim to desire become a real possibility.

My aim in this book, however, is not to compare prevalent male and female styles of selfhood. But neither do I believe that we can skip over the question of gender identity, with all its painful confusions, so as to reach some universal "humanism," as though we should or could neatly transcend our bodies and our histories. Whatever our sexual preference and phase of life, we never grow beyond or above but always *with* and *through* our gender identities. Both the problems of the separate self and the promises of an alternative extend, but very differently, to men as well as women.

What alternative can there be? Surely talk of "less separation," "more relation," or gender "balance" will not suffice. For such compromises will inevitably defer to conventional and thus androcentric sensibilities. The crisis of subjectivity in this century and the ground-swell of the women's movement demand more than a few considerate shifts of rhetoric and lifestyle. What is required is nothing less than our lives. In the meantime, thinking broadly and feeling deeply through all our disciplines and experiences, interests and fields, does help to shape the profile of the possible. It follows that the rhetoric of this book, as at once feminist and interdisciplinary, excludes no one who does not want to be excluded.

In the first chapter we encounter a familiar dyad, whose members I will call the 'separative self' and the 'soluble self.' Traditionally, this is that complementary pair known as man and woman, a pair in which his selfhood is bought at the price of hers. I will engage Simone de Beauvoir's classic analysis of the patriarchal subordination of women as objects of male subjects. Even in her unique blend of feminism and existentialism we will recognize in her concept of subjectivity certain androcentric presuppositions, which I finally trace to the theology of transcendence.

Chapter 2, in a more mythic mood, will summon various she-monsters. We will discern how the old mythic monster carries the lost power of the female, defeated by the self-assertions of the patriarchal hero. Repressed inwardly, in the psyches of both men and women, and oppressed outwardly, in the institutions of the public world, the monster-energy takes exception to the norms of manhood and threatens a furious return of the repressed. Fabulous beasts come back to protest the matricidal syndrome in which the major occidental religious traditions—Hebrew, Greek and Christian—are steeped.

Then we will plunge, in Chapter 3, into a depth psychological investigation of the hero's motive-force. Freud and Jung offer infra-patriarchal accounts of the hero's misogynist masculinity, his defensive ego-structure, his matricidal and patricidal needs. These explanations themselves still express the androcentric bias; they may serve ultimately, though differently, to justify the heroic ego. We will rely upon a feminist analysis of separation and relation, which we take above all from the work of Nancy Chodorow, to move us further toward a connective self restricted neither to "feminine" psychology nor to patriarchal acculturation.

In the fourth chapter, our endeavor waxes cosmological. Connective selves, far from depending upon any peculiarities of feminine psychology, display a deep affinity with all beings. To discern this "all" requires a twist of metaphysics, not through regression to traditional metaphysical deductions but through an expansion of our vision. The vision depends as much upon feeling as upon analysis. Indeed, feeling shows itself to be the vehicle of all connection as we move into an interpretive use of the "process philosophy" of Alfred North Whitehead. Fluidity and interpermeability, long associated with the monstrous and feminine, show themselves to be the character of every being: every entity in the universe can be described as a process of interconnection with every other being.

In the last chapter, the image of the web comes finally to the fore. Poetry and myth pull us toward a new religious sense that can be called arachnean, allowing us to articulate something like a feminist ontology of self. Here I shall propose four non-polar conceptual dyads: being one/being many, being public/being private, being body/being soul and being here/being now. These form a complex rhythm out of which connective and fluid selves compose themselves and their worlds.

The web of their interactions is what we are starting to weave together. Let us experiment with that sense of relation that begins even here and now: with this moment's feelings and our own bodies, with the weight of the book and the pulse in the fingers. Let us imagine the radical choreography of all sentient beings. Perhaps we can at the same time begin to retrieve, in the name of connection, those freedoms and solitudes often held under the guardianship of separate selfhood. But then our subjectivity will never be the same.

ONE
_____

The Separate and the Soluble

For to weave is not merely to predestine (anthropologically),
and to join together differing realities (cosmologically) but
also to *create*, to make something of one's own substance as
the spider does in spinning its web.
—Mircea Eliade, *Patterns in Comparative Religions*

But I waste my heart away in longing for Odysseus; so they
speed on my marriage and I weave a web of wiles. . . . In the
daytime I would weave the mighty web, and in the night un-
ravel the same.
—Penelope in *The Odyssey*, trans. S. H. Butcher.

IN THE CLASSIC WESTERN EPIC, Penelope waits while Odysseus
wanders. As he intrudes, escapes and seduces his way through time
and space, he creates an ego of epic independence, positing it over
and against a world of dangerous opponents. Enemies and elements, monsters and magical ladies exist only to strengthen his self-
identity and to test the powers of his autonomy. After his separation
from home, he completes the archetypal hero's journey by returning
to faithful Penelope. Having created nothing, she merely remains:
intact, yet "wasting away." Daily weaving and unweaving her tapestry, she has preserved herself—but is it a self?—for him, in a fixed
space, in a cyclical time. He is loosed; she is bound. To be "loosed
away from" is the etymology of the Absolute: that which is complete in itself, independent of and separate from everything else.
Thus Simone de Beauvoir's now-classic thesis: "He is the Subject,

he is the Absolute—she is the Other."[1] But would Penelope, as she binds and looses the threads of daily survival, want to be the Absolute—even were her fate, like her shuttle, in her own hands?

The classical pair personifies a familiar pattern. We encounter it in endless tales of errant knights and wandering cowboys, adventuring against an emotional background of waiting women: "In song and story the young man is seen departing adventurously . . . she is locked in a tower, a palace, a garden, a cave, she is chained to a rock, a captive, sound asleep: she waits."[2] Most of us know this complementary dyad through the less heroic familiarity of familial history. Even more intimately, we know it because we have not altogether escaped *being* it. The pattern congeals into two different sorts of self, completely dependent upon each other; but the task of one is to assert its apparent independence, the task of the other to support that appearance. If now the Other is asserting her independence, she will want to avoid setting herself loose only to find herself bound up in the subjectivity of the (apparently) separate and supreme ego. And if he begins to extricate himself from the politics of the "male ego," one hopes he does not resort to passive dependency. Moreover, if we wed both sets of gender roles to produce what is sometimes called androgyny, we may simply redouble the force of the stereotypes by internalizing their complementarity.[3]

No-one's Separation

An occasional antihero notwithstanding, the myth of the warrior-hero has dominated Western imagining of what it is to be a "man," that is, a full human being. Within the most sublimated contexts, far from any battlefield, the Homeric heroes continued in the mind of every schoolboy to savage their opponents, while Christian soldiers marched onward against each other and other enemies of the Lord. The archetypal hero fashions human personality in his own image, projecting an ego armored against the outer world and the inner depths. His philosophical descendant is the separate, self-enclosed subject, remaining self-identical throughout its exploits in time. Its relations do not affect its essence. Indeed, to sustain its sense of independence, such a subject is always liberating itself from its bonds as though from bondage. Intimacy, emotion and the influence of the Other arouse its worst anxieties, for somehow it must keep relation external to its own being, its "self." It proves its excellence through the tests of separation, establishing a mobile autonomy as its virtue (where *vir* means "man"). Virility lies above all in impermeability.

A contemporary male here recalls his education in the integrity of separateness: "I was raised to be authentic, to be my own man. I was told that the way to success was to be self-possessed, to love difficulty and isolation, independence and self-sufficiency, as the strength of not needing others. I discovered the philosophy of authenticity as if I had lived it all along."[4] A philosophical economist, Wikse here brings into play the economics of the separate self: it is its own property, possessing itself. We may add that its Other, its complementary opposite, must also be possessed; for this independent ego is in fact dependent upon its array of waiting and attendant Others, largely women. Thus the Greek word *ousia,* from the verb *to be,* traditionally translated as "substance," denoted at once "reality" and "realty": Odysseus reclaimed his own substance upon his return to Ithaca, where wife and real estate awaited him.

Man's self-possession seems to have required woman as his property. So the theft of woman warrants war. Helen's beauty launched a thousand ships—in defense of the system of masculine self-possession. If Menelaus loses her, the heroic integrity of all Greeks fails. Wikse reports how in childhood an American myth formed his sense of authenticity. His father regularly narrated to him the Saga of Cowboy Jack, a wandering good guy who saves the town but steers clear of all attachments—so that he can go on wandering and saving. Certainly the self-identity of the heroic ego involves impressive disciplines of self-denial in the pursuit of its successful career. (The static self-sacrifice of the waiting woman pales by contrast.)

But is the self-denial of the heroic ego simultaneously other-denial: a repression of its own deep interrelatedness with everything else, and a suppression of the legitimate claims of any others? However much the ego feels single and apart, this feeling may represent not truth but denial. It is less precise to call this ego separate than *separative,* implying an activity or an intention rather than any fundamental state of being. The separative self is identifiable historically, but neither essentially nor necessarily, with males and the masculine. Its sense of itself as separate, as over against the world, the Other, and even its own body, endows it with its identity. It is *this,* not *that.*

Virginia Woolf's character Louis (an exceptional male) bemoans the prevalence of separateness:

These attempts to say, 'I am this, I am that,' which we make coming together, like separated parts of one body and soul, are false. Something has been left out from fear. Something has been altered, from vanity. We have tried to accentuate differences. From the desire to be separate we have laid stress upon our faults, and what is particular to us.[5]

Fear and vanity motivate both males and females, but within the culture of sexist complementarity it motivates them differently. As a self-shaping, primary force, this accent on differentness is part of the cultivation of the heroic ego. Continuous, self–imposed exposure to fear and a defiant vanity seem fundamental to the character of the hero. But his woman's fear is of *him,* and her vanity reflects her image in his eyes. Thus her difference from him is often little more than a reaction to him, a secondary role formation.

Fortunately, even the *Odyssey* contains—however subtextually—certain ironies that belie the defiant self-identity of the male ego on its journey and the sheer passivity of the female at her immobile loom. Irony, as the incongruous juxtaposition of what is said with what is true, provides a possible methodological perspective for approaching androcentric traditions and texts. According to Kierkegaard "irony is the incitement to subjectivity."[6] An ironic perspective is inspired, if not intended, by the *Odyssey's* most classic pun: The monstrous Cyclop (son of Earth and rebel against the order of Zeus) asks Odysseus his name. Odysseus knows the Cyclop will then call for help from his one-eyed friends and so tells him: "No-one is my name." No One, *oudeis,* puns upon the word *Odysseus.* After escaping, Odysseus hurls his real name at the Cyclop expressly to contribute to the fame of that name and so to his own immortality. On the surface of the text, these are ironies enough.

But a deeper incongruity suggests itself. The last laugh may be on our hero and on the kind of ego he so splendidly embodies. Perhaps Odysseus told the truth when he meant to dissemble. For if such a subjectivity ultimately loses itself in its own bid for fame, name and immortality, then here it inadvertently names its repressed anxiety: "No-one is my name." I am not important. Not real. Not one. Not *one*. Not a self-possessed monad. By this account, the hero illustrates what Kierkegaard calls the "despair of defiance," which he equates with "the despair of manliness."[7] "That self which he despairingly wills to be is a self which he is not (for to will to be that self which one truly is, is indeed the opposite of despair)." An authentic self wills to be what it is. And so if Odysseus calls out that he is No-one, does he in his very defiance voice the despair of a yet unacknowledged self-contradiction? What if the controlling ethos of heroic egoism, foisted upon millenia of males (and lately upon white middle-class professional females) smacks of an unrecognized self-doubt? After all, it received its ultimate modern rationalization as the Cartesian ego, a concept that was forged in the depths of self-doubt. Descartes divided human reality into two independent substances, cogitating ego and lifeless matter, while meditating in solitude about whether he existed at all.

Incitement to a fresh notion of the self and its subjectivity may prove the only solution—though not as just one more argument against dualism or substantialism. But the stubbornly entrenched presupposition of the separateness of selves militates even below consciousness against any alternative. For as we will see, it is fortified by the even more massive self-defenses of patriarchy itself.

Women in Waiting

What of Penelope's self? Of late she has been disrupting the static fidelity of her ancient persona; she has been exploring the apparently endless psychic and social ripples of her peculiar ontological status in history: woman's self as no self of her own, and thus a false, an owned, self, somehow not quite a self at all. She seems dispersed, diffused, defused, meant to glory in her being-for-him, named even by his name. In her devoted anonymity, she has collaborated in his self-deception, fostering in him that covert dependency upon her by which he sustains his sense of independence. In our epoch the incongruities mount as she encounters old "feminine" inauthenticities in tandem with her new temptation to a "masculine" defiance. Inasmuch as economic self-sufficiency has become an option for women (though the prospect remains bleak for all but middle-class white career women), the separative urge to claim "I am this," "I am that," becomes harder to resist.

Kierkegaard defines sin as despair, the despair summoned by the failure to be who we are, by the desperate attempt of the self to escape being itself. He goes on to distinguish between specifically "masculine" and "feminine" forms of despair. If the masculine sin is "potentiated defiance"—a refusal to accept the ultimate terms of selfhood—the feminine analogue is "potentiated weakness." Kierkegaard perceptively links woman's weakened sense of self to her self-loss in service to others, that is, to her devotion. He recognizes that the traditional feminine devotion is a sin, not a virtue, because it is a form of despair and self-abnegation: "by devotion (the word literally means giving away) she has lost herself."[8]

Kierkegaard might seem to be anticipating the contemporary re-evaluation of sin by feminist theology. Theologians Valerie Saiving, Judith Plaskow and Sue Dunfee demonstrate how the traditional notions of sin as pride and self-assertion serve to reinforce the subordination of women, whose temptations *as* women lie in the realm of "underdevelopment or negation of the self."[9] But unfortunately Kierkegaard, who like most thinkers cannot distinguish between the effects of patriarchal culture and woman's nature, only turns the screws tighter, as the above passage in its fuller context reveals:

But the fact that devotion is woman's nature comes again to evidence in despair. By devotion she has lost herself, and only thus is she happy, only thus is she herself; a woman who is happy without devotion, that is, without giving herself away (to whatever it may be she gives herself) is un-womanly.[10]

While he correctly exposes the despair concealed in women's devotion, he at the same time sentences us to self-loss as the very condition of our happiness! This typically androcentric pronouncement on women's "nature," mistaking a femininity required by masculine arrogance for some feminine essence, renders the intolerable inevitable. Such a relapse into essentialism eclipses Kierkegaard's own existentialism, injecting it with a certain bad faith. Moreover for the masculine sin there is no comparable double-bind. One does not read that a man must commit the despair of defiance in order to be manly.

If in Danish, *devotion* means "to be given away," we find that the archaic definition of the English word is "doom." Women know the doom of devotion all too intimately: a mother who has sacrificed untold possibilities of self-development to see to her children's opportunities observes them retreating emotionally when she most needs support because they resent her history of selflessness for its implicit demand; or a woman who devoted herself to the support of her husband's ego and career now finds herself cast off as he discovers the excitement of self-assertive women (not depleted by his own need); or a daughter who feels her success subtly poisoned by sorrow at her mother's unrealized potential. In these stereotypical but still typical situations, women trapped between stages of a culture that is only begrudgingly changing sometimes feel scorned by feminism as well—as though their despair is indeed sinful. The generations of devoted and desperate women haunt us like a chorus of furies.

Psychologist Maggie Scarf offers the case of a wife and mother who, within an externally ideal family situation, is a near victim of suicide in her late forties. This woman expresses the feminine despair with precision: "I've got no identity in particular. . . . I'm not *anybody*, you know, not really a person. I've surrendered that part to Bob."[11] Her self was his to receive but not to return. Thus, while Odysseus calls himself No-one only by virtue of being a public someone, the woman is someone only by virtue of being no one; that is, of belonging to him. If this is Penelope's irony, it has incited only the subjectivity of the possessed: just by being owned can she gain her own public identity. She encounters herself always already as someone else's. If even at sea his image retains its separate solidity, hers, even in its grounded fixity, suggests the deliquescence and dispersion of any selfhood.

Let us designate this sort of self, neither necessarily nor essentially but historically embodied by women, the *soluble self*. In the classical dyad, it complements the separative self, which works upon it as a solvent. Women's tendency to dissolve emotionally and devotionally into the other is a subjective structure internalized by individual women, but imposed by the superstructure of men. Woman is to wait: for her very self, her self-definition, and the advent of the hero who will bring her joy. Simone de Beauvoir captures the self-contradicting state of women's passivity:

Now, what peculiarly signalizes the situation of woman is
that she—a free and autonomous being like all human crea-

13

tures—nevertheless finds herself living in a world where men compel her to assume the status of the Other. They propose to stabilize her as object and to doom her to immanence since her transcendence is to be overshadowed and forever transcended by another ego (*conscience*) which is essential and sovereign.[12]

In de Beauvoir's thought, "immanence" means to exist within an already established reality, to remain within any *status quo ante*. For her, immanence designates the ultimate in human doom, the stagnant acquiescence in given conditions resulting thus in the failure of freedom; one has given oneself over to the given, the past, "nature," the path of least resistance. Authentic subjectivity, by contrast, arises "through exploits or projects that serve as a mode of transcendence."[13]

For de Beauvoir as for Sartre, this secularized sense of transcendence implies no religious movement upward toward a God or a Heaven, but keeps its feet—moving—on the ground. Existential authenticity occurs as we step beyond static patterns into the pursuit of creative projects. But Penelope at her loom, weaving, unweaving, reweaving the same fabric every day, creates nothing. Woman's subjectivity becomes objectified in such a futile cycle, characteristic of our assigned activity throughout history: "The domestic labors that fell to her lot because they were reconcilable with the cares of maternity imprisoned her in repetition and immanence; they were repeated from day to day in an identical form, which was perpetuated almost without change from century to century; they produced nothing new."[14] Mere repetition produces only the objectification of the one who repeats. Subjectivity is ground down in the routines of survival, where nothing new takes place. To take part in history, in the creation of our worlds, is to transcend ourselves and so to realize novel possibilities. The voice of transcendence—"Behold, I am doing a new thing" (Isa. 43:19)—articulates the heroic history of men, not the domestic heritage of women.

For de Beauvoir, as for the Hegelian-Sartrian tradition as a whole, all class, race or mass oppression stems from the reduction of the Other to immanence, that is, to the status of object. Women's oppression is the most universal instance of such objectification. Though we will shortly challenge a certain presupposition at work in her particular opposition of immanence and transcendence, de

Beauvoir's rich analysis and documentation of women's objectification stands as irrefutable.

As women we know well the cast of Sleeping Beauties, Snow Whites and servile Cinderellas sustaining a mythos of feminine passivity intact through the ages. The imagining of our futures has been channeled into a soporific hope for the redeeming prince. In his embrace, adolescent passivity melts into maternal devotion: this womanhood grows from waiting for its self to giving its self away. Its ontology is—at least partly—that of the object, the object of the hero's adventure. His the agency, hers the patience.

Complicity and Relation

Now that her patience has been waning, the question arises—why have so many women so long supported this self-negation? Have we not worked as the main accomplices in our own oppression? As de Beauvoir poses the problem: "Why is it that women do not dispute male sovereignty? No subject will readily volunteer to become the Object, the inessential; it is not the Other, who in defining himself (or itself) as the Other, establishes the One. The Other is posed as such by the One in defining himself as the One."[15] One answer to the question excuses women of complicity: the arrangement suited not only the economic intentions but the "ontological and moral pretensions" of the brawnier group. Women put up with this self-negation because they had no choice. Untold violence awaited women who stepped out of bounds and into selfhood. This level of historical explanation is certainly true as far as it goes.

De Beauvoir's answer, however, challenges us to look beyond the sheer fact of our victimization. All consciousness, according to her existential analysis, is constantly tempted to collapse into immanence. Therefore woman's particular entrapment, decorated with promises of magical love-happiness, has offered a seductive alternative to authenticity. It potentiates weakness by suggesting that not only can the male shoulder for us our burdens of freedom and decision, but he will share with us the bounties of his prestige. While both men and women are tempted to betray their freedom, women have been offered a ready-made and socially sanctioned context for self-abdication. Indeed, men sometimes seem, ironically, to resent women's option to remain dependent, to hide from the world and so from themselves (though in the meantime few men have taken the househusband option, and fewer women than at any period since World War II have even the option of economic dependency). Thus de Beauvoir calls women to take responsibility for ourselves and for our status in society.

The question of woman's complicity in patriarchal patterns becomes ever more pressing an issue, at once private and public, of the self, of who we are to *become*. For women's self-negating subjectivity continues to issue from the old habits even as public opportunities seem to increase. What in *us* threatens to hold us back? What keeps whispering the rhetoric of female inferiority in our inner ear? The external situation has loosened up, and a few men here and there speak for the downfall of patriarchy. Patriarchy, however, is still erect, if failing. Many middle-class women have been entering into its power elite, its activities. The question of the old female complicity with male dominance must now be asked in conjunction with the question of "co-optation"—a new form of seduction by the sovereign structures.

In complicity women embody patriarchal definitions of the feminine self; in co-optation women embody patriarchal definitions of the normative self (i.e., man's). Both produce "male-identified" women, but in the first instance through complementarity, in the second through imitation. Thus the double bind of woman's self-nullifying self is now doubled again; she appends to her female emotional base the anxieties of the traditionally masculine-separative self. Furthermore, entrance into cultural and professional roles once reserved for men appears to be—and indeed has required—authentic rebellion against our old compliance. And so it is an especially unpleasant irony to discern depths of cooptation circulating through the apparent channels of liberation. So let us first look more closely at the original form of woman's identification by the male, in the complicity of her soluble selfhood.

Something more than mere cowardice, more even than immanence, must be at work in woman's complicity. Else how could it be so nearly universal in history? Some other bait must have always tempted her to relinquish the "free being" she is. Her subjectivity in the state of androcentric oppression cannot be exhaustively explained as an interplay of objectification by men and acquiescence in the given. Hers is a state of *relational* entrapment. She does not merely give something up—her self, authenticity, responsibility. What is it she wants and seeks for herself? Isn't it the gilded promise of love? But embedded in her love nest, her castle, her condo, she has seen this love locking the door on her. Nonetheless, though she might err in the choice and be coerced by the form of relation, her commitment to the value of relation itself should be neither condemned nor too lightly attributed to sexist socialization.

Love after all remains a real possibility, a true experience, a mode of transcendence in which the reality of the other belies all self-encapsulation. Therefore, she was not just misleading herself, surrendering existential responsibility and sacrificing self. The bitter perplexity of her situation is that love, which has the capacity to release and refine an unlimited strength of interconnection, instead shrinks her fabric of relations and so her self to a domestic minimum.

Her unconscious ontology of relation has made her prey, it would seem, to a savage irony. Her fabric of love turns against her, trapping her in its strong fibers. As her field of relations is attenuated, so is she. The political, intellectual and spiritual possibilities of relation fade, leaving her nothing but the hopelessly overcharged intensities of the personal and the domestic. Thus her complicity seems in the first instance less an act of cowardice than a confusion at the edge of consciousness. Betrayal in and by relationship, when relation spins the very context of her spirit, con–fuses literally: she cannot differentiate loved individuals from the cultural trap, nor her self from either, particularly if she is not yet maturely launched into her life's creative work. The love that had promised to expand her horizons typically comes instead to tailor her dimensions to the needs of her beloved. For if he wants her dependency—however much he resents it—in order to believe in his own independence, and if the surrounding culture signals to both of them that his exploits of transcendence are to be supported by her faithful acquiescence, then the fusion of her identity in his will seem the only "loving" option.

In order not to betray relation, she succumbs to the betrayal of her creativity by relationship. But then she no longer experiences her *self* enough to love another. And if he extracts her selfless devotion, he no longer experiences that reciprocity without which love dies. For whatever else it may be, love is an interconnection full of reciprocal resistance: if it leads to a merger of beings the activity of loving that can only take place between distinct subjectivities extinguishes itself in a passive state of security. But while his ego will step free, hers will stay in its selfless solution. Then it is that the culpable complicity de Beauvoir diagnoses sets in. Woman's solubility—the lurking shadow of her connectivity—will damp down her capacity for creative projects. And with children the institution of the family situation can siphon all her energy into feats of survival on behalf of these necessarily dependent beings. For some women, unquestioning complicity with the patriarchal dyad that has claimed them may now seem the strongest self-assertion available to them. Soon the self-loss is accompanied by an array of resentful hostilities and embittered manipulations. For solubility does not pass long as sweet compliance.

No wonder the channels of transcendence—of activity and creativity in an open world—beckon like salvation to women. But these channels, because they have been shaped and controlled for millenia by males, can only conduct andromorphic modes of transcendence: that is, egocentric forms of world-making dependent on dependent women. Moving beyond complicity with our oppression, we find ourselves mired in imitations of our oppressors. But we must challenge even de Beauvoir here: might her very denigration of immanence and the exaltation of transcendence already imply a subtle form of co-optation? Does a transcendence which is opposed to immanence not echo the defiance of the wandering warrior? Does such a lop-sided stress on transcendence perhaps confuse all that bonds with bondage? To deny the legitimate claims of the immanent Other may be tantamount to denying what I am made of, what I make myself of, and what connects me to the world. For does not the immanent world—the world *in* me, and which I am *in*—disclose a vast network of relations? The given, the past, the body, the Other can indeed fix me in their demands and terms, and thereby stifle the vibrancy of transcendence. But immanence is surely not itself the evil. Immanence is the way relations are part of who I am. Stagnation results from failing to "do a new thing" with and within the field of relations. Either to acquiesce in the shrunken tapestry of relations (complicity) or to deny the internal influence of relations in favor of sheer transcendence (co-optation) may leave the work of Penelope unredeemed.

Fundamental Hostility and the Second Sex

When we turn a more sympathetic ear to the realm of the immanent, we begin to question de Beauvoir's account of the interplay between the transcendent subject and its inessential object. De Beauvoir cannot locate transcendence in any interdependence with immanence itself, as, say, a transformation of all that is within me and which I am within. Immanence for her is neither a revelatory "within" nor an inner presence of the other, but a failure to get beyond one's habitual self, to become a subject, to exercise transcendence. But this is more than a semantic issue of definition. There is no place for the immanence of others within myself if I can only establish myself as "the One" by posing "the Other" as the inessential. For if the others are part of me, they are essential to who I am, as I shall argue in chapter 4.

Any problem for de Beauvoir's thinking about oppression is a problem for feminism as a whole. This is true not simply because of the pervasiveness of de Beauvoir's influence but because of the persuasive force of the ideas themselves: they remain foundational, irreplaceable, always illuminating. My object here is not to find fault with de Beauvoir so much as to ask what causes her—or anyone—to set up the opposition of subject and object as she does. I ask this not so much to analyze de Beauvoir's own thought as to learn how a certain root presupposition shapes her ideas even as it shapes the very culture she criticizes. This presupposition about the nature of the self weakens the liberating force of her initial analysis, I believe, by foisting upon it an unnecessary masculinism. By catching such a presupposition at work we may learn to recognize its persistence in our own perspectives. And in this recognition we confront an intimate basis for the co-optation of women's thinking and women's selves.

De Beauvoir states the terms of her analysis of oppression clearly. Not only do male subjects make objects of women; all oppression consists in the objectification of one group by another. Women, she believes, are exceptional as an oppressed group because they have largely failed to overthrow, or even to resist, their own objectification. But such objectification is grounded in the nature of all human reality; for all subjects, in order to become subjects, require an alien. "Otherness is a fundamental category of human thought." [16] De Beauvoir derives this axiom from Claude Lévi-Strauss, in his translation of Hegelian categories into an analysis of all human culture. Here is de Beauvoir's key generalization: "We find in consciousness itself a fundamental hostility toward every other consciousness; as the subject can be posed only in being opposed—he sets himself up as the essential as opposed to the other, the inessential, the object." [17]

The One requires the Other, which the One "posits," that is, unilaterally positions, *as* that Other. The aggression of such positing, whereby the other is set apart and separated off from the self, is undeniable: it is truly op-position. Transcendence then becomes a function of ontological hostility. With the help of the Hegelian tradition, de Beauvoir implicitly exposes the character of all subject-object dualism: the static dichotomy of Cartesian substances gives way in Hegelian–existential thought to an active opposition. The traditional dualism seems to have functioned as a cover for the hostile character of Western subjectivity. Existential analysis replaces the traditional substantial self, which simply and ever *is,* with a dynamic consciousness that *has become.* Philosophy is indebted to Sartrian thought for the recognition of the "bad faith" (*mauvais foi*) at work in the traditional idea of the self-identically enduring subject, which bases its authenticity on an essential unity, always already given, as an object. (Bad faith according to Sartre is the art of forming contradictory concepts, that is, of conceiving of oneself at one and the same time as a totally free subject and as an objectified other—and pretending not to know the difference.) The Cartesian self-objectifying subject, believing itself already an individual, thus evades responsibility for what it is and does, that is, for its existence.

Nonetheless the fundamental dualism of presupposing the separation of subject from object straddles the distinction between the Cartesian and existential schemes and persists in *The Second Sex.* In the existential case the opposition is based on aggression; in the Cartesian, on essentially different natures. Yet perhaps de Beauvoir herself treats the "fundamental hostility" as a sort of nature, a given, an ineluctable structure of consciousness. What if such oppositional consciousness, however pervasive, need not characterize all relations? What if hostility is not fundamental, but institutionalized by patriarchal social forces? Then does the presupposition of aggression as the constant dynamic of transcendence not itself evince "bad faith"?

Of course de Beauvoir is not glorifying belligerence. She advocates a respectful "reciprocity" of authentic subjects. Yet it is difficult not to hear resonances of Freud's view of the ego, in *Civilization and Its Discontents:* "Aggressiveness ... reigned almost without limit in primitive times ... and forms the basis of every relation of affection and love among people." [18] For Freud the aggression is based on an instinct that precedes and pervades all culture; for de Beauvoir, who develops a powerful feminist critique of Freudian determinism, the hostility is basic to all subjective consciousness and so by inference to all culture. As George Steiner writes:

It is surely notable that the theory of personality, as it develops from Hegel to Nietzsche and Freud ... is essentially a theory of aggression. Hegel defines identity against the identity of others. Where it is ontologically realized, consciousness of the full self will imply the subjection, perhaps the destruction, of another. [19]

In other words, according to this theory of aggression—within the tradition in which de Beauvoir positions *The Second Sex*—the patriarchal problem is not so much that men exercise a fundamental hostility toward women, but that women do not exercise it themselves. In failing to oppose the Other, women cannot "authentically assume a subjective attitude."

In the attempt to claim the rights of subjectivity, to become more vigorously creative selves, women are much helped by de Beauvoir's demand for transcendence not only of every past and patriarchal bond, but for transcendence as the very means of becoming. Tension, difference, conflict—without which there is no creation, no revolution, no development—represent means of transcendence women have tended to evade. Even the presupposition of a hostile duality energizes necessary strengths for women, such as self-defense, self-assertion, courage, adventurousness and honesty. Women who would overcome the inhibition of their own power do indeed risk this hostility and do not obsequiously belabor the distinctions between aggression and assertiveness or rage and confrontation.

The historically accumulated skills of the second sex, arising from activities of nurture and intimacy, may possess more integrity than de Beauvoir admits. But they will not, as Jean Baker Miller puts it, "get you to the top at General Motors. . . . They will not even provide you with a self-determined, authentic, effective life." As a feminist therapist concerned with encouraging and radicalizing some of those traits de Beauvoir would associate with immanence, Miller is still aware, as any woman must be, that "the characteristics most highly developed in women and perhaps most essential to human beings are *the* very characteristics that are specifically dysfunctional for success in the world as it is."[20] And creation of new worlds presupposes, dangerously, some sort of success in the world-as-it-already-is on the part of the would-be creators. It would be presumptuous to believe myself capable of any success without both obvious and subtle co-optation by the politics of the dominant, separative self. These dilemmas of pragmatic and particular strategy keep us edging along the fine line between self-compromising co-optation and constructive subversion of the system.

The larger question remains: Do we *want* to set ourselves up as the essential, the subjective Absolute? What price would we pay—if such a self-stance were to embody our criterion of authenticity? Can its dichotomous oppositionalism, however effective, ultimately empower women to be ourselves, or will it lead to a new self-contradiction?

The Sex That Kills

The internal tension of de Beauvoir's account, and of the oppositionalism it assumes and furthers, becomes graphic in her account of the Neolithic origins of culture. Placed early in *The Second Sex*, this historical analysis represents a crucial foundation for her thesis as a whole; it concerns the impressive historical universality of women's oppression and of women's complicity in that oppression. Women as a class, she argues, differ from other oppressed groups by virtue of lacking a historical religion or culture of their own and therefore even the memory of a "subjective existence." So she claims that the Neolithic images of a Great Goddess constitute no exception to woman's oppression: "slave or idol, it was never she who chose her lot."[21] Peremptorily dismissing any matriarchal hypothesis, she accepts unquestioningly Lévi-Strauss's insistence upon the anthropological universality of male dominance and the exchange of women as objects. The early agricultural communities become in her hands a vivid metaphor of feminine sub-subjectivity: "In no domain whatever did she create; she maintained the life of the tribe by giving it children and bread, nothing more. She remained doomed to immanence, incarnating only the static aspect of society, closed in on itself." [22] All activity that produces or sustains life rates, then, as immanence, as less than fully human, because bound to biological necessities. The production of pots and fabrics belongs to the same sedentary round of subcreative preservation. De Beauvoir continues by contrasting with woman's work the activities of the male:

Man went on monopolizing the functions which threw open that society toward nature and toward the rest of humanity. The only employments worthy of him were war, hunting, and fishing; he made conquest of foreign booty and bestowed it on the tribe; war, hunting and fishing represented an expansion of existence, its projection toward the world. The male remained alone the incarnation of transcendence. [23]

In other words, activities that give life are unworthy, whereas activities that kill express transcendence! We see here a concrete illustration of the "fundamental hostility" of the ex-istential, out-going subject. Odysseus—indeed any warrior—is its perfect embodiment. The spear seems to rise up in de Beauvoir's own analysis as the symbol of transcendence, making manifest the phallic-aggressive energy of this outwardbound, projectile subject. Warfare becomes the sine qua non for world openness. Indeed it is difficult not to interpolate into such passages the phallus as the true symbol of transcendence, or in the psychoanalyst Lacan's words, as "supreme signifier." [24] Ironic as it is to encounter this phallocentrism in a feminist classic—one in fact that contains a brilliant refutation of penis envy—de Beauvoir is not herself speaking ironically. Here she summarizes the thesis: "The worst curse that was laid upon woman was that she should be excluded from these warlike forays. For it is *not in giving life but in risking life* that man is raised above the animal; that is why superiority has been accorded in humanity not to the sex that brings forth but to that which kills" (my emphasis). [25]

But let us set the matter of the warrior's ethos aside for the mo-

23

ment. (Writing in France in the pre-Hiroshima world, as World War II came to a close, de Beauvoir and other heroes of the Resistance would not incline toward pacifism.) She is surely right to emphasize the importance of the element of risk for all creative subjectivity. Without voluntary risk, one merely repeats. Nothing ventured, nothing gained. But how does risking life in the hunt and the kill set "man" above any carnivorous animal? Surely this preoccupation with marking "man" off from the animal expresses the same old anti-ecological hierarchy that subordinates woman (along with nature and body) to man. The hunt surely subserves the ends of survival as much as does foodgathering or agriculture.[26] When women make agriculture possible in the Neolithic period, after the Ice Age decimation of the great herds of bison, their culture interweaves ritual and work in a seasonal religion of death and rebirth. Does this fecund imagery count as less creatively human because the work was less violent and risked fewer lives? (De Beauvoir here ignores the risk to female life in childbearing because, we may presume, it is "natural" and so involuntary; by contrast the hunt and warfare, though pursued for the sake of survival and in common with animals, is understood as superior to "nature.") Yet risk is hardly absent from Neolithic agriculture, when the life of the entire community depends upon lunar calculations of growing seasons and a few handfuls of seeds. The very etymology of *risk* witnesses to the original experience of agriculture: *risk* stems from Germanic and Latin roots meaning "sickle" and "scythe." De Beauvoir's interpretation of the Neolithic age exposes the false pair of alternatives that can come to shape even feminist thought. Women are either to continue in the subjectivity of a life-maintaining tedium or to aspire to a life-destroying heroism. My challenge here directs itself not at the historical plausibility of de Beauvoir's account of prehistory but at the way her description of the Neolithic polarization of the sexes highlights her own unpalatable presupposition of the hostile structure of any truly human subject.

Another account of the Neolithic and Chalcolithic ages is gaining force. The work of archeologist Marija Gimbutas, set forth in *The Goddesses and Gods of Old Europe: Myths and Cult Images*, makes significant headway in redescribing these millenia. For her evidence Gimbutas draws upon archeological artifacts, especially figurines whose imagery she has classed and translated. (As this era is preliterate, its evidence has heretofore been ruled academically out of court.) She argues on the basis of archeological evidence for a "pre-Indo-European culture of Europe, a culture matrifocal and probably matrilinear, agricultural and sedentary, egalitarian and peaceful." [27] Here as in Anatolia (in Turkey) there is evidence of neither male dominance nor a strict matriarchy, if that means a mirror reversal of patriarchy. Rather, the artifacts point to a matri-local, matrilinear and symbolically matricentric society focussed upon the worship of a Great Goddess, "the creative principle as Source and Giver of All," and an accompanying prestige of women. Yet images of males coexisted with her markedly varied forms. Moreover, the Goddess is not yet predominantly figured as earth mother or sex symbol at this stage; biological femininity is transformed into formal symbols celebrating world generation rather than merely glorifying fertility. These goddesses often take on the characteristics of bird and snake, perennial images of transcendent heights and underworld depths. We encounter a "symbolic, conceptual art not given to physical naturalism." Far from a culture relegating women or goddesses to the realm of mere biology, the Neolithic, in its artistry, suggests a creative interplay of the immanent and the transcendent. "The primary purpose was to transform and spiritualize the body and to surpass the elementary and corporeal." [28] In short, the agricultural age evokes the spiritual and the social power of women, with no indication that men were correspondingly degraded or oppressed.

These ancient cultures were gradually superseded by the invading hordes carrying the sort of subjectivity de Beauvoir has represented at once as male and as normative. While de Beauvoir collapses two phases into one epoch, Gimbutas claims that Neolithic Old Europe

contrasted sharply with the ensuing proto-Indo-European culture which was patriarchal, stratified, pastoral, mobile and war-oriented, superimposed on all Europe, except the southern and western fringes, in the course of three waves of infiltration from the Russian steppe, between 4500 and 2500 B.C. During and after this period the female deities . . . were largely replaced by the predominantly male divinities of the Indo-Europeans. [29]

We belong to the culture of these conquerors, whose activities do not signify the prerogative or even the primordial choice of any generic "male," but of a set of migrants who emerged victorious. Thus it should not come as a surprise to encounter powerful affinities of the Western ideals of human subjectivity as expansive, aggressive, and dynamic with the early history of mobile, invasive, war-oriented prototypes.

It turns out that our opening personification of this supervening ego ideal in Odysseus has deep historical roots. For the age of mythic heroes (3000 B.C.E. to 1500 B.C.E.) is precisely the epoch of the transition from the Neolithic and early Bronze Age cultures to the establishment of the Indo-European invaders in Europe and the Semitic conquerors in the Near East. The heroic age, which Homer already recalls with nostalgia, is the period in which the wandering warriors extirpate the matricentric images of a nonheroic and prepatriarchal culture. A process of "mythological defamation" would systematically transmute the images of female power into the monster, the enemy and the amazon.[30]

The Self-Absolving Absolute

The hero-warrior lives a transcendence without immanence, a separative oneness based on opposition to the Other. With de Beauvoir we acknowledge that the very structure of subjective freedom must be *achieved*, for by definition it cannot be something already given. But then why should we receive the subject-object opposition itself as though *it* is a given? We may with her appreciate a dynamic account of the genesis of subjectivity; but nonetheless we must doubt the desirability or possibility of the subject's achievement of absolute independence from nature or from others. For we begin to suspect that the ideal of autonomous self-assertion is implicated in a sort of ontological belligerence, and we see that the hostility, glorified by the image of the warrior, discloses after all a specific historical beginning and so no universality.

In contrast to the soluble self, which dissolves into relation, the separative self makes itself the absolute in that it absolves itself from relation. It brooks no other subjects and so it turns them into the nonsubjective other, the object, whenever it can. But does it not in fact require these objects, as though to complete something missing in itself? What would it be that it misses? What lack in itself could motivate its violence of conquest and dominance?

Perhaps we can gain a clue to the motives of objectification if we reexamine the notion of immanence. If the other enters my experience, then it enters as an influence upon me: it makes a difference, and so I am no longer quite the same. But influence, to be more precise, is not working *upon* me so much as *into* me; in-fluence is that which flows in. If the other flows into the self, then the other is immanent to the self, to the inside being of that self. This is the philosophical meaning of internal rather than external relations: relations between different subjects that are internal to what those subjects *are*—part of their very essence, for good or for ill. But then a self has no shield to protect it from others, no hard bronze off of which influences bounce like intercepted arrows. The in-flowing other must feel to a defensive ego like an aggressive intrusion, a threat to its self-containment. So it will redouble its fortifications and can justify its own aggression as defense. Indeed it will declare itself an absolute in the original sense of the word: to be "cut loose" from—the other, we presume, who faced with the self-absolutizing I soon appears as the alien Other. Relation to others, once ousted from the self's inside and so experienced as external, must be *kept* outside by a policy of psychic isolationism. Thus the ego denies the streams of influence entering into it and tries to control—and so to possess—their sources. Only by subduing and possessing the Other can it feel truly in possession of itself. Externalizing relation, it in fact projects both the threats and comforts of relationship onto the Other. Then woman, as man's most intimately threatening yet most comfortingly controlled Other, is there to fill his lack: the lack of immanent relations—of the sense of an intimate interconnection—with the world. But the lack is in a way as illusory as his absoluteness—because willy-nilly each subject exists in interdependence with its world. And so in a bizarre sense, by objectifying the Other the subject compensates for a lack that it does not really have—for it is only the feeling, not the reality, of isolation that cuts it off from the in-flowing other.

Where does the cycle begin? Later chapters may shed light on causes, both mythic and psychological. For now let us claim that any fundamental opposition of self and other serves the double purpose of establishing the self's sense of its inner independence from influence and compensating for the haunting fear that the independence is illusory. As it cannot embrace interdependence, it ironically comes to depend upon the dependent Other, in reality or fantasy.

This Other, especially as Woman, is then understandably subject alternately to adoration and abhorrence: she symbolizes at once what he misses and what he dreads.

In its gender history, we are for example all too familiar with the phenomenon of dependent women supporting the so-called male ego. While these women (and few of us have not been among them) are deriving their sense of identity from his, they are consciously shoring up what they know to be an illusion: his sense of his own strength and independence. Exchanging knowing winks, devoted women have exercised the peculiar bad faith of getting their own sense of self from a masculine Absolute that the women themselves are helping to invent. Without the endless supply of flattery and motherly solicitude, how long would the so-called male ego keep up its feeling of absoluteness? So the feminine bad faith perfectly complements and sustains the masculine bad faith of an ego rendering itself absolute in the first place.

Why does the normative ego structure of our culture—the male ego—lend itself so readily to a dyadic dependency when its self-image insists upon a singularity, a stable unity? Let us inquire into the foundations of this odd two-in-oneness, in which the only absolute, complete in itself, is the pair made up of the apparently independent and the apparently dependent selves. This two-in-oneness need not refer to sociologically defined couples, as for example marriage partners; it may refer as well to the parent-child relation or to an internalization of the idealized parent relation; indeed, it may refer to any external or internal dyad characterized by an exclusive and hierarchical symbiosis.

Let me suggest that the very notion of self discloses a paradoxical internal division. The word self connotes a reflexive act: the self as subject functions simultaneously as its own object. George Herbert Mead summarizes this structure succinctly: "the characteristic of the self as an object to itself . . . is represented in the word 'self,' which is a reflexive and indicates that which can be both subject and object." [31] But can it really? Or has this subject exercised upon itself the heroic dichotomy? In order to assure itself of its own existence, it splits itself in two, bending back upon itself. "Bending back"—as light bounces back from a mirror—is the original meaning of *reflexive* or *reflective;* in the Western tradition, the capacity of selves to turn themselves and the rest of the universe into objects of reflection has formed the definition of the nonanimally human, of the rational soul.

The Opaque Blade

It is significant that the ability of mirrors to reflect is based upon their opacity. This distinguishes them from windows, transparent or translucent. Opacity, as impenetrability by light, suggests the external relations of atomic individuals. The windowless monad of Leibniz, for example, mirrors the universe within its own self-enclosure. The monad experiences no interpenetration with the actual world. As another image of external relations, the sexual metaphor of absolute maleness (precisely as "cut off from") suggests the castration anxiety Freud found in the civilized male psyche. The oedipal conflict produces, as chapter 3 will show, the separative ego. The *fear* of castration already "cuts off" male from world. Thus reflexivity replays the *failure* to penetrate, to reach into, the others as they also reach into us. It is the failure of intimate penetration which motivates phallic conquest and preserves an aggressive narcissism.

In his early essay "The Transcendence of the Ego," Sartre describes the notion of reflexivity precisely in terms of opacity. Criticizing the Cartesian tradition, he argues that the ego to which the dualism of reflexivity gives rise—the transcendental ego of idealism—has "no raison d'être." If it existed, it would "be a sort of center of opacity. . . . This superfluous *I* would be a hindrance . . . would tear consciousness from itself; it would divide consciousness; it would slide into every consciousness like an opaque blade." [32] But such an opacity does in fact characterize the mode of subjective existence we have called separative; it is no mere error in theory. Reflexive consciousness reflects itself accurately in Cartesian categories. Sartre argues that such an opaque blade cannot do justice to the lively phenomena of awareness. He advocates instead an "unreflected consciousness," one that precedes any division into a separate ego and an external object and therefore cannot be an object for itself. By contrast, the Cartesian habit turns consciousness into a substantial monad in which, Sartre claims, the I lives as an "inhabitant." "Consciousness is then no longer a spontaneity; it bears within itself the germ of opaqueness."[33] On this basis Sartre can demonstrate that spontaneity, as the predualistic relation to the other, is lost through the enduring self-identity of any underlying subject. The Cartesian subject, as "thinking thing" that walls itself into a formal self-identity to which it always transcendentally returns, represents perhaps the most sophisticated product of disconnection. The separative self, we might say, reflects back on itself as a defense against any unreflected, unpremeditated spontaneity. We have linked the separative self with the Odyssean complex. But does Penelope not seem more an "inhabitant" than Odysseus? Perhaps it is through the very restlessness of his travels that the rigid stability of self-enclosure establishes itself. The ultimate return to the waiting woman—the stable home—symbolizes the bending back of reflexivity to the sameness of its origin. The Odyssean subject is recognized as the same one and no other—the same self-identical subject. Let us recall the fundamental hostility that originally characterized the separative subjectivity of the heroic ego. It is through nothing other than his masterful aggression that Odysseus, in his climactic return, is recognized as himself, indeed proves himself master of his own "substance". By the wielding of his famous bow and the massacre of his competitors, his identity is reestablished in perfect reflexivity.

"Like an opaque blade" indeed, the consciousness of the warrior ego slices through the subtle membranes connecting itself to both the outer others and its own past (where it is uncomfortably other to itself). Thus isolated in its journey of transcendence, it must then posit the other as object and twist itself into a strange transcendental posture of self-objectification. The objectification of itself and of the other establishes its formal unity with itself, its oneness as something enduringly the same.

Inasmuch as the patriarchal male has wielded the opaque blade of a disconnective ego, the attendant female has served both as cause of and reward for his hostility. Penelope, whose fidelity lay not in any integrity of self but in waiting for her man's return, keeping herself defined purely in terms of his identity, is the Good Woman, his reward, herself rewarded only by his return. But there are always Bad Women available as scapegoats. The homecoming of this hero involves a macabre housecleaning in which Odysseus makes all the female servants who had been reportedly seduced by the suitors clean out their lovers' bloody remains. Then he has the women themselves peremptorily hanged, not even bothering to witness their execution.[34] In the household economy of this returned "inhabitant," being possessed by the rival males counted as gross infidelity to the one true master, a threat to his self-possession.

The hero's need to posit the submissive other, be it male opponent or female property, seems to make up for the lack, the despair implicit in his triumphant defiance—the fundamental anxiety that he may be no one. The self-identity of the separative ego is in fact a self-delusion. It is philosophically "superfluous" because it is existentially a hoax. The inner and outer violence with which the opaque blade flashes and flails about expresses a fear of ineffectuality, of impotence. The sword cannot cut itself: for this piece of Zen wisdom we may be grateful; but the sword has already chopped the world to pieces trying. Wars aside, even the most serene rationalism enacts the subtle violence of reflexivity, of a separate and independent substance cut off from the world. Truly reflexive self-knowledge would imply that there is no difference between the I who knows and the me who is known. But if the self endures as exactly the same for even that microcosmic interval—the interval in which the light bounces back from the mirror—self is then a frozen substance. Its changes appear external and accidental by contrast to its fixed essence; in this way it blocks awareness of the influent effects of the world, the others. For if the other can get into oneself, one's self must become another. It does not remain the same *one*. Rather, it has the continuity of indissoluble ties to its own history, as it has to the world. But if it can appear to remain the same, it will seem transcendent, even absolute, in its impenetrability. Its reflex action generates a chain reaction of self-identifications: I am what I am what I . . . (This is precisely the Popeye chain of karmic bondage first diagnosed by Gautama the Buddha.)

Another way of stating the Odyssean irony is this: In the bending back of its voyaging transcendence upon itself, it collapses into its own immanence. Thus for Sartre the transcendental ego (not to be confused with the transcendence *of* the ego) belongs to the metaphysics of mere immanence—of acquiescence in the given, the past, the illusion of an unchanging inhabitant. Penelope seems with all waiting wives to maintain for him the aliveness, the habitability, of this illusion. He can always find himself in his return. Or so he thinks. He can project doubts about the absoluteness of his own ego onto the available crowd of dispensable others—the suitors and the slaughtered women at home, the sirens, lovers, monsters and enemies abroad. His own difference (gained in twenty years of wandering) from his previous self, projected onto the apparently external members of his "substance"—his property—can thus be literally subtracted from existence. He thereby attains the static unity of the self-divided.

The reliance of this analysis upon Sartre for the critique of the reflexively self-identical ego might seem a bit misleading, even confusing. After all, I began this chain of thought by disagreeing with a presupposition of de Beauvoir, whose existentialism developed in tandem with that of Sartre. Her insistence upon the belligerent transcendence of the ego, by which it at once transcends itself and objectifies the Other, derives from her Sartrian existentialism. The declaration of transcendence, over and against the relational or the immanent, is Sartre's. But this involves a hostile positing of the Other as external object, which seems to belie his own view as given in "The Transcendence of the Ego," where he underlines the role of a spontaneous, prereflexive and nonoppositional consciousness.

A bit of intellectual history helps disperse the perplexity. Only after this early essay had been written did Sartre and de Beauvoir together attend over several years Kojeve's lectures on Hegelian philosophy.[35] Kojeve was stressing the role of opposition, bifurcation and aggression in the Hegelian system, exemplified by Hegel's insistence upon the historical necessity of the master-slave relation. Though Sartre and de Beauvoir continued to develop the critique of any substantial or "transcendental" ego, the Hegelian notion of opposition became for them the model of authentic transcendence. If we are to come to grips with the presuppositions of patriarchy itself, this historical change of mind does not, as a specific example of the large problem, count as trivial. Rather, it suggests how powerfully in our culture the idea of opposition insinuates itself into that of a free subject. Already in "The Transcendence of the Ego," a vulnerability to this dualistic thinking appears. For evidently, Sartre can only conceive of the nonreflecting consciousness as self-consciousness from the start. But it would seem that such self-awareness already contains the germs of the sort of reflexive dualism he opposes. This dualism underlies at once the Cartesian reflexivity he criticizes and the Hegelian hostility he later espouses.

With all this talk of transcendence, we cannot ignore the theological underpinnings of Western subjectivity. Though de Beauvoir and Sartre may have managed to secularize transcendence and the Absolute without any religious remainder, for Hegel the Absolute was after all God. A foray into theology will help to illumine the sources of the separative sensibility in our culture.

The Embarrassment of God

Classical Christian theology, from Augustine through Luther, has envisioned sinners as human beings who are curved back in on themselves, *homo incurvatus in seipsum*. This tradition long pre-dates the formally reflexive sense of modernity; indeed, Luther locates it in scripture, which, he says, "describes man as curved in upon himself to such an extent that he bends not only physical but spiritual goods toward himself, seeking himself in all things."[36] Does this curvature of the ego, by which it bends all things back into itself, not bear a striking resemblance to the reflexive narcissism that turns the world into its mirror? If we here take the sexist language at its—unintended—face value, we may read the doctrine as a confession: "the *man* is curved in upon *him*self, seeking *him*self in all things." (This suggests a peaceful methodology for reading androcentric texts: we might systematically approach them as they present themselves, as treatises on masculine experience.)

It is as though Luther, writing in the margin between the medieval and the modern worlds, subliminally senses the increasing self-enclosure that Descartes's self-objectifying ego would within a century successfully rationalize. Thus Luther's critique of the self-centered self picks up the erstwhile radicalism of Augustine's battle against Pelagianism (the "heresy" that declared the human will capable of changing itself for the good, apart from the direct intervention of divine grace). We can only agree with Luther regarding such a self-encapsulated ego, that "it knows only . . . what is good, honorable and useful for itself, but not what is good for God and for others." That is, because the separative ego is only externally related to the other, it can define its good only in separation from a whole in which self and others are inextricably connected. But Luther, of course, does not mean to address a specific brand of individuality, a patriarchal male-identified ego, but ahistorically aims his polemic at universal "human nature." "Now this curvedness is natural; it is a natural defect and a natural evil. Hence, man gets no help from the powers of his nature, but he is in need of some more effective help from the outside. And this is love." [37] This love is strictly a gift of grace, to which nature is radically opposed. This notion of love as "from the outside" may receive some support from the psychoanalytic aim to replace narcissistic self-love with object love. But when love, as divine grace, is rendered an external and unnatural force, how is it love? The dichotomy between the internal and the external is here reinforced by the opposition of the natural and the divine. So the division of self from the world and "God" builds a mighty fortress indeed. By a sort of vicious circularity, Luther buttresses the very self-enclosure he decries.

Kierkegaard, himself a Lutheran, differentiates sin, as we saw earlier, into two modes of despair or dread—into an arrogant "masculine" defiance and a devoted "feminine" self-loss. Accommodating as it does both members of the dyad of the separative and the soluble, his version holds more promise. In *Concluding Unscientific Postscript,* he summarizes the common element of all sin: "The inwardness of sin, as dread in the existing individual, is the greatest possible and most painful possible distance from the truth, when truth is subjectivity." [38] Rather than a matter of self-interest per se, or merely too much self, sin reveals itself as self-alienation and indeed too little self. A false sense of self shrinks subjectivity: a view that can support—if kept free of Kierkegaard's own sexism—woman's need for more rather than less self. His exceptional awareness of selfhood remains squarely within the classical theological continuum in which the self finds itself only in self-transcendence, that is, in the God-relation. Yet the Kierkegaardian link between subjectivity and existence—in "the existing individual"—provided a profound stimulus for twentieth-century existentialism of the secular sort we have examined. But discourse on "sin" maintains the accountability of human life before God; "sin is a decisive expression for the religious mode of existence." [39] (We must remember that at least for Kierkegaard, consciousness of sin is distinguished from consciousness of guilt; that is, sin in this sense should not lead to any guilt trip or simple sense of ethical inadequacy, but is a matter of "fearful freedom.")

If we ask, however, what this God-relation is like, indeed whether it is a relational relation at all, we encounter the intuition that only love answers the sinfulness of our ineffectual freedom. Kierkegaard's solution is this: "It is the last enthusiastic cry in which the finite spirit appeals to God . . . : 'I cannot understand Thee, but still I will love Thee . . . even if it seemed to me as if Thou didst not love me, I will nevertheless love Thee.' "[40] This resembles Luther's more primitive emphasis on loving God unconditionally even at the price of eternal separation from God: "Now, all who truly love God and revere him as a father and friend, not from natural capacity but only through the Holy Spirit . . . submit freely to the will of God whatever it may be, even for hell and eternal death, if God should will it."[41] Luther knows that one so well attuned to this God "cannot possibly be forever outside God." The point for both theologians is a supremely unconditional trust—Kierkegaard's famous "leap of faith." But while we cannot miss the courageous radicalism of this spirit, what sort of love-relationship does it espouse? A satiric passage from Kierkegaard is revealing. To one who "seeks slyly to slip the thought into his dealings with God, that God needs him just a little," he retorts: "But this is stupidity, for God needs no man. It would otherwise be a highly embarrassing thing to be a creator, if the result was that the creator came to depend upon the creature."[42]

But why should this be? Why is it so stupid, so embarrassing, to imagine a creator interdependent with the creation? Quite clearly because this God is to stay absolutely self-sufficient, independent of the world. He has created and so reigns in utter omnipotence. "God may require everything of every human being, everything and for nothing." Our love is absolute dependence; his love an infinite transcendence. In our culture this God could only take the pronoun *he*. For is this not the ultimately separate subject, before whom all humanity (male and female) tremble, emasculated and dissolved into the role of the feminine dependent? Thus traditionally the soul, especially in the mystic tradition, is feminine, melting into the unity of ecstatic subservience to a masculine image. This would be traditionally the pole of religious experience Tillich characterizes as "participative," the mystical merger of the individual with God, who is experienced as the infinite Whole. At the other pole, "individualization" generates a relation of divine-human dialogue in which the divine and the human remain strictly separate. This latter, characteristically orthodox or neo-orthodox dichotomy sounds more like a patriarchal man-to-man relation, yet the hierarchical grade is so steep here that the human male is reduced to complete dependence upon the Holy One.[43]

ONE

One might readily come to doubt the lovingness of this deity. For the doctrine of divine self-sufficiency (aseity, or the creator's independence from the creature) is bound up with a concept of power that seems antithetical to love. First, God is traditionally seen as omnipotent, all-powerful, all-controlling, and so ultimately responsible for all evil or unjust suffering. Theodicy aside, human freedom, incapable of the good on its own, seems to be allotted us so that we can incriminate ourselves. Thus, "nature" can only seek itself, sinfully, in all things. "Grace," says Luther by way of contrast, "is not content unless it sees God in and above all it sees." But grace, of course, is nothing other than the action of God. In other words, God loves God in us, if we are graced. Yet it is *human* nature that is blamed for self-loving!

Furthermore, divine self-sufficiency depends upon divine impassionability—that is, God's inability to feel. For if God could be moved by feeling for the creatures, God would not be the purely active cause of all things, the Unmoved Mover. In the history of Christian thought the Aristotelian metaphysics quite consistently triumphs over scriptural metaphors, which portray a God sometimes sorrowing and raging in the vulnerability of love. The Lord and Creator of the Universe must be spared the embarrassment of influence—at least in the view of theologians who themselves suffer from Bloom's "anxiety of influence." The attribute of impassionability is itself a consequence of divine immutability: for to feel is to be moved, and to be moved is to be changed. No tenet of Christian theology has stood so firmly—and with so little scriptural justification—as the divine unchangingness. Since Plato, change has been taken to imply imperfection: a perfect being is eternally—already—all that it can be. Or in Aquinas's language, God's essence is strictly identical with God's existence: this is the meaning of the divine infinity. Hegel challenges the self-sufficient infinity of God, claiming that God needs the world for God's own self-actualization, and so draws down on his philosophy Kierkegaard's masterful satires of the "system." For Kierkegaard was hurling the epithet "stupid" especially at Hegelian presumption for believing that God might in any way need us. It is not for Hegel's approximation of the dialectic to a relation of aggressive dominance and subjugation that Kierkegaard ever criticizes him.

Western thought has been riveted to the ideal of unchanging perfection, in which all God's attributes merge in a crystalline "sim-

36

plicity." Yet theology could not afford to subtract love from the list of perfections. After all, apart from the power fixations of the ecclesial hierarchies, the Christian movement derived its persuasive power, human appeal, and salutory tenderness from love (*agape*) as its raison d'être. One may read much of theological history as a conscious and convoluted attempt to compress the warming intuition that God is love into the cold, hard diamond of divine immutability. Impervious to effects or affects caused by the world, the absolute separateness of deity has symbolized the separative aspirations of a Mankind created in His image.

For instance, Aquinas, taking his cue from Aristotle, claims that God "loves without passion."[44] That is, God loves without compassion: "To sorrow, therefore, over the misery of others belongs not to God, but it does most properly belong to Him to dispel that misery."[45] That is, the divine agape-love contains no passive moment, no reception of the other's feelings. It is strictly an action of the will. This mode of love is generalized to all agapic relation: "To love anything is nothing else than to will good to that thing."[46] Love is a matter of acting *upon*, the action of a controlling and unilateral will. Anselm had earlier struggled with the same dilemma: "how art thou . . . compassionate, and, at the same time, passionless?" He needs his deity to be caring and solves the paradox by claiming: "Thou art compassionate in terms of our experience, and not compassionate in terms of thy being."[47] As David Griffin, interpreting this tradition, paraphrases Anselm: "In other words, God only *seems* to us to be compassionate; he is not *really* compassionate."[48] This is more than a claim that we cannot know God's essence; it is a claim that God's essence is separate, not from his own existence but from his relations to the world. This is the supreme case of external relatedness. Indeed this is the ultimate separate subject, eternally self-sufficient, immune to the influence of those others, whom he has created. He is sundered from the natural universe by the transcendent exclusivity of his being. Grace is unilateral and therefore all that he "saves"—takes into his own life eternally— are those wills conformed *by* his will, *to* his will. There is no ontological input from others. Despite scripture and piety suggesting a more emotionally engaged relation, this One is shaped by Aristotle's idea of the deity absorbed in eternal self-contemplation (the *nous noein*).

Thus the God of the fathers, or God the Father, reveals a pure structure of reflexive selfhood: self-knowing rendered infinite and exact by his own immutability. Because he cannot be affected, he is the perfect object to himself: his self-objectification circulates around the eternal self-enclosure of his self-identity. But a bizarre double standard confronts us here: the traditional God is the absolute instance of the traditional sin. Who is more "curved in upon himself" than this separate—not merely separative—supersubject? Embarrassed by feeling, could this deity be other than a magnified He?

Man's Spirit, Woman's Nature

The present inquiry concerns itself with doctrines of God only inasmuch as they shed light on our images of self. And they do. The traditional perfections of God read like a catalog of the heroic ego's ideals for himself. At this level a Feuerbachian analysis of "man's" projections and illusions would be in order. Furthermore, in the language of theological imagination, the human self was created in the image of its God, but sin is said to obscure or even demolish that imago. Classical theology decries self-enclosure as sin; let me suggest, however, that self-enclosure—with its accompanying arrogance, isolation and dominance—is precisely what the *imago dei* came to convey! Things are all turned around here. This reading is no call for a dismissal of Christian theology, but for its conversion—its "turning again." In the persistent Christian emphasis on love (though separatively defined), in the recognition that the separative self-enclosure is sin (though falsely generalized to "nature" and to women), there certainly survives a useful source for patriarchal autocritique. But for reasons the rest of this book will probe, the association in this epoch between separatism and masculinity is so tight that as long as God is imagined in mainly masculine metaphors, there is simply no chance for conversion to a fundamentally relational spirituality. And the reverse holds equally true: as long as divinity is externalized by the traditional perfections of self-sufficiency, omnipotence, impassibility and immutability, "God"— even were she made in name and image a woman, an androgyne, or a neuter—will support the oppression of women. In other words, moving to gender-inclusive, nongendered or female language and imagery for the deity is essential to the viability of God–talk, but insufficient.

As long as separation itself is deified, women of faith will end up in the doubly dependent role of subjugation to God and the male, who is himself subjugated to God. For the separative transcendence has arisen to express and sustain patriarchal manhood. If we understand "God" to be not merely the object of theological reflection and religious devotion, but also a symbol for a cultural superstructure, we realize that theism and atheism do not represent the important alternatives. Selfhood is so much a response to what we deify, what in Tillich's phrase is our "ultimate concern," that our metaphors of deity reveal the images of our own genesis. What sort of deity, what imagery of the ultimate? This question takes precedence over any debate between theism and atheism. If for women most forms of theism prove to be oppressive or regressive choices, it is also true that atheism is usually a banal reductionism. To liberate the divine of the patriarchal images and impulses that have been projected into it does not necessarily mean to kill God. But we still operate out of a culture whoses religions have all come to subserve the purposes of patriarchy. Or, as Mary Daly puts it: "Patriarchy is itself the prevailing religion of the entire planet. . . . All of the so-called religions legitimating patriarchy are mere sects subsumed under its vast umbrella/canopy."[49] So we can only experimentally, experientially imagine what sense of the sacred, with what (if any) ontological status, might survive the retraction of those massive projections whereby patriarchy has maintained its own apotheosis. Wrestling with theological presuppositions—whether from the inside or the outside of Jewish and Christian institutions remains also a secondary question—is already a mode of critical imagining, and so of self-recreation.

How does relation to this divine self-sufficiency, this transcendent independence, shape actual concepts of self? A brief look at a celebrated twentieth-century theologian, Reinhold Niebuhr, will unveil the involvement of theology in creating the separative self. In his theological anthropology (anthropology here refers as in philosophy to the study of the human subject), the human dimension of transcendence comes back into focus.

Niebuhr cites Kierkegaard, whose paradoxes were a great inspiration to him, with esteem: "The more consciousness, the more self . . . the self is the conscious synthesis of the limited and the unlim-

ited." [50] Niebuhr has earned great acclaim for his notion of sin as
the pride by which the finite mistakes itself for the infinite. His
astute analyses of political history as the playing field of collective
egotisms won him unparalleled status as ethical theologian to the
nation. But among feminist theologians his doctrine of sin has
gained him a special infamy. As noted earlier, feminist theology has
shown—I believe definitively—that the traditional definitions of sin
as pride, arrogance, self-interest and other forms of exaggerated
self-esteem miss the mark in the case of women, who in this culture
suffer from too little self-esteem, indeed too little self. So when
women, who are already prone to deny themselves for the sake of
relationship, are taught to deny themselves for the sake of God,
theology redoubles the message that for women any strong selfhood
is selfish. In her superb analysis of Niebuhr and Tillich, Judith Plaskow develops Saiving's earlier critique of classical notions of sin:
"Defining sin's religious dimension as rebellion against God and its
moral dimension as pride, Niebuhr not only fails to convey the
nature of women's sin, however; he actually turns it into a virtue."
For "women's sin is precisely the failure to turn toward the self." [51]
That is, we fail to come into our subjectivity in the existential sense,
or to claim what Niebuhr calls the "spiritual stature" of the human
"height of self-transcendence." [52]

This is in Niebuhr no accidental sexism, as his explicit position
on women's destiny—in *The Nature and Destiny of Man*—demonstrates. Intending to criticize "male arrogance," he states that
"the relation between the sexes is governed on the one hand by the
natural fact of sex differentiation and on the other by the spiritual
fact of human freedom." [53] So far he remains aligned with his axiom
that the human being "stands at the juncture of nature and spirit," [54]
suggesting a more wholesome view of nature than could Luther.
(Indeed, he criticizes Luther for the exaggeration of the opposition:
"free-will is denied to the point of offering man an excuse for his
sin." [55] But at another point he specifies *woman's* relation to "nature": "The natural fact that the woman bears the child binds her
to the child and partially limits the freedom of her choice in the
development of various potentialities of character not related to the
vocation of motherhood." [56] This statement is of course historically
quite accurate. But here his message is marked by a lethal confusion
between nature and history: "A rationalistic feminism is undoubt-
edly inclined to transgress inexorable bounds set by nature. Any

premature fixation of certain historical standards in regard to the family will inevitably tend to reinforce male arrogance and to retard justified efforts on the part of the female to achieve such freedom as is not incompatible with *the primary function of motherhood"* (my emphasis).[57]

Niebuhr gives with one hand and takes away with the other. He confuses the matter of biological-maternal capacity with that of a maternal vocation. But vocation was in Christian tradition the con-cretization of spiritual calling. For women he subsumes with one blow the freedom of the spirit's potential under the biological ne-cessities of a "primary function." The unique human individuality Niebuhr so cherishes as the legacy of Christian faith remains barely applicable to women, who all share the same vocation. Yet Niebuhr, part of an unbroken lineage of Christian preachers of maternal vo-cation, never attributes to males any comparably distinctive biolog-ical limits. Men merely share with women the general fact of fini-tude, but retain their freedom of individual vocation. If it is true of the normative human that *he* "is at the juncture of spirit and na-ture," he has forced woman off the path and into nature.

Our interest lies less in exposing such explicit and typical sexism, already the subject of a whole tradition of criticism, than in dis-cerning the relation of this sexism to Niebuhr's basic concept of self. The self for Niebuhr is coterminous with the human spirit and with creation in God's image and is distinguished above all by its capacity for self-transcendence. Human selfhood implies a "special capacity of standing continually outside itself in terms of indefinite regression."[58] This Kirkegaardian sense of always standing beyond the given self and so surpassing any status quo ante puts into psy-chological focus the dynamically historical energy of the biblical worldview. Process theologian John Cobb has identified this self-transcendence as the very "structure of Christian existence." Like Niebuhr, Cobb defines spirit as "the radically self-transcending character of human existence that emerged in the Christian com-munity."[59] This dynamic of creative, self-surpassing spirit is, as we saw earlier, crucial to de Beauvoir's contribution to feminist theory. Certainly women getting unstuck and living vigorously partake of such self-transcendence.

But now let us see just how Niebuhr's concept of self-transcend-ence defines human existence: "Man is the only animal which can make itself its own object. This capacity for self-transcendence . . .

is the basis of discrete individuality, for this self-consciousness involves consciousness of the world as 'the other.' "[60] Self-transcendence, in other words, is equated with self-objectification, and spirit with reflexive self-identity. Niebuhr explicitly affirms the ability to make oneself an object and to divide oneself from the "others." "Human consciousness involves the sharp distinction between the self and the totality of the world. Self-knowledge is thus the basis of discrete individuality."[61]

To transcend, then, is to separate. How odd that the author of *The Nature and Destiny of Man*, which features an extended, often brilliant, critique of modernity, never spots the mote in his own eye: he has reduced self-transcendence to Cartesian reflexivity. He decries the "autonomous individual" of the modern epoch for having trespassed "the limits set in the Christian religion,"[62] yet both the Cartesian and the Kantian edifices of autonomy are built on the foundation of the self-objectifying and separate ego. But Niebuhr merely clinches a tendency we traced already in orthodox forms of theology and indeed—as the next chapter will unfold—in the mythology of the masculine hero.

On this basis Niebuhr can explain sin as the perpetual temptation of an infinitely self-transcending creature to mistake itself for the Infinite creator. Impressed by its own self-objectifying capacity, it forgets it is also animal and so mistakes itself for God. But nowhere in this traditional critique of human pride does Niebuhr recognize that the ego's discreteness is the foundation of its egocentricity. So indeed theology again makes into the God-imaged self that separative "curvedness" that is at the same time the classic sin. The sin of pride derives precisely from the self-enclosure of a separate self, paradoxically seen as the self's virtue. In that case, no wonder theology finds sin "original"—it expresses an ineluctably self-perpetuating cycle: self-objectification in the image of a separate God resulting inevitably in an opaque self-preoccupation called evil. For strict self-objectification freezes the self in its own tracks: the knower is reflexively reduced to the known.

Once again we encounter a transcendence without immanence. Interpreting the biblical tradition, Niebuhr claims that "the most important characteristic of a religion of revelation is this twofold emphasis upon the transcendence of God and upon His intimate relation to the world."[63] One would expect to hear God's transcendence coupled with God's immanence: Niebuhr's consistent substitution of "intimate relation to" for "immanence in" the world is in this context obviously intended to guarantee God's separateness from the world. And upon this discrete independence of Creator from Creature the entire scheme of self-transcendence hangs: there is to be no interrelation of beings, no blurring of the boundaries between God and world, self and God, self and Other. God's curving in on himself comes full circle, in the continuing creation of discrete, self-reflecting selves in the image of the God they keep creating.

Nonetheless, we are indebted to Niebuhr's interpretation of the sin of pride for the inside light it sheds on the predominant ideal of the separative self. The inapplicability of his concept of sin to woman's situation is symptomatic of the deep sexism he inherits from the tradition. So the separative-dualist theology would remain inhospitable to women, even if the explicitly sexist comments were deleted, the sin of pride relegated to masculine psychology, and a corollary concept of the sin of self-loss for women developed.[64]

Niebuhr's critique of human pride and greed, forged in the prophetic tradition, did lend him the powerful political voice for which he is rightly so admired today. Yet the vulnerability of his renowned "Christian realism" to conservative use bears directly on the present thesis. Harvey Cox recalls the fear in the 1950s that Niebuhr, who once ran for office on a Socialist ticket, was becoming a "cold warrior": "he suggested that although right-wing despotisms were indeed unjust, they did not destroy the roots of an open society, but communism always does."[65] However well Niebuhr turns his critique against capitalist modes of collective egoism, his theory of the discrete individual as the locus of freedom would quite naturally lead to such surprizing outbursts of anticommunist rhetoric, since all forms of socialism, whatever their particular merits or distortions, derive their motive force from the idea of the intrinsically social individual, that is, one whose individuality is realized only in solidarity with the whole. Though Niebuhr accounts well for the collective institutionalization of arrogance and greed, even his doctrine of sin rests upon an individualistic anthropology of the spirit.

Lost and Finding

The politics of individualism is not accidentally sprung from a theology of sheer transcendence. Both express the power plays of patriarchal masculinity, a masculinity that we begin to suspect of a chronic separatism. The virtually uninterrupted maleness of the metaphors of God coalesces with the equally unbroken masculinity of the normative "human" subject. For they are created in each other's image. In the reflexivity of his own acknowledged sin, Man mirrors the immutable transcendence of his God. And so as human transcendence opens into an unlimited sphere of possibilities, it is sealed back into self-objectification, mirroring the self-objectification of God the Father. What we may now call woman's sin of solubility and man's sin of separation are within patriarchal religion touted as virtues—however self-contradictory the system that supports them.

Two self-mirrorings mirroring each other: how can we even see woman—and ourselves as women—in the glare of all this reflexivity? Her narcissism will not take the form of self-reflection but of selflessness; she is objectified less by her ego than by his. The woman gazing into the mirror is often not seeing herself, but an Other defined by his desires. Her identity, dissolved in his, magnifies the male into the successful patriarch. "Women," in the words of Virginia Woolf, "have served all these centuries as looking-glasses possessing the magic and delicious power of reflecting the figure of man at twice its natural size." [66] In other words, woman's support of his ego sustains his god-likeness, which together they amplify into the Infinite, thus assuring an endless return of the same cycle. For after all, the ego of the patriarchal God must be flattered ("glorified," "magnified") like that of the patriarchal male, in order, we suspect, to obscure the possible interdependence of the divine and the mundane—and so of all beings upon each other. If, as I claimed, the separative ego expels the world from himself, projecting the sphere of immanence onto the fleshly woman below him, he simultaneously projects his transcendence onto an otherworldly spirit above him. But for the disturbing promise of its ironies, the apotheosis of patriarchy might have remained secure. That "God" is the supreme embodiment of "sin," that before Him "man" is reduced to the role of woman, eventuates in the death of this God. But if the mirrors have shattered, leaving the androcentric cycle defiantly and desperately confused, the living subjectivity, even mired in its immanence, has not died. Beyond separation or dissolution, there may be a selfhood transcending the cycle of the wandering hero and the waiting woman.

Odysseus was long lost on his journey. Being lost may belong to the reflexive arc. Marguerite Duras distinguishes feminine selflessness from the self-loss of the male, which she likens to the loss of childhood memories: "Just as when you are grown up you forget the child you once were. You no longer know anything about that. Men have gotten lost in the same way, whereas women have never known what they were. So they aren't lost." [67] Finding oneself seems to present no very meaningful aim for a woman. Nor does the solution of the classical religions, summed up in Norman O. Brown's classic pronouncement: "get lost." [68] Woman seems not so much lost as transposed into someone else's kingdom. Its rules do not quite make sense, and she improvises in private. She has treated men like children—"they're just like children" reverberates through the discourse of women as they feed the pretense of the male ego. He finds himself, his forgotten self, his lost child, his first home, in returning to her. She lets him in, never having closed herself to the influent energies of the world. Neither having found nor lost herself in his embrace, but rather not yet having quite become, she has been given over to him as Penelope gives herself over to Ulysses. In her sedentary spinning, we witness the drag of immanence.

Then what does it mean to say that women have never known what they were? Her lack of self-knowledge reflects her under-achieved self. But we may also acknowledge that her lack of self-knowledge protects, perversely, a lack of self-objectification. A refusal to turn herself into an object—at least, an object to herself—accompanies her failure to turn the Other into the object. She does to neither self nor other what the dominant other has done to her and to himself. If she has avoided the reflexive subjectivity, so much the better. Perhaps she bears today some new sense of self, some integrity which obviates the divisive complementarities. As though in allusion to *The Odyssey,* Mary Daly merges and so revolutionizes the activities of Penelope and Odysseus: "This Spinning/Voyaging is multiform expression of integrity." [69] Beyond the dyadic polarizations, not a simple unity but a multifarious variety seems to beckon.

The epic polarization of our creative spontaneities into sedentary feminine spinning (immanence without transcendence) and restless masculine roving (transcendence without immanence) has lost its credibility. Yet woman's new sense of self only now begins to take form and voice. She no longer waits weaving in private. The creation of her self has become a public matter. It seems imperative in a world fearful of a man-made doom that she not emulate the subjective style of the traditional male; the implications of becoming a woman-identified woman ramify far beyond the immediate personalities and projects of individual women. For the various guises of the heroic male ego are wearing thin, deconstructing themselves in a mounting crisis of subjectivity, a crisis at once global, theological and psychological. The center does not hold: the inhabitant essence has been evacuated, decentered. New clothes for the emperor no longer conceal his condition. Certainly we as women do not want to don his cast-off robes. Something unprecedented is needed. The ironies of the old are, indeed, inciting a new subjectivity.

Of Men and Monsters

Gorgons, unruly gorgons,
With eyes that start, with curls that hiss—

Once
I listened to the father's lies,
Took their false advice:
I mustn't look at you, I'd turn to
Stone.

But now I meet your clear furious stare and
It is my natural self that I become.
Yes, as I dare to name your fury
Mine.
Long asleep,
It writhes awake.
  —Barbara Deming, "A Song for Gorgons"

Whatever does not resemble its parents is already in a way a
monster, for in these cases nature has . . . deviated from the
generic type. The first beginning of this deviation is when a
female is produced . . .
  —Aristotle, *Genesis of Animals,* trans.
  Charles Young

I am a monster
And I am proud.
  —Robin Morgan, "Monster"

47

WOMAN ACCORDING TO ARISTOTLE is the beginning of the category of monster. She is a deviant from the generic human type. (No
wonder *man* counts as generic language!) But Aristotle's logic articulates more than simple misogyny or outdated biology. Our understanding of the bond between the general separation of self from
other and the specific objectification of women will be enhanced as
we listen for the mythic undertones of Aristotle's doctrine of the
female as monster.[1] The idea is embedded in his larger understanding of individuals as independent, enduring substances—a view
that would provide the basis for the bulk of Western thought until
at least the eighteenth century. Augustine inherited and developed
the dogma of God as three persons in one substance; Aquinas fine-
tuned Aristotle's substantial individual; and Descartes separated
mental from physical substance. We will return to this history in a
subsequent chapter. Now let us surmise that the separative individuality—variously exhibited in chapter 1 as pagan hero and as
Christian God—is just what Aristotle meant by his "generic type."

The female, according to Aristotle, deviates from this generic
type because she does not resemble her parents: a perplexing doctrine, since parents, one might have thought, come in two sexes.
There are echoes here of Apollo's resounding claim in Aeschylus'
Eumenides that "the parent is he who mounts." The Apollonian
argument only carries the day when underwritten by the Olympian
goddess Athena (who, we recall, functioned as Odysseus' guide). In
an act which stands as archetype of all female co-optation, she offers her own origin as evidence that a father can give birth unaided:
"There is no mother anywhere who gave me birth, / And, but for
marriage, I am always for the male / With all my heart."[2] The Zeus-
born Goddess casts the deciding vote against Orestes' conviction
for matricide and thus in favor of the new Athenian system of paternal supremacy. Aeschylus, according to Robert Graves, "was
writing religious propaganda: Orestes' absolution records the final
triumph of patriarchy."[3] Or as the classicist Jane Harrison put it
earlier, "The outrageous myth of the birth of Athena from the head
of Zeus is but the religious representation, the emphasis, and over-
emphasis, of a patrilinear social structure." With a discreet indignation, Harrison continues: "As, in the old matrilinear days,
Kronos the father was ignored, so, by the turn of the wheel, the
motherhood of the mother is obscured, even denied; but with far

less justice, for the facts of motherhood have been always patent."⁴
Athena becomes "a diagram of motherless birth."

The stage is set for Aristotle's motherless metaphysics of the monstrous female. "Females are weaker and colder in nature, and it is necessary to regard the female status as a deformity, though a natural one."⁵ Thus women gain at least the status of necessary and natural, rather than random and unnatural, monsters. How does Aristotle justify his implicit claim that the mother is no genuine parent while acknowledging (unlike Athena) her necessary function in the procreative act? Here his doctrine of substance insists itself. Substance, *ousia,* meaning that which really is, refers for Aristotle to the concrete individual, defined as "that which is neither predicable of a subject *nor present in* a subject; for instance, the individual man or horse" (my emphasis).⁶ The substantial individual is thus something that cannot be *inside* of (i.e., immanent to) another—something that by its own integrity remains independent, an ontological "outsider," even if literally or physically placed in another subject. Moreover, substance takes the shape of a soul/body compound in the human species. Aristotle means thereby to avoid the soul/body dichotomy (for which he criticized Plato), arguing that only together do soul and body compose the individual. The soul counts as the formal cause, giving form and definition to the substance of the body that it in-forms. Yet this promisingly nondualistic definition serves him as a support for a radical gender dualism.

In Aristotle's biology, soul has particularly to do with "heat"; the reportedly colder female measures many degrees less soulful than the male. Furthermore, the male substance, particularly as sperm, is described as dry, a quality Aristotle associates with the active principle and contrasts with woman and the ovum as wet and cold. So she seems already fishy, akin to sea monsters, indeed to the sea itself.

But the essential linkage of Aristotle's doctrine of procreation and monstrosity with the idea of the substantial individual comes in the following proposition: "While the body is from the female, it is the soul that is from the male, for the soul is the reality [substance] of a particular body."⁷ The male, by imparting the soul to the offspring, endows it with its true being; the female provides only body, the passive matter that waits to be informed by the defining power of the masculine soul, which is active and intellective. Because the soul is the formal cause, the male in fact engenders the form of the human being: in the case of daughters (monsters), the mother has managed to deform the species. Women deviate from the normative human type because they lack "active" intellectual souls, possessing only lower "passive" intelligences. Inadequately informed themselves, lacking the power to contribute form to the offspring of their bodies, women fall short of the full actuality of a substantial individual.

Insubstantial, soluble, our humanness retreats to the margins. Women, lacking real ontological independence, remain exceptions to the norm. If true and separate substance cannot be "present in a subject," in another, women, we may infer, are beings who *are* in others. Women are in others as others are in us.

Monster

A monster is defined as "a fabulous being compounded of elements from various human or animal forms." [9] Monsters mix the media of nature. Furthermore, any plant, fetus, or object, indeed any deformity or enormity, can be called a monster. Monsters, "deviating from the norm in appearance or structure," (*American Heritage Dictionary*), count as deformed, not conforming to the "nature" of any species. No wonder monsters appear dangerously deranged to the Western mind, disarranging and rearranging in their own complexity the components of any settled "nature." Let us note the original meaning of the term monster: *monstrum* in Latin is a "portent," and the verb *monstrare* means "to show" (as in "de-monstrate"), while *monere* of the same root means "to warn." What then do the ancient monsters portend for our present purposes?

Sirens, sea serpents, and sphinxes, dragons, dwarves and giants, harpies and horrors of every imaginable combination,—a world of monsters clamors for our attention. Let us call upon a classical Greek monster. Her story will lead us beyond Greek shores to an oceanic school of monsters whose tales merge with those of all women of the Western world. Let us recall Medusa: she whose name comes from the word for ruler (*medon*), who dwelt with her two sisters on an island "beyond famous Ocean, in the most remote quarter night-ward," [10] granddaughter of the goddess Earth. We know her as the hideous gray-skinned hag with the head of writhing snakes. To look at her was to turn to stone.

Yet originally, we read, she and her sister Gorgons were gorgeous. Ovid recounts that "of all the beauties she possessed, none was more striking than her lovely hair. . . . But, so they say, the lord of the sea robbed her of her virginity in the temple of Athena. Zeus's daughter turned her back, hiding her modest face behind her aegis: and to punish the Gorgon for her deed, she changed her hair into revolting snakes." [11] Virginal Athena punished the raped maiden rather than the rapist Poseidon, and the poet displays no indignation. Medusa's punishing deformity represents therefore an inflicted monstrosity, a deformation. The symptom of her dangerous affliction is the hairlike growth of literally petrifying serpents. If as James Hillman says, "myth lives vividly in our symptoms," [12] it would seem equally true that when it comes to monsters, symptoms live vividly in our myths. He suggests elsewhere that "we owe our symptoms an immense debt": [13] a thesis worthy of consideration as we discern to whom the symptom and thus the debt truly belongs.

As the myth unfolds, it turns out (as do indeed all classic monster tales) to be not Medusa's story at all, but the story of the hero. By the time the tale takes written shape, the monster seems to exist only for the glory of the warrior who slaughters her. Indeed, without monsters to kill, the hero would fail to instantiate his generic type; he depends upon his defeat of her deformity to achieve heroic form. Perseus, whose name means destroyer, conceived during Zeus's visit to Danaë in the guise of a shower of gold, is the shining hero who vanquishes the Medusa. Heroes typically have miraculous births as sons of god—the divine father, in union with a mortal virgin. Under the tutelage of none other than Athena (a patroness of many heroes) Perseus arrives at the Gorgons' island with a mirror-bright shield and a strategy, both conferred by his goddess. "Everywhere," as Ovid tells it, "all through the fields and along the roadways he saw statues of men and beasts, whom the sight of the Gorgon had changed from their true selves into stone." But he looked not at her, but at her mirrored image on the polished bronze. "While she and her snakes were wrapped in deep slumber, he severed her head from her shoulders. The fleet-winged Pegasus and his brother were born then, children of the Gorgon's blood." [14] Perseus snatched her head, stuffed it in a magic wallet and fled. Thus was the world saved from her disease. But the symptom itself persists:

the severed head retained the power of petrification, a formidable weapon in the hands of Perseus until he offered it to Athena. "To this day, in order to terrify her enemies and numb them with fear, the goddess wears as a breastplate the snakes that were her own creation."

Athena combines the images of monster and hero: she wears the *snakes* upon her own *armor*. As patron goddess of the hero Perseus, she functions as soul guide for his journey of destruction, even guiding his arm, according to one account, as he decapitates Medusa. As virgin, born with armor and war cry from Zeus's head, Athena epitomizes the possibilities of a higher, that is, a purely male-identified, femininity within the rule of the father god. She is the warrior-intellectual, doubly stripped of female sexuality: there is no mother with whom she might identify and so identify herself as woman. No embarrassing aromas of maternity emanate from her image. More thoroughly even than the Virgin Mary, she is cleansed of sexuality. And like the birth of Eve from Adam's rib, her birth fulfills the fantasy of womb envy, legitimating male dominance by glorifying paternity. As divine daddy's girl, Athena becomes the soul sister of heroes, born of the archetype of the spiritual father. She is a feminine principle inhabiting the patriarchal psyche and its society. But why does the sight of the Gorgon so threaten Athena and her heroes? What are they afraid to see? And how can we account for this anima figure's specific animosity for Medusa? After all, Medusa's monstrosity was Athena's own creation. There is a complex mechanism of displacement at work as Athena reportedly causes, kills and then wears as her own the snakes that are the primary symptom of the Medusa syndrome.

Serpentine Sisterhood

Long before its descent into the demonic and the monstrous, the serpent wound its way through the symbolisms of the Near and Middle East, Crete and Mycenaean Greece, as an integral aspect of the worship of a female deity. Sometimes the snake was her consort, but more frequently her manifestation. The familiar Cretan figurines of goddesses or priestesses with snakes coiled about their arms or bodies, the Egyptian Cobra Goddess Ua Zit, the serpent-entwined staff of Ishtar, the python associated with the oracular priestess, the Pythia of Delphi, point to the serpent's sacred connection with the prepatriarchal imagery of the goddess. The common contemporary designation of the serpent as a phallic symbol cooperating with orgiastic priestesses in a "fertility cult" misses the mark. According to Merlin Stone, "it appears to have been primarily revered as a female in the Near and Middle East and generally linked to wisdom and prophetic counsel rather than fertility and growth as is so often suggested." [15] Yet its oracles and visions, while nonreducible to biological process, do express profound attunement to the cycles of nature. The impressive ability of the serpent to renew itself by sloughing its skin situates its symbolic wisdom in the mysteries of death and rebirth. [16]

The serpent power predates the myth systems of patriarchy: Neolithic art from the eighth millenium B.C.E. onward undulates with images of the cosmic serpent, intertwined with waves and female bodies, and depicting the energy of perpetual creation. [17] Thus Joseph Campbell finds in its devaluation and demonization an image of the fall of all the "demons that formerly had symbolized the force of the cosmic order itself, the dark mystery of time, which licks up hero deeds like dust: the force of the never-dying serpent, sloughing lives like skins." [18] Yet its darkness exists in rhythmic counterpoise to its light, as Campbell acknowledges when he symbolizes with the serpent image the entire prepatriarchal world:

In the older mother myths and rites the light and darker aspects of the mixed thing that is life had been honored equally and together, whereas in the later, male-oriented, patriarchal myths, all that is good and noble was attributed to the new, heroic master gods, leaving to the native nature powers the character only of darkness—to which, also, a negative moral judgment was now added. For, as a great body of evidence shows, the social as well as mythic orders of the two contrasting ways of life were opposed. [19]

The biblical figure of Eve, "Mother of All the Living," and her association with her serpent colleague, will shortly bring home to us through the long Christian history of her own degradation the continuing fate of the serpent goddess.

Of the goddess Athena, we discover that her power far predates that of the patriarchal city-state whose inspirational emblem she became. She belongs originally to the earlier culture of the pre-Hellenic peoples, of which only distorted vestiges, lame or monstrous, seep through the symbolic overlay of the triumphant, Zeus-worshiping, Achaean and Dorian invaders. According to Stone, the vestigial derivatives of the Egyptian and Cretan Serpent Goddess in Greece were nowhere more evident than in the figure of Athena. "Her serpent continually appeared in legends, drawings and sculptures. In some statues it peered out from beneath Her great bronze shield or stood by Her side." [20] A special building stood on the Acropolis beside her temple, the Erechtheum, to house her snake. "But the snake of the Greek Goddess of Wisdom, who was revered on the majestic heights of the Athenian Acropolis, was not a creation of the classical Greek period. Despite the Indo-European Greek legend that suggests Athena was born from the head of Zeus, the worship of the Goddess had arrived on the Acropolis long before—with the Cretan Goddess of the Mycenaean settlements." [21] In this perspective the serpents on her aegis commemorate the old serpentine power: the myth of their donation by Perseus begins to show itself as a late attempt to explain away the lingering reminders of the overthrown order. For Athena, alone among the goddesses of the classical pantheon, retained the old association—and yet paradoxically, perhaps as a defensive mechanism controlling the old power, functioned as patron anima for Athenian culture. Similarly, the story of her birth from Zeus's head appears, as Jane Harrison put it over half a century ago, "a desperate theological expedient to rid her of her matriarchal conditions." [22]

Campbell, upon whom Stone and many feminist theorists rely, subsumes all religious and cultural history under this dramatic dialectic of two world orders, that of the original mother myths and that of the conquering heroes with their supreme father. He is, however, often criticized, with some justification, for the oversimplification and ahistoricism of his Jung-derived "monomyth." Classicist Gilbert Murray's interpretation of pre-Olympian Greece better typifies the mainstream interpretation of the serpent-symbol: speaking of the original role of the "sacred breasts," he refers to "the old superhuman snake, who reappears so ubiquitously throughout Greece, the regular symbol of the underworld powers, especially the hero or dead ancestor." [23] While Murray agrees that the snake "is a type of new birth because he throws off his old skin and renews himself," "he" is made a mere primitive antetype of the masculine hero. The epoch itself is described with condescension: of its oracles, Murray tells us that "like most manifestations of early religion, they throve upon human terror: the more blind the terror, the stronger became their hold. In such an atmosphere the lowest and most beastlike elements of humanity tended to come to the front in drowning the voice of criticism and of civilization, that is, of reason and of mercy." [24] This is history from the vantage point of the victor: what had provoked awe in the older religion is now seen as the ignorant device of manipulative terror, to be rooted out by Olympian and other "sons of light," for whom the serpent's underworld will eventually appear as hell.

Stone's and Campbell's alternative perspective, with its challenge to the still-dominant heroes and its broad sense of symbolic interconnection, remains irreplaceable. We begin to see the Western transmogrification of the snake into Satan as a central symptom of the demonizing of all nonpatriarchal powers.

The Matrimonstrous Displacement

The serpentine symptom, which returns manifold to Athena with Perseus' gift of Medusa's head, was originally Athena's own symbol. What diagnosis might account for it? In the earliest account of Athena's birth from Zeus's head, Hesiod divulges a fact of critical significance: contrary to Athena's classical self-understanding, she does indeed have a mother. After the defeat of the race of Titans, children of the goddess Earth and previous inhabitants of heaven, the order of Zeus rises to its ascendancy. We may presume that the violence of supersession mirrors theologically the overthrow of the pre-Indo-European, goddess-venerating peoples. But the lingering matrifocal presence, never so cleanly extirpated by the new Greek order as by Hebrew monotheism, had to be assimilated. Therefore Zeus's first act after the conquest of the monster Typhoeus (the Greek mother goddess's progeny and last resort in the face of the final defeat of her cosmos) is telling. He seduces, or rapes (according to Pindar), Metis, the Titan goddess of wisdom. In Hesiod's account, his "conquest" results in her pregnancy.

But when now at length she was about to give birth to
Athena, gleaming-eyed goddess, then it was that having by

deceit beguiled her mind with flattering words, he placed her within his own belly. . . . For of her it was fated that wise children should be born: first the glancing-eyed Tritronian maiden, having equal might and prudent counsel with her sire.[26]

Metis then is the mother of Athena. Zeus clearly manages to usurp—indeed, to assimilate orally into himself—Wisdom by swallowing and holding her captive in his belly. Here we find the locus classicus of "the feminine within" or the "gut feeling"![27] Thus he means to prevent the birth of her powerful and wise daughter Athena and so to break the old chain of female wisdom. When she is born, after his splitting headache, it is truly a matter of re-birth: not the rebirth from the dead skins of the outgrown past as ritualized in the matrifocal serpent power, but rebirth through the father by which the female heritage of the daughter is obliterated.[28] (As Campbell points out, this is a case of Freudian "displacement upward," where creativity is transferred from penis or womb to head.) Athena herself remembers no mother.

The repression that sustains Athena's forgotten origin renders her the perfect patriarchal maiden, the dutiful daughter and mouthpiece of the father. Yet a nagging anxiety adheres to her status, for after all, the beginning of the deviation that makes a *monster* is simply to be a female. Her denial of her mother, echoed philosophically in Aristotle's assumption that the "parent" is male, cannot undo the fact of her gender. (This is a problem that many Christian virgins, aspiring to the spiritual masculinity that sainthood represented, would later face.) The anxiety produced by her repressive amnesia seems to account for the projection of her own snake symptom—her idiosyncratic affiliation with the old serpentine power—onto a shadow figure Medusa. Thus she doubly displaces her female origins: positively from the mother to the father, and negatively from the female as self to the female as Other. Medusa functions as a classic Jungian shadow for her on three counts: because Athena has created Medusa's monstrosity by her own irrational anger, because Medusa's punishment is completely incommensurate with the deed, and because Medusa is a figure of the same sex and life stage as Athena.

And who is this Medusa? Her two sisters complete the old triune form of the prepatriarchal Goddess, a triune form that Athena herself had earlier assumed (associated with the three phases of the moon and the three stages of woman's life as maiden, mother and crone). But most telling of all, the name Medusa, a feminine form for *ruler,* stems from the same Sanskrit root *medha* meaning "wisdom," from which comes the Greek *metis,* translated "prudent counsel." The repressed Mother and the shadowy Other merge at the roots. Metis and Medusa are one. It follows that the reborn Athena has accomplished through her heroic accomplice Perseus a secret matricide. Rather than confronting Medusa as her mother, rather than facing the struggle to claim her own woman power, she simply sends her heroic animus figure out to slaughter the monster. If Athena is to function as the ultimate personification of *patriarchal* wisdom, an epiphenomenon of Zeus in whose culture wisdom remains a male prerogative, she must deny any femaleness not defined and sanctioned by the male. But does such unsanctioned femaleness transmit itself still through our bonds to mothers? We know how troubled, overstressed and ambivalent these bonds inevitably become within the constrictions of the patriarchal family unit. Indeed, we know our mothers very often as the most formidable Athena figures. In the next chapter this ambivalence, as analyzed by theorists such as Dinnerstein and Chodorow, will be explored.

The *monstrum* of Athena's denial portends the psychological practice of all women who will function successfully within their particular patriarchal profession. Many of us have experienced our mother, or rather her imago (her introject), within us as raging, petrifying monsters who threaten to paralyze us in our worldly adventures. Moreover, "education requires the development of Athena qualities," as Jungian analyst Jean Bolen suggests, "be it for business, academy, or church." Indeed, Western education has always been Athenian. Bolen points to Phyllis Schlafly's brilliant and successful opposition to the ERA as an extreme example of Athena's hostility toward other women: "Schlafly, whose biographer called her The Sweetheart of the Silent Majority, is a contemporary Athena in the role of an archetypal father's daughter, defending patriarchal values." [29]

Yet even among feminists we know Athena—in our sudden animosities toward the maternal, in the disappointing divisions in the woman's movement, in our occasional aggression toward ourselves *as* woman. When she fails to shape our very selves, she may lurk defensively, along with the Medusa-mother, in our shadows.

Athenian productivity derives from a mind detached from its body. Of course there is no indication that Metis/Medusa's "prudent counsel" ever centered on sexual processes. But perhaps it would teach us with Adrienne Rich "to think through the body." [29] Medusa's severed head takes on new meaning. The heroic culture, known for its dissemination of dichotomies, requires perpetual decapitations. It specializes in the business of separating heads from bodies, especially when it confronts women of power. It is not clear that creative selfhood can survive the act of "dichotomy"—literally, "cutting in two."

As Athena represents the way of the woman whose liberation consists in emulation of the male, she is "born" wearing armor. Beyond its affinities to the apparel of contemporary success (whether the female executive suit or the hard ruffles of "ladylikeness"), armor protects the illusion of the separate self. It symbolizes our status as objects. Defending against all permeability—doubly denied by the virginity of this goddess—armor symbolizes the artificially rigid boundaries the warrior wears between him(her)self and the Other, the opposite, the opponent, the world over and against the self. Yet paradoxically the Schlafly-style woman fights to enforce "femininity," that is, the soluble selfhood in women that is the necessary support system for men. Of course, herself male-identified, the Schlafly-woman resembles traditional females only in a studied persona of lady-likeness. She knows, like Athena, that patriarchal society can afford, indeed needs, the rare exception like herself who eschews the female role in order to campaign for the Fathers full time.

The monstrous rage expressed in the image of the Gorgon's head, the primal fury of a power suppressed and repressed, cut off from our own bodies and minds, can indeed be hung on the defensive shield of the armored woman, turned often against other women, just as often against men, and usually against ourselves. Such a second-order, decapitated rage makes scapegoats of those closest to us, rather than directing itself at the larger situations of patriarchal injustice.[30] But the rage depicted on the Gorgoneion-mask has deeper wellsprings, shared with the ancient Furies. These Furies, who embody the insatiable resentment of the superceded Mothers, haunt the patriarchal order, becoming in their suppression regressive and vengeful, defined by opposition.

Robert Graves suggests that the Hellenic Furies are a vestigial form of the Triple Goddess, whose "priestesses will have worn menacing Gorgon masks to frighten away profane visitors."[31] While this explanation rather reductively derives an entire myth from a relic, it does suggest a more positive and protective role for the Gorgon's rage. However, Graves presupposes (as do most mythographers, notably Eliade) a sharp division between the sacred and the profane. Such a bifurcation of experience seems to typify not so much the culture of the archaic Goddess, but the culture that opposed spirit to body, life to death, male to female. Once operating within the parameters of such dualisms, the vestigial forms of Goddess reverence might well have required such a prophylactic Gorgoneion. But the fearful mask suggests another use (as do gargoyles, halloween pumpkins and all manner of protective demon-masks): not to "frighten away," but to make visible and forefront fear itself—to "face" fear. Only thus is the sacred-and-profane confrontation with Deming's "natural self" of women, and surely of all persons, possible.

Erich Neumann makes the classic archetypal case for the Gorgon figure as the "Terrible Mother," the eternal dark side of the "Great Round" or "Archetypal Feminine" who (in men and women) threatens to destroy the ego consciousness. "The petrifying gaze of Medusa belongs to the province of the terrible Great Goddess, for to be rigid is to be dead. This effect of the terrible stands in opposition to the mobility of the life-stream . . . ; it is a psychic expression for petrifaction and sclerosis. The Gorgon is the counterpart of the life-womb; she is the womb of death."[32] Neumann is right to recognize in the Medusa a transpersonal mother symbol and well captures her role within the Olympian environment. But his account is ahistorical; he himself petrifies Medusa, freezing her into a static terror, the image of some intrinsic feminine darkness for which there is no comparable masculine analogue (the "terrible" or "bad" father images seem by contrast to lack any terrifying presence). Her link with death was not always deadly.

Woodward, in *Perseus: A Study in Greek Art and Legend,* offers a historically and culturally more enlightening account of Medusa's background. Referring to the Gorgon image on a sixth-century temple of Artemis, the author comments:

It may seem odd that this uncouth, grimacing figure should be given the place of honor on the temple pediment, but the idea behind it takes us back to a time long before these Gorgon-figures were identified with the creatures of the Perseus legend. With her attendant lions, she embodies the great Nature Spirit of primitive belief, who appears in early Asiatic and Ionian works of art as a goddess, with birds, lions, or snakes heraldically set on either side of her.[33]

If the Gorgon energy originally expresses a "Nature Spirit"—the Great Goddess herself—it is only in the Perseus-Athena constellation that Medusa becomes the Terrible Mother. Her power is originally life-giving and generative—a "womb of death" perhaps only when it comes to the birth of the patriarchal hero? She need no longer express the static archetype of the Terrible Mother—as though the rage of the feminine is not a response to its oppression and repression, but an eternal and inevitable expression of its essence.[34] "The Gorgon," writes Emily Culpepper, "has much vital, literally life-saving information to teach women about anger, rage, power and the release of the determined aggressiveness sometimes needed for survival."[35] The Gorgon in her very darkness inspires self-disclosure, as May Sarton's "The Muse as Medusa" suggests:

I turn my face around! It is my face.
That frozen rage is what I must explore—
Oh secret, self-enclosed, and ravaged place!
This is the gift I thank Medusa for.[36]

Perseus the Ego

As Athena shares after all in the ancient Goddess power of her forgotten mother Metis/Medusa, the monstrosity with which she endows Medusa seems symptomatic of Athena's own repression: Athena's dread shadow of her own mother-identified past, projected by her onto the Gorgon. But Athena, herself once a mode of the Great Goddess, actually can be seen as serving, in the guise of anima figure for patriarchal Athens, as a symptom of its heroes. She is not living there her own subjective truth (i.e., the subjectivity of real Athenian women). To love Athena well—and how many of us have not cherished this powerful image of intellect and independence—is to connect with her deeper past, her truer self. However graciously Perseus attributes inspiration, guidance and protection to his patron goddess (itself a telltale title, as *patronus* derives from "father"), to him accrues the real agency and glory in Medusa's slaughter. May we surmise that in some sense the monstrosity of the monster results from the state of being that Perseus embodies? To achieve self-definition as a hero, he treats the archaic serpentine power as monstrous. He must eradicate its primary symptom, the Gorgon. Graves suggests that the destruction of the Gorgon means, historically, that "the Hellenes overran the goddess' chief shrines." Analyzing Perseus' feat and the simultaneous birth of Pegasus in conjunction with Bellerophon's use of the winged horse to kill another monster, the Chimera, Graves claims that "both feats record the usurpation by Hellenic invaders of the Moon-goddess's powers, and are unified in an archaic Boetian vase-painting of a Gorgon-headed mare. This mare is the Moon-goddess, whose calendar-symbol was the Chimaera; and the Gorgon-head is a prophylactic mask, worn by her priestesses to scare away the uninitiated, which the Hellenes stripped from them." [37] To the initiated, that is, those taking the wisdom of the goddess as their own starting point, the serpent mask would not, as I suggested above, have evoked a sense of terror and alienation but of mystery and invitation. Massive historical patterns more than timeless truths are summarized by this and kindred tales:

There occurred in the early thirteenth century B.C. an actual historic rupture, a sort of sociological trauma, which has been registered in this myth, much as what Freud terms the latent content of a neurosis is registered in the manifest content of a dream: Registered yet hidden, registered in the unconscious yet unknown or misconstrued by the conscious mind. [38]

The rupture, however unclear its historicity remains, symbolizes the transition of world orders. An older order of the goddess seeps into the myths of the hero, producing in the dominant masculine world "an essential duplicity, the consequences of which cannot be disregarded or suppressed." [39] A pervasive fearfulness, a sense of threat, motivates the heroic psyche, resembling what existentialism univer-

salizes as *angst*. Converting this ontological anxiety into particularized fears—such as fear of this monster—affords momentary
relief by triumph over a specific cause.

Perhaps not only on the surface is the hero, rather than Athena,
the true matricide. For he constructs his self-identity by this violent
defeat of the values and claims of the female power. Speaking of the
"paternal principle," Jung claims that "its first creative act of liberation is matricide." [40] This axiom, which we will analyze in the
next chapter, bears a peculiar resemblance to de Beauvoir's identification of creative subjectivity with warrior activity. While Jungians usually assume that such a violation of "the Mother" was necessary for the development of "ego-consciousness," they generally
recognize (quite apart from feminist concern) that too high a price
has been paid for the hero's own good. Thus Campbell offers an
insightful account of the psychology of Perseus' relation to Mother
Medusa:

Mother Nature, Mother Eve, Mother Mistress-of-the-World
is there to be dealt with all the time, and the more sternly
she is cut down, the more frightening will her Gorgoneum
be. This may cause her matricidal son to achieve a lot of ex-
tremely spectacular escape work; but, oh, my! What a Sheol
he will know—and yet not know—within, where his para-
dise should have been! [41]

Let us say it this way: it is by "killing" the monster that the male
establishes her monstrosity and his heroism. But as monster she is
his symptom, *his* dread and *his* monstrosity. Yet she is also symbol
of the lost selfhood of which her one time power was an outer sign.

Neumann also notes the importance of Perseus' flight: "The main
feature is not, as one might think, the killing of the Gorgon, but the
hero's headlong flight from the pursuing sisters." [42] Neumann shows
how "the hero's flight and escape . . . testify very clearly to the overpowering character of the Great Mother." [43] No doubt. Is not all
separation escape? But when Neumann adds that "he is barely man
enough to kill her," one suspects a quite different Jungianism from
Campbell's. Indeed, Neumann selects the story of Perseus as the
epitomizing "paradigm of the hero myth," and so of the historical
and individual development of ego consciousness: *"through the
masculinization of consciousness and emancipation of ego-*

consciousness the ego becomes the 'hero' " (my emphasis). In both men and women this is emancipation from the mother, and in both, the masculine hero symbolizes consciousness: "Consciousness, as such, is masculine even in women, just as the unconscious is feminine in men."[44]

Deferring psychological comment on this implication of analytic psychology, we may note how neatly Neumann's gender contortions illustrate de Beauvoir's thesis that masculinity has been identified with humanity. Consciousness itself is taken to be "masculine," and—this is crucial for my thesis—masculine in the sense of heroic, matricidal and ego-centered. Neumann's own androcentrism should astonish us far less than the accuracy with which it fits the Western experience of selfhood. Furthermore, it dresses in twentieth-century psychosymbolic clothing Aristotle's biological postulates on the male as active intelligence and the female as monster. Neumann's interpretation—which captures the ideology of the myth—presents the warrior, soaring away on Pegasus, as the human norm: "the hero Perseus espouses the spiritual side, he is the winged one, and the gods of the spirit [Athena and Hermes] are his allies in the fight with the unconscious."[45] In Perseus we revisit the spirituality of pure transcendence to see more clearly revealed than ever the intrinsic belligerence, escapism and egocentricity of the androcentric paradigm.

Regarding the strict reflexivity of the androcentric self, we note in the Perseus myth the importance of the mirror-shield. A perfect representation of the reflecting ego, it is at once defensive and aggressive, at once opaque and mirroring, at once reflected and unable to *look*. Neumann's interpretation of the image is interesting: "he would not be strong enough to gaze directly upon the petrifying face of the uroborus, the Great Round of unconsciousness, so he raises its image to consciousness and kills it 'by reflection.' "[46] This sounds like a fine description of the use of the intellect in patriarchal thinking—killing "by reflection" what one is too cowardly to face.

Philip Slater, in *The Glory of Hera*, offers an interesting response to both Perseus and Neumann, set in his monumental psychoanalytic exposé of the misogynist narcissism of Athenian Greek culture. He notes the farcical character of the story in which Perseus has "two gods aiding him, a superfluity of magic implements, a sleeping enemy at whom he cannot even look, and a goddess guiding his hand to actually commit the act. Has there ever been so helpless and dependent a hero?"[47] This irony supports our earlier suspicion that in Perseus' hostile defiance, the separative ego is hiding from himself the impossibility of his own autonomy. From his more Freudian perspective, Slater supports Neumann's contention that Medusa symbolizes the mother. As evidence, Slater cites Aeschylus, who has the chorus inspire Orestes to slay his mother by exhorting him to "hold in thy breast such heart as Perseus had."[48] But he expresses skepticism toward Neumann's discovery of "soaring creative forces" in Perseus. Slater finds Perseus "a singularly unattractive hero," with "no special virtues or capabilities save the ability to do as he is told and to utilize in an obvious way the implements he is given. He is a phallic nine-year-old's hero par excellence." As to the symbolization of consciousness: "In the first place, Perseus' act of 'raising the image to consciousness' is rather too half-hearted to serve as a prototype of truth-seeking confrontation. Consciousness would be represented by looking *directly* at the object."[49] Unfortunately, Slater does not link the prophylactic mirror to phallic narcissism. We might say that Perseus looks in the mirror and indeed does not see his ego image—this narcissism yields no true self-knowledge. The mythic mirror however presents him with that Medusa-reality (in self or other) that he ought to face. Instead he strikes out with phallic aggression, *fearful* in both senses of the word. Slater makes the image serve brilliantly to criticize Neumannian Jungianism:

I am struck with the fact that it is precisely this contentment with mirror images which limits the utility of Jungian theories. . . . Any influence by real family or personal experiences, or real social structures, must be denied, so that the myth can preserve some of its mysterious quality. . . . The 'archetype' is the Athena's shield of Jungian analysis.[50]

We will have reason to return to this ground of dispute between Jungian and Freudian approaches. Slater's point aids in the needed deconstruction of the archetypal method of eternalizing patriarchal images. Freezing archetypes into immutability only produces a psychological version of the theological eternity supporting an endless cycle of narcissistic self-enclosure. However, Slater's own analysis, "that the Medusa head *is* a symbol of maternal genitalia,"[51] seems sometimes so literal as to send one running back again in search of

64

that "mysterious quality." Need we trade mystery for honesty? Mystery is not mystification. The irreducibility of the mythic metaphor is shown precisely in its ability at once to glorify and undermine the hero; even in their patriarchal captivity, myths cannot conceal the larger story.

We are trying to situate the mythic symptom back where it belongs, in the psychology of the hero. There it might offer its oracle, its *monstrum*, most effectively. Neumann is correct when he claims that "the most striking feature in the figure of Athena is the defeat of the old mother goddess by the new, feminine, spiritual principle." [52] Athena as accomplice to matricide is no more herself than are any women in her guise. Enacting the co-optation we feared in chapter 1—the seduction by institutional favors—she stands far from her own authenticity. She, along with her sister-mother Medusa, is a patriarchal objectification, a by-product. But unlike Medusa, who is not co-opted, Athena offers a support system, the dependent upon whom the Fathers can depend. Though she still has "all the characteristics of the Great Cretan goddess . . . the primordial power of the female has been subdued by her; she now wears the Gorgon's head as a trophy upon her shield." [53] Neumann lauds where we deplore; yet our object is not to restore the primordial goddess but to emancipate ourselves from the effects of a culture based on emancipation from her. Getting free of the onus of feminine monstrosity cannot mean for us more monster-slaying. It means returning the symptomatic attribute of deformity to the culture hero who produced it, while reclaiming the Medusa-power for the woman-identified.

It is interesting to learn that the heroic ego represses and opposes not only the symptom of the mother-monster, but *any* symptom whatsoever. At least this is the claim of James Hillman, whose "archetypal psychology" (as distinguished from "analytic") remains remarkably free of Jungian dogmatism. "For our concern is with the symptom, that thing so foreign to the ego, that thing which ends the rule of the hero—who, as Emerson said, is he who is immovably centered." [54] "Immovably centered," we might add, because reflected in the image of an impassionable transcendence—which Perseus in relation to his father, Zeus, only begins to incarnate. Hillman himself systematically links the heroic mythology—even in its polytheistic setting—with "monotheistic psychology," which not only the Judeo-Christian traditions but also Campbell's monomyth exemplify. That which fixates on its own oneness, its immutable center, cannot tolerate the plurality of images within itself. As they try to bear their messages, the heroic ego cannot look, cannot hear. So they become (or already were?) his symptoms, pressed down into the unconscious, which Hillman prefers to name the Underworld.[55] As the hero is severed from the realm of dreams, of death, of the hosts of images he cannot control, he will not tolerate the underworld messengers, the Medusas, and works all the more violently to repress them. Though part of "his" personality, the "symptom" will not bow to his rule.

Unlike Neumann and other mainstream Jungians, Hillman does not sanction the heroic mode—or any single image—as necessary to the "development of consciousness" in individuals or in culture. He recognizes in Western ego consciousness the prime enemy of the "soul-making" he advocates. "Soul," he says, "refers to the *deepening* of events into experiences";[56] "the significance soul makes possible, whether in love or religious concern, derives from its special *relation with death*."[57] We shall see that the heroic ego's aversion to the underworld, indeed to all depth, is inseparably linked to his monster-killing compulsions. Our guess that the swashbuckling male hero inspires by his power drive the entire subjectivity of the One against the Many, of the self-identical, other-opposing dualist, receives notable support from Hillman's "psychologizing." "For what sort of mind working with what sort of issue is the ideology of oppositionalism so useful?" he asks (in the context of his later critique of the Jungian dogma of opposites). "The apparent answer is *the heroic ego who divides so he can conquer.* Antithetical thinking, found by Alfred Adler to be a neurotic habit of mind, belongs to the will to power" (my emphasis).[58] We may infer that the heroic neurosis of patriarchal culture, hacking away at its own symptomatic monstrosities, is self-divided precisely in its immovable egocentricity—always two in its oneness, and so not surprisingly self-reflected. Hillman adds an inadvertent twist to the mirror image: "If our civilization suffers from *hybris,* from ego inflation and *superbia,* psychology has done its part. It has been looking at soul in the ego's mirror, never seeing psyche, always seeing man."[59] This critique of humanism—and perhaps of Perseus' shield—holds good for Freudian as well as Jungian trends. How male is this "man"? While Hillman is perhaps no feminist, he early advocates anima as culture's lost soul, not as mere complement to masculinity. In a way that prefigures *Revisioning Psychology,* his critique of the heroic consciousness, Hillman's essay "On Psychological Femininity" in *The Myth of Analysis* richly documents the history of biological, medical and psychological woman hating. The book concludes: "It is so difficult to imagine, to conceive, to experience consciousness apart from its old identifications, its structural bedrock of misogyny, that we can hardly even intuit what this bisexual God might hold in store for the regeneration of psychic life." [60] Whether or not we would now be intuiting a "bisexual God" (whom he himself does not long pursue), Hillman's work helps expose this misogynist bedrock underlying the basic Western sense of self-consciousness.

Memories and Monoliths

The serpentine growth shows itself thus to be a metasymptom, symbolic of the unconscious teleology of any symptom in its attempt to remind the anxiously heroic ego of what it has denied. Does it perhaps disallow his triumphant separatism? Hack as he might at the internal connections between life and death, present and past, head and body, male and female, self and other, god and cosmos, the immanence of the world abides. The monster returns, and reminds. Remonstratively, does she come to commemorate repressed connections or the repression of connection itself? The word *monster* stems from that root, *mens,* out of which springs the entire family of memory words: to remember, to remind, *anamnesis,* to commemorate. The portentous images of mythic monsters disclose as irresistibly as dreams the displaced and denied possibilities of a nonpatriarchal and nondualistic self. And as we learn from Edward Casey's *Remembering: A Phenomenological Study* "commemoration is ineluctably a matter of participation, and in this very capacity it calls upon us not as separate beings but as always already intertwined." [61] Myth, with its ritual enactments, is always a matter of commemoration and so of coparticipation. But if we wish no longer to participate in the heroic myth, which almost every institution in our civilization ritually reenacts daily, then we can only join in what the monster commemorates by commemorating the monster. We can thus subvert the hero myth without ever forgetting how irrascibly it persists among us.

To participate, to take part in one another, recalls the forgotten reality of an influent self: a self flowing into the others, feeling the others flow into self. For in our reciprocal influencing, we commemorate one another. Like the serpents wound about the Hermetic caduceus, which itself commemorates the older staff of Ishtar, the image of relational intertwining works healingly upon the neurosis of the separative ego. Unlike an Aristotelian substance, such a being is always immanent in others. Lacking an immovable center, its oneness is full of the many. Yet while giving the lie to sheer separation, participation need not deny the difference of self and other. As later chapters will tell, difference is not the same as separation. True individuals can intertwine best. Serpentine fluidity is not aqueous solubility, but a well-defined rhythm of inner and outer interactions.

The copulative vipers of the caduceus eventually came to serve the god of healing, Asclepios. He is said to have obtained with Athena's aid the blood from Medusa's veins, "both from her left side and from her right. With the former he slays, but with the latter he cures and brings back to life." [62] To de-monstrate Medusa: in the blood of the goddess, even extracted and abstracted from her body, the powers of birth and death are "always already intertwined," undulating in rhythms of becoming and perishing, of intimacy and introversion, which woman's own body ritually commemorates in the lunar ebb and flow of the menstrual tide. An alternative mythos begins to arise: the forgotten and remembered goddess is becoming neither more nor less than a contemporary metaphor for—among other things—the empowerment of a postpatriarchal, participative personality.

By these rhythms, remembered or not, individuals participate in each other. But according to Aristotle, to be an individual is precisely not to participate in other individuals; thus such intertwining counts as insubstantial, "accidental" and passive. The serpentine powers of regeneration can seem only monstrous to the "immovably centered" hero. The Perseus ego imitates—and creates—Aristotle's Unmoved Mover. But if the heroic ego already seeks immovability—precisely in his adventurous mobility—why is Medusa's gaze lethal to him? The petrifying effect of the goddess's visage upon the hero would capture him in his own desire: she would only return to him the truth of his own unmoving immortality. Her gaze simply realizes for him his self-image, "a superman image of a God-man" as Hillman analyzes it, "who dominates our ego's fantasies of itself as a hero in marble without hurt or blemish, carved of one solid piece, perpetually balanced upon its center of gravity." [63] The irony of the hero, who in his Odyssean adventures seeks a static immortality, seems to require the she-monster as a scapegoat for his own self-contradiction. Monsters, recall, are beings composed of Others; they are intrinsically composite individuals; the hero, by contrast, sees himself as "of a piece," *monolithos* (single stone) and ultimately *a-tomos* (indivisible). Hereupon rests the metaphysical doctrine of the simplicity of substance, which would later come to define the Christian God.

Perseus' deed seems to free him from any self-knowledge the Gorgon might have to offer; however, in his hands the head of serpent locks becomes the deadliest of weapons, turning opponents and bystanders en masse into rocks. This act suggests the heroic objectification of the world, of the others. Any deeper meaning of rockiness—as living stone, biblical or alchemical, or as the poet Grahn's mother rock[64]—is lost to the legend itself. Whereas we never hear of Athena using the Medusa's head destructively, Perseus now manifests the snake symptom, cut off from the body of the goddess, as sheer evil. Today the warrior threatens to vent his repressed rage on everything that lives, keeping masses petrified by the image of nuclear holocaust—of an entire planet, our living stone, becoming dead rock.

The Monster and the Maiden

Let us follow Perseus a bit further in his journey. The story as classically told will yield no moral, at least none that demoralizes the heroic ego it glorifies. But it will momentarily net for us an entire nest of monsters who swim beneath Western heroic culture. And at the same time it reveals another anima figure, one who symbolizes the main manifestation of the nonmaternal "feminine" within the patriarchal world and soul.

As Ovid tells it, Perseus, on his way home, comes across a beautiful woman chained naked and bejeweled to a sea cliff. Against the horizon, a monster approaches. Because the Ethiopian queen had boasted of her own and her daughter's beauty, the fifty mermaid Nereids have appealed to their protector Poseidon, who has in turn unleashed on the kingdom a female sea monster cum flood. An oracle has advised that Andromeda, the daughter of the royal couple, be exposed on the rock as a sacrifice to assuage the angry sea-forces.[65] Emboldened by his defeat of Medusa, Perseus sizes up the situation and seizes the moment. He makes a quick bargain with the distraught parents:

There will be time enough for weeping later, but there is only a little time in which to help her. If I ask for this girl as Perseus the Son of Jupiter or as Perseus the slayer of the snake-haired Gorgon, I would indeed be preferred above all others as your son-in-law, and now, if only the gods will favor me, I shall try to add my helpfulness to my other qualities. That she be mine, if she is rescued by my courage, is the only condition I make.[66]

Of course no one asks Andromeda whether she might prefer to take her chances with the monster than face life with a well-muscled braggard. Ovid comments, "Her parents accepted the bargain—for who would hesitate to accept?—and promised him also a kingdom as her dowry." Perseus accomplishes the slaughter with gory aplomb, "and the girl, now freed from her chains, came forward, the prize and reason for his deed of daring."[67]

Andromeda is one of the first of the long mythological string of such passive princesses—a maiden awaiting the hero who will rescue her from the dragon, hopelessly alluring in her helplessness. In the psychology of women she has symbolized the fantasy of salvation by marriage to the "divine" prince, who seizes her from the chains of her childhood relation to her parents (her oedipal triangle) and who by killing the monster overcomes her regressive identification with her mother. That the mother's deed has brought on the monster in the first place suggests a displacement of the mother's own womb-watery monstrosity onto the sea creature. In the psychology of the male, rescuing the damsel in distress has been almost as important as slaying monsters in his realization of his own generic type. Without monsters to kill and maidens to rescue, the hero would be no hero. Neumann describes the relation between monster, captive and hero as a constellation necessary to the development of ego consciousness in both its individual and historical dimensions.

The transformation which the male undergoes in the course of the dragon fight includes a change in his relation to the female, symbolically expressed in the liberation of the captive from the dragon's power. In other words, the feminine image extricates itself from the grip of the Terrible Mother, a process known in analytical psychology as the crystallization of the anima from the mother archetype.[68]

This theory belongs to Neumann's basic masculinization of all consciousness, as a variant on his general advocacy of Great Mother murder. Apart from his prescriptions, he offers valuable descriptions of the chain of images producing the masculine, heroic ego. But elements of this mythologem require different interpretation. For instance, *Andro-meda* means "ruler of men"—an incongruous name for a passive princess. Indeed, the name tacitly commemorates the Ethiopian analogue of the Libyan *Med*usa, "wise woman" and "ruler." Graves presents a hypothesis intriguing in its correlation of images.

Andromeda's story has probably been deduced from a Palestinian icon of the Sun-god Marduk . . . mounted on his white horse and killing the sea monster Tiamat. . . . In the same icon, the jewelled, naked Andromeda, standing chained to a rock, is Aphrodite, or Ishtar, or Astarte, the lecherous sea-goddess, 'ruler of men'. . . . But she is not waiting to be rescued: Marduk has bound her there himself, after killing her emanation, Tiamat the sea-serpent, to prevent further mischief.[69]

Rereading the tale this way corroborates the hypothesis that monster and maiden are both carved from the mother archetype but exactly reverses the narrative flow of both the myth and Neumann's interpretation. Perseus and Marduk both distinguish themselves as monster-killing heroes. In the older Near Eastern imagery, however, the erotic anima does not crystallize from the terrible mother, but rather the mother-monster from the erotic goddess; the goddess is not saved by the hero for marriage *to* him, but in fact is chained to the rock *by* him. Goddess and sea monster are of the same stuff. So here we seem to find ourselves once again with Aristotle, for whom any woman, no matter how well formed, counts as a deformity, a necessary instance of passive monstrosity.

Does her deformity consist simply in the fact that she is powerful and that her power threatens the many domains of masculine dominion? Does the simple fact of her ancient authority mark her as a monster? Does the wise rulership to which her names bear witness root more in a historical queenship—matrilineal or matriarchal, Amazon or simply pre-Indo-European—or more in the psycho-physical-social primordiality of the power of mother in each person's origins?

The ancient serpent power insinuates itself again. Sea monsters are often described as sea serpents, suggesting simply bloated versions of the serpent that was from Neolithic times associated with water more than with earth (cf. Gimbutas). Sea monsters enter into easy homology with the maternal, at least from the vantage point of an insecure ego still attempting to separate itself from her swelling, devouring, disappearing saltwatery womb. (As we will see, many sea serpents and other monsters are of male gender; this will not contradict the fundamental meaning of monstrosity. Even for Aristotle, women belong to but hardly exhaust the category of the monstrous.) The identity of the sacrificial maiden with the sea monster to whom she will be sacrificed pertains to an anxiety de Beauvoir has analyzed: the masculine fear that his passive princess, his maiden-wife, will turn back into the overpowering Mother he only just escaped. "His normal sexuality tends to dissociate Mother from Wife. He feels repugnance for the mysterious alchemies of life, whereas his own life is nourished and delighted with the savory fruits of the earth; he wishes to take them for his own; he covets Venus newly risen from the wave." [70] The mother conjures for him the uncontrollability of nature, its overpowering, disconcerting threat to finite human projects. In winning the maiden, by contrast, the male has domesticated nature, which she embodies for him lyrically, tamely tantalizing in her lightly lingering wildness. "Man expects something other than the assuagement of instinctive cravings through the possession of a woman: she is the privileged object through which he subdues nature." [71] But then the symbolism of his bloody conquest of the monster and of his—not unsanguinary— "conquest" of the virgin appear increasingly indistinguishable. Both mother and maiden-wife (whom we find later impossibly combined in the Virgin Mary) appear as Other, incarnating the nonsubjective energies of the physical world. Yet if the maiden makes the transition to mother that has been required of her, as her "true vocation," she frightens and repels him. No wonder women become anorexic, fearful that they might swell into the hated sea monster.[72]

From another perspective, however, the merger of the one sacrificed with the one to whom she is sacrificed intimates a typical cycle of deity. (As God the Father receives the sacrifice of God the Son.) To follow the cycle to its source, let us pinpoint a moment when the Goddess becomes the monster, for there her original Divinity may still shine through the patriarchal myth.

May He Still Conquer Tiamat!

Let us re-member dismembered Tiamat, the First Mother of the Babylonian creation epic, the *Enuma Elish,* which dates from the time of Babylon's rise to political supremacy (2057–1758 B.C.E.) The divine hero Marduk, of the rising warrior class of rulers, annihilates Tiamat in a mighty combat and, by dismembering her carcass, creates his cosmos of her pieces. *Tiamat* means "the primeval waters, the precreation chaos, the salt waters, the ocean"; she embodies that space-time "when there was no heaven, no earth, no height, no depth, no name," "when there were no gods."[73] She is no-thing, and in her all things exist potentially. She symbolizes something like the state of immanence, yet surely not as stagnation but as an all-encompassing inwardness. In her undisturbed and highly relational integrity, she enjoys an intercourse of primordial wetness with her spouse Apsu (the fresh waters). Their union generates the beginnings of difference itself: "In the waters gods were created, in the waters silt precipitated." Their uroboric intermingling results in the first generation of form, of consciousness. It is not statically fixed, but creative. Then we hear that "discord broke out among the gods, though they were brothers, warring and jarring in the belly of Tiamat, heaven shook, it reeled with the surge of the dance; Apsu could not silence the clamor, their behavior was bad, overbearing and proud."[74] Sibling rivalry, divine restlessness, new possibilities madly unleashed and competing for actualization, then the first discordant strains of the patriarchal wardance that seizes the world at approximately the point of this epic's composition: whatever the overdetermining causes of the disturbance, the final result is the slaughter of Tiamat by one of the "brothers." And by the time Marduk, the Babylonian culture hero, slays his (Great-Great-Grand-) Mother, she appears as a huge serpentine monster and breeder of monsters of all kinds. Observing how the demotion of this cosmic creatrix into "the old Hag, the first mother"[75] takes place may lend us the needed "deep background"[76] of the heroic pattern of monster-making/monster-slaying.

Though Tiamat emerges as the greatest obstacle to the warrior's rise to supremacy, vastly more threatening than her spouse Apsu, the narrative demonstrates the overtly oedipal friction between generations of males. He announces: "Their manners revolt me, day and night without remission we suffer. My will is to destroy them ... we shall have peace at last and we will sleep again."[77] Apsu, prefiguring the irritable twentieth-century father home from work, symbolizes the paternalism of an old order resisting transformation in order to conserve its somnolent harmony. He functions as "the tyrant Holdfast" against whom, according to the early work of Campbell,[78] the hero arises as the anarchic principle of change. Whitehead lends cosmological generality to the impulse: "Each new epoch enters upon its career by waging unrelenting war upon the aesthetic gods of its immediate predecessor."[79]

As precise a piece of psychological characterization as literature can provide, the text poignantly narrates Tiamat's very different response to the disturbance of "oceanic feeling."

When Tiamat heard, she was stung, she writhed in lonely desolation, her heart worked in secret passion, Tiamat said,
'Why must we destroy the children that we made? If their ways are troublesome, let us wait a little while.'[80]

Not the maternal but the paternal uroboros[81] shows itself intolerant of change and discord. Whitehead's characterization of divine relatedness as the patient operation "of a tender care that nothing be lost"[82] fits well this mother Goddess willing to suffer the rebellious uproar of adolescent confusion, of the new which has not yet found its constructive equilibrium. But this divine dimension of tender patience soon tragically disappears, transmuted into fury when the young males, out of fear, actually kill her primordial mate. Now the text launches its full-fledged mythic defamation of the old mother Goddess, whereby, according to Campbell, the gods of one order become the demons and monsters to be defeated by the next. Ancient splendors are turned into nagging terrors. The young gods now appear justified to unleash a torment of storms upon the surviving members of the older generation, who are able to convince Tiamat to fight back both in defense and in vengeance. So now we read that "the Old Hag, the first mother, mothers a new brood," among which are included "enormous serpents with cutting fangs, chock-full of venom instead of blood, snarling dragons wearing glory like gods" (perhaps they *had* been gods).[83] This monster birthing exactly parallels the reaction of the goddess Earth in Hesiod's theogony, who when confronted with the defeat of her divine children, the Titans, by the invading order of Zeus, gives birth to the cosmically scaled horror, Typhöon, and other monsters.

The rebels are now understandably terrified at all this procreative preparation for their overthrow: note how well the text motivates matriphobia. The wisest among them, hearing "how the Tiamat-tempest was rising," proposes a nonviolent strategy: "I will meet Tiamat and calm her spirit, when her heart brims over she will hear my words, and if not mine then yours may appease the waters." But his approach, realistic in the light of Tiamat's earlier tender-heartedness, fails because it is not even tried. This is a crucial moment. The heroes will not give peace a chance: "when he saw her whole strategy he could not face her, but he came back cringing." [84]

Still another deity, "the true hero, an irresistible onslaught, a strong God" is urged to try the same tactic and fails for the same reason. One senses the wry irony of the anonymous bard. These true heroes are so terrified by the maternal power that they refuse to *face* it. While in Greek myth Perseus' refusal literally to "face" the petrifying monster counts as strategic courage, this older epic exposes the failure to confront her as simple cowardice. It is at this moment that young Marduk strides in and cunningly reassures his fellow gods with his bravura. His defiant masculinity now inaugurates an unprecedented misogyny: "I will accomplish what you long for most in your heart. . . . *Only a female thing,* only Tiamat flies at you with all her contrivance. You shall soon straddle Tiamat's neck" (my emphasis).[85] A classic moment: we see the collective matriphobia converted to matricidal aggression. When Marduk mocks her femaleness as a weakness, his snoolish[86] fellows are much heartened; there is no more talk of persuading Tiamat to relent; the effeminate methods such as peace-talks and negotiation are circumvented for the sake of the clean kill. After much political plotting to assure his own ultimate supremacy, structurally resembling Zeus's overthrow of the primal, mother-identified powers, Marduk proves his skill. Entering fully armed into battle with a Tiamat now manifestly sea-monstrous, he vanquishes her by driving the violent winds into her body. At the end of a most satisfactory slaughter, "The lord rested; he gazed at the huge body, pondering how to use it, what to create from the dead carcass. He split it apart like a cockle-shell; with the upper half he constructed the arc of sky, he pulled down the bar and set a watch on the waters, so they should never escape." [87]

This brutal construction work creates the cosmos: after dividing her in half, he proceeds to form the specific parts of the universe from the pieces of her corpse. "Thus the creative act," writes Paul Ricoeur, "which distinguishes, separates, measures, and puts in order, is inseparable from the criminal act that puts an end to the life of the oldest gods, inseparable from a deicide inherent in the divine." [88] Ricoeur's idea of an inherent deicide seems to impute a universal inevitability to this identification of creation with destruction. But assuming for the moment that his intention is phenomenological and thus descriptive, he aids our understanding of the normative impact of this sort of narrative theogony, which he considers "the first 'type' of myth concerning the origin and the end of evil." [89] It represents not only the paradigmatic defeat of chaos (which is equated by the myth and by Ricoeur with evil), but justification for the massive political violence initiated by the Sumero-Akkadian kingdoms.

Creation is a victory over an Enemy older than the creator; that Enemy, immanent in the divine, will be represented in history by all the enemies whom the king in his turn, as servant of the god, will have as his mission to destroy. Thus Violence is in the origin of things, in the principle that establishes while it destroys. [90]

Thus Ricoeur traces the ultimate historical outcome of this species of myth in "a theology of war founded on the identification of the Enemy with the powers that the god has vanquished and continues to vanquish in the drama of creation." [91] As Ricoeur himself so skillfully argues, each stage of symbolism bleeds into the next. We may infer that this archaic myth of combat still pulsates deep within the spirit of civilization, for the "theology of war" continues to inspire the greatest expenditure of human resources on our planet today. But Ricoeur ignores the fact—highlighted in narrative and ritual by the relative insignificance of Apsu's murder—that the primordial enemy is a woman and that the cosmos established by her destruction is not accidentally a patriarchy. Splicing this fact together with his interpretation yields support for Mary Daly's pungent postulate: "The primordial, universal object of attack in all phallocratic wars is the Self in every woman."[92] In some sense every enemy of the hero (even other heroes) embodies the first Other, his primeval opposite who is the female self.

The salient fact of Tiamat's sex helps also to explain the bizarre paranoia of a cosmogony in which creation means the conquest of an "Enemy older than the creator." Who could constitute such a preexistent threat but a Mother, indeed "the First Mother"? For it is the mother who literally exists before the ego, as historically the Mother Goddess precedes the primacy of masculine deity. Viewed retroactively, from the vantage point of an ego bent on separation and preeminence, the power of her a priori presence can only seem monstrous. So is the patriarchal self born in combat.

Because the cosmogenic conflict was ritually reenacted as the central yearly drama of Babylonian culture, Ricoeur names it the "Ritual vision of the world": "every historical drama, every historical conflict, must be attached by a bond of *re-enactment* of the cultural-ritual type to the drama of creation."[93] In this bond of "re-enactment" lies the link between myth and history.

The history of religion places the cosmological dismemberment in the context of the universal motif of sacrifice, by which the universe returns periodically to chaos and, according to Mircea Eliade, regenerates itself by the "annulment of time" in an "eternal return." But while in agricultural societies the voluntary sacrifice of a victim in emulation of the periodic decomposition of nature reflects the eternal return of nature, the involuntary and bellicose sacrifice of Tiamat must be distinguished from images of sacrifice associated with the natural process of decay, which feeds life of its own accord.[94] Eliade's account of the ritual repetition of the cosmogonic sacrifice, though it fails to make this distinction, sheds further light on the psychocultural import of the slaughter, which, while depicted as once-for-all, must be reenacted at every Babylonian New

Year's celebration: "It repeated, it actualized, the cosmogony, the passage from chaos to cosmos. The mythical event was present: 'May he continue to conquer Tiamat and shorten her days!' the celebrant exclaimed. The combat, the victory, and the Creation took place *at that very moment.*" [95] In other words, the slaughter is a way of life. As the woman-identified powers of "chaos" will continually recrudesce, they must repeatedly be killed. The matricide, we begin to realize, constitutes the central act of the heroic lifestyle, the ritual gesture in which the patriarchal ego must participate at every moment—at *this* very moment. "The combat, the victory, and the Creation" constitute the theological psychology of the West. The covert slaughter of the mother is this culture's bond of reenactment.

The De-faced Other

Mary Daly has called patriarchy "the Religion of Reversals." [96] So we see the *Enuma Elish* translating the First Mother into the ultimate destroyer, the Creator-Goddess into the Monster of Chaos, a generation of cowards into the heavenly heroes, and murder into creativity. Reversing the reversals, we read a different story: as he refuses to face Her, the warrior-hero represses and oppresses the woman-identified energies (in himself, in others, in nature), thus turning them into a raging monstrosity. The repressed, when it returns, is always vengeful, and the return of the oppressed (as in feminism today) poses a threat of revolutionary magnitude. The separative ego feels creative chaos as regressive disorder, and depth as an atmosphere of death. Or so the hero justifies the slaughter whereby he attempts to establish his dominion eternally. No longer—he hopes—need he confront primordial depths. Once she is declared monster, he makes himself master. Dead, she now functions as the facelessly inhuman, the *prima materia,* the defaced stuff, upon which his transcendent andromorphism enacts its new creation. In the meantime, the suppressed rage of woman, devouring others through emotional manipulation and herself through depression, keeps dissolving the sea monster in her own sea.

At the level of myth, the hero makes the woman inert and makes his world *out* of her (fleeing immanence at any cost, let alone co-creativity). He then passes her on to the level of classical ontology, where the philosopher receives her as already deactivated and can fantasize the superior value of the active male seed. As the divine hero creates, so the human male procreates, in an action for which she provides the inert matter: "If, then, the male stands for the effective and active, and the female, considered as female, for the passive, it follows that what the female would contribute to the semen of the male would not be semen but material for the semen to work upon." [97]

"Thus mythology," Hillman claims in discussing this tradition of biological misogyny, "cannot help becoming metapsychology, indispensable to any ontological description of psychology." [98] The mythology of the heroic warrior becomes the subtler metapsychology of the active and effective male agent. An intellectual lineage, extending through Thomas Aquinas and Freud, will transmit this ancient mythos of the independently potent male substance. The female contributes the objective material to be worked upon by the transcendent subject.

The heroic agency of the masculine principle still reverberates, freed of procreative metaphors, in the modern ideal of an autonomous subject. Women understandably adopt this ideal in order to elude our own insubstantiality, our monstrosity. Monsters may be said to represent for the West the sheerly immanent—the force of nature, past, and otherness become alien, resisting the exploits of the transcendently belligerent ego. Every self, according to the model we questioned in Chapter 1, posits the Other as an object, an opponent, in order to become *itself;* the transformation of women and other aliens into monsters illustrates all too well this process of oppositional transcendence. To externalize any other as an object, means ultimately to create a monster: for the other has been denied its claims both to authentic subjectivity and to intimate participation, and so made less than human.

But let us not forget the theological sources of this transcendence. For it is the Christian tradition, in its conjunctions with Aristotelian philosophy, that bridges the long gap between ancient cosmogonies and atheological existentialism, and that claims world-creating transcendence for human subjectivity. We shall see how the mythic paradigm of the dragon-defeating hero penetrates later Western culture through the biblical images of the Creator.

The Face of the Deep

In the first of the two creation accounts in the Book of Genesis, "when God began to create the heaven and the earth," a very different, quite non-Babylonian, mood prevails. No primeval intercourse and oedipal rivalry, no monsters, combat, and crushed she-carcass litter the cosmic scene. By definition a monotheistic myth of origin contains no originating relations. For opposite the divine One there can be no Others: neither consort nor combatant shares the scene. The priestly account depicts with peaceful orderliness the picture of an unimpeded Will, a unilateral action.

But the surface differences do not tell the whole story. We learn that the biblical authors are indebted to Mesopotamian models, and in particular to the *Enuma Elish,* for both form and content of the early Genesis chapters. Concerning the parallels between Genesis 1 and the *Enuma Elish,* E. A. Speiser writes: "There is not only a striking correspondence in various details, but—what is even more significant—the order of events is the same, which is enough to preclude any likelihood of coincidence. The relationship is duly recognized by all informed students, no matter how orthodox their personal beliefs may be." [99]

Opportunities for Mesopotamian input extend from the period of the (official) patriarchs through that of Babylonian exile, so historically it is not surprising to find considerable influence. Here is Heidel's classic tabulation of the structural relations:

Enuma Elish	Genesis
1. Divine spirit and cosmic matter are coexistent and coeternal.	1. Divine spirit creates cosmic matter and exists independently of it.
2. Primeval chaos; Ti'amat enveloped in darkness.	2. The earth a desolate waste, with darkness covering the deep (*tehom*).
3. Light enamating from the gods.	3. Light created.
4. The creation of the firmament.	4. The creation of the firmament.
5. The creation of dry land.	5. The creation of dry land.
6. The creation of luminaries.	6. The creation of luminaries.

7. The creation of man.	7. The creation of man.
8. The gods rest and celebrate.	8. God rests and sanctifies the seventh day.[100]

These similarities underlying the differences are often explained as a Hebrew strategy for subverting the Babylonian myth. Genesis 1 can be read as a monotheistic polemic against creation by either procreation or combat. Then the similarities serve only as a foil for the difference, articulated as the speech of the One God. The Word takes the place both of warrior's weapons and woman's womb. Far beyond the sovereignty of Marduk—who is the supreme but never the only deity—the God of Genesis emerges as transcendent in precisely the sense explored in the previous chapter, as that which at once posits—literally *creates*—the other as Other and stands *independently* over against it. God's others are then the natural universe, humanity in general, and some exclusively chosen people in particular, Israel or Church, who mirror his exclusivity back to him. While God may come and go in his world at will, he is not ontologically *in* it, not a part of it, not immanent. He exists before it, and has no precreation peers. It is absolutely dependent upon him for its origin and for its salvation. Fishbane well describes the distance from the earlier, polytheistic ontology.

In this worldview, the gods are immanent and near, and there is a deep harmony linking man and god and world. This harmony is truly ontological. . . . Is not mankind created out of the very bodies of Tiamat's cohorts in *Enuma Elish*, even as the world is itself carved out of her dessicated hulk? The same energies flow throughout all being; . . . all is linked, and every level of being ontologically 'mirrors' all others.[101]

The worldview of Israel, by contrast, emphasizes separation and will:

Elohim is unengendered; there is neither theogony nor combat . . . no panerotic or pandivine aspect to the orderly creation by Elohim. Later psalmists would underscore this vision with their emphasis that creation ever praises God, and that his creative Spirit enlivens and nurtures all life. . . . But such a god is distinct from nature, which neither contains him nor exhausts his power. It is 'will' which characterizes such a god. Such a one, says Gerardus van der Leeuw, is a Father—beneficent perhaps—but not a mother.[102]

Fishbane's opposition of a polytheistic, immanentist worldview to the monotheistic transcendence does justice to Israel's self-understanding as well as to the pagan sensibility. However, that he overdraws the case for what he calls "mythic monism" and its harmony is immediately evident in his own example. We have an *Enuma Elish* bursting not only with a plural diversity of figures, unsuitably called "monism," but with divisiveness and fragmentation. Any "harmony" is established at the cost of violence, and the links "mirroring" the levels of being are homologies of warfare. Furthermore, his association of the *Enuma Elish* with "the Mothers" is itself an instance of "reversal." It ignores the myth's sanctification of matriphobia and matricide, and so obliterates the difference between polytheisms—between prepatriarchal vestiges of "the Mothers" and their patriarchal defamation. Too impressed by the actual presence of female deity, he uncritically assimilates misogynist to truly matricentric uses of the Goddess. Yet he helps us differentiate between the polytheistic and the monotheistic forms of patriarchy. Moreover his antithesis remains quite valid at the level of ontology.

But let us reverse approaches and come to grips with the deeper similarity. Otherwise, how shall we account for the patriarchal continuity between the cultures and their myths? To return to the text: "In the beginning God created the heavens and the earth. The earth was without form and void, and darkness was upon the face of the deep; and the Wind (or Spirit) of God was moving over the face of the waters" (Gen. 1:1, 2. R.S.V.). *"Tohu,"* we learn, "is related to the Hebrew loan word *tehom,* the 'deep' or heavenly ocean-chaos that is held back . . . so that it might not destroy all creation."[103] *Tehom,* "deep," is in turn the Hebrew rendition of *Tiamat.* Of course the scripture brooks no conscious remembrance of any other deity; but the fact that nowhere in the Hebrew Bible is the grammatically feminine *Tehom* preceded, like normal Hebrew nouns, by an article seems secretly to commemorate its status as a proper noun: the name of the First Mother.

Western civilization is steeped in the liturgical solemnity of these opening verses—these Deeps. It is she—Tehom/Tiamat—who renders the chapter poetically efficacious. Without her dark, stirring potentialities, would the subsequent saying-and-separating elicit any emotional interest? Indeed the text's metaphoric power drops as soon as the light is turned on, the dis-spirited natural universe set in place, the mysterious shadow of the abyss apparently vanquished. Interest rises again only on the sixth day, with the creation of humanity in the male and female image of Elohim (a plural form for the One God), who speak(s) as "we" and so distantly recalls the primordial Babylonian parents. But the scene presents a masculine God (though sexually inactive and ontologically solitary), a "Deep" rendered completely abstract, and the wind (*spiritus*) of God in context reminiscent of the winds with which Marduk defeated Tiamat. The older mythic figures are more than superficially present:

> Somewhere in the back of the minds of the writers of Genesis is the Tiamat world of dark and storm, and the story of the masculine warrior-god who creates the cosmos from out of chaos, splitting the dragon-mother's corpse as the initial act of creation. The transparent image of Marduk is thus superimposed upon Yahweh.[104]

Just how far back in their minds we cannot say. And whether the complete elimination of the Goddess in Judaism and Christianity is ultimately preferable to the cyclical polytheistic epic of her bloody defeat and humiliation we must leave at present undecided.

An open defamation of the serpent power of the female attends the Yahwist myth that the editors put in second place, in which Eve comes forth almost Athenalike from the body of a male. Adam, like Zeus when he gave birth through the head, usurps the female prerogative of childbearing. But for Yahweh himself, usurpation remains unnecessary. For as the priestly account establishes, a monotheistic male deity does not procreate (even through his head!). Unlike Athena, Eve is stripped of any lingering divinity. While the etymology of her name remains subject to dispute, it commemorates a Goddess to those who have ears to hear: the Yahwist himself links her name, *hawwah*, with the Hebrew *hay* (living), calling her "Mother of All the Living." Another scholar suggests a reading that will remind us of the Gorgon herself: "Not in the Hebrew preserved in the Bible but in the cognate Arabic and Aramaic languages a word related to *hawwah* means "serpent." [105] The old kinship of female deity with her serpent-familiar and the fluid boundary between God and World, female and male, self and other, which their bond insinuates, is both metaphysically portrayed and theologically betrayed by the text. The curse that alienates her from the serpent utters a suppressed truth: that of the brokenness of the All Mother, leaving women frightened of our own power and divided against our Selves. But the story of Eden has already been well treated by feminist advocates of Eve of both biblical and post-traditional orientation.[106]

In the Genesis passages, Yahweh's warrior attributes are sublimated to a more dignified father image. But the passages that demonstrate unmistakably the affinities between the biblical God and the Babylonian Marduk occur in the poetic and prophetic traditions.

... Who is mighty as thou art, YHWH?
Thou dost rule the raging of the sea ...
Thou didst crush Rahab like a carcass.

(Ps. 89:6010.)

In the liturgical poetry, the monsters themselves reappear—Leviathan and Rahab (who are usually male) and Deep herself. Poetic license seems in the psalms to banish priestly inhibitions concerning the vestigial polytheism accruing to such primeval creatures and to the cosmic battle in which they are crushed. In the following verses, Isaiah recalls the primeval water wars, trying to rouse the old divine warrior to come to the support of Israel in its state of national emergency.

Awake, awake, put on your strength, O arm of YHWH
Awake, as you did long ago, in days gone by.
Was it not you
who hacked the Rahab in pieces and ran the dragon through?
Was it not you
Who dried up the sea, the waters of the great abyss Tehom
and made the ocean depths a path for the ransomed?

(Is. 51:9–10)

Through a subtle parallelism of metaphors, the Exodus passage through the Red Sea, with its message of historical liberation, coalesces with the prehistoric sea battle. How interesting, however, that the prophet feels that the divine warrior is asleep, perhaps not to be awakened. It is as if Yahweh has returned to some primordial slumber in the arms of Tehom. Isaiah's mythic commemoration of primeval and historical heroism nonetheless provides the basis for an apocalyptic hope:

On that day YHWH will punish
with his cruel sword, his mighty and powerful sword,
Leviathan that twisting sea-serpent,
that writhing serpent Leviathan,
and slay the monster of the deep.

(Isa. 26:1)

True to the mythic sense of recurrence, the memory of the monster's first dismemberment only provides the basis for another dismemberment—the kill was neither once and for all, but takes place in a pre- and post-temporal space in which the divine warrior establishes his celestial supremacy. Yet the eschatological consciousness is linear and quite opposite the cyclic slaughter of the *Enuma Elish*. The construction of Western historical consciousness stretches between the mythic extremities of alpha and omega, radically at odds with Deep's tidal temporality. The end of history threatened/promised by the prophecy of a final battle with the Deep seems to portend some ultimate defeat of all that the warrior opposes: the "evil" of the Other, of the unconscious, of all objectified enemies, of the mother-identified powers, of the goddess herself. If today we find ourselves in an age too content with the shallows even to sing the dangers, let alone the blessings, of the Deep, the message of severance and supremacy dominates in demythologized form. Today the "mighty and powerful sword," in its apotheosis as nuclear warhead, has cut free even of the divine warrior. So the enemy has become a completely invisible Other, not even confronted man-to-man on a battlefield.[107] Fearing to lose face, the contemporary warlords do not face the Deep at all.

Theological Re-monstration

In the ancient poetry of the primeval battle, we sense the mythic impulse powering the more austere imagery of Genesis 1. As in

chapter 1 of this book, we could claim that a dynamic hostility
motivates the apparently fixed dualisms of the philosophical tradition; we see a subtle belligerence at work behind the serene transcendence of the priestly scenario. In the biblical tradition the transcendence belongs to the Lord alone, and only indirectly to those
created in his image. But gradually (impeded by the healthy Hebrew
commitment to the corporate nature of human life) the heroic image of the Exclusive One collaborates with the metaphysics of independent substance to bring about the modern individual divided
against self and world. Monotheism does attempt to overcome fragmentation and division. But because monotheism so far has con-
veyed itself as a competitive exclusion, it could only turn in upon
itself and against any prior Mother.

Huge pieces of history begin to fall into place: it is the heroic-
matricidal impulse that provides the common denominator of the
misogyny of Greece and of the Near and Middle East. The ubiqui-
tous image of the patriarchal warrior, in his polytheist as well as
Hebrew manifestation, belies the tradition of an absolutely unique
revelation in the form of biblical monotheism. There is nothing
unique about the masculine and misogynist divine warrior. Of
course misogyny in itself cannot be understood as the sole deter-
minant of the hero. The hero vanquishes many enemies besides the
monster-mother. But the point remains: misogyny and heroic masculinity are indistinguishable. In their coalition with the myths or
the theologies of the absolutely independent One, they will give rise
to the separative ego and his soluble counterpart. For it is again a
matter of creation in the image of a god. The ancient images of the
divine warrior provide the mythic loam out of which history could
fashion the bricks of Hebrew Torah, Christian doctrine and Greek
metaphysics. These images form a common foundation upon which
the later synthesis of classical with biblical thought erects itself. In
this sense the monster-defeating misogynist deity aligns the otherwise divergent cultures of Athens and Jerusalem. Might this deep-
seated warrior image explain the perturbing fact that however else
these and other cultures seem to vary, a theological and social structure of male dominance rises as our planet's great cultural universal? If so, this has interesting theoretical implications. For instance,
consider the God-world dichotomy, which biblical faith fails to re-
solve (generating tension pushing toward an apocalyptic end). It
can be seen to parallel the mind-matter dualism that Greek sub-

stantialism perpetuates—if viewed, that is, from the vantage point of the critique of the fundamental subject-object separation. A deep gynophobia fuels the underlying momentum of all dualistic hierarchies, with their one-upmanship that results in the increasing separation of the one up from the many down, of the one from the many.

Our thesis retains its bioptic focus, for sexism and separatism make a pair and cannot be understood apart from each other. Thus in Greece the open belligerence of the archaic warrior, Zeus or Perseus, turns into the closed circle of the One God, whom Aristotle defines in the supremely separatist terms of the Unmoved Mover. Serene, self-contemplating, this apotheosis of Reason has transcended the mindless megalomania of the warrior. Eastward, in the Levantine basin, the brutal cosmocrat Marduk bequeaths his patrimony to the Hebrew creator. Yahweh Elohim presents the more dignified image of the paternal ruler and judge who inspires the authentic hope for a community of justice. There is no need to dismiss the legitimate breakthroughs of reason or revelation that these two traditions continue to facilitate, even among feminists. But whether more derived from Greek reason or from Hebrew will, an order prevails that is sustained by the incessant rituals of heroic matricide. No wonder both the Greek and the Hebrew deities achieve an image of absolute independence from their worlds. They thus fulfill the heroic ego's impossible wish for an impenetrable dominion—and for the final conquest of the too penetrable, permeating forcefield of femaleness.

Nor is it surprising that these two quite opposite images of pure independence—the one of a settled, indeed eternal, self-objectification, the other of a dynamically historical power—should merge in Christian theology. The early Christian intuition of incarnation—of inspirited flesh, of the divinely human—might have counteracted the dualisms of both traditions. The bold emphasis on Love, stemming from Hebrew and Judaic sources, might have led to a different outcome, creating a transforming community of equals. The Platonic Eros, the Aristotelian organicism, could have collaborated to undermine the gods of power and impermeability. But these scattered seeds fell upon hard ground indeed: the misogynist complex of separation and control was hardly shaken. In his fear of Medusa's gaze, the hero still turns all to stone—and so the stony common ground of the Western tradition, be it rationalism, biblicism, militarism, technologism, or some combination, has

TWO

reached today's alarming state of sterility. We fear our planet's literal petrification, its ultimate objectification, as Perseus the son of god swings the severed head recklessly about. We are threatened by an absolute transcendence of life: the world transformed, in a twinkling, into eternal hardness. For would-be heroes with hardened hearts have arrogated unto themselves even the apocalyptic prerogatives of the Judeo-Christian God.

The Medusa's unfaced look remains the warrior's symptom, and all of our best hope—if he could face her. In his depths, his Tiamat, his Tehom, swims still the First Mother. Perhaps her movement can become redemptive; perhaps the women's movement is redeeming her in time.

Remembering Ahead

Quite naturally, the human imitates its image of the divine. But quite unnaturally, antinaturally—with heroic artifice—the divine became the male alone. Human "heroes" imitate and incarnate divine ones, and soon even the matter of myth or of theology becomes irrelevant, unconscious, whether accepted or rejected. Then we cannot even wrestle with the assailants or the angels of the tradition. But the image keeps working with mythic force. Marduk's victory, Yahweh's triumph over the Deep, Perseus' confrontation by destruction of the Gorgon—these manifest the root-metaphor of heroic achievement. The defeat of the "female thing" eventuates in the paradigm of the radically separative self.

The simple oneness of the modern substantial individual endlessly recapitulates the separative-matricidal impulse of the hero: it eliminates, decapitates and manipulates whatever it excludes from the tense panoply of its own limits. Thus increasingly it becomes an empty oneness, an individual without content. The monolithic simplicity of the heroic individual arises precisely in opposition to the intricate complexity that the divine warrior names—in his defensive attempt to simplify and conquer—"chaos" and "monster."

When, however, we demythologize—that is, place in its mythical context—the presupposition of the transcendent independence of the ego, we are already reclaiming the values of immanence for feminist use. De Beauvoir's position on immanence incarnates the intellectual Athena, as we easily do. Alternatively, we may recycle

88

the monstrous. As merely monstrous—that is, as the deformity created and defeated by the self-formative action of the warrior—she
becomes captive of her own rage, and victim of the triumphant
warrior.

We began this chapter by asking what the monster—an intrinsically portentous creature—promises. Monster, we recall, denotes a
fabulous composite, a fabled ontological mix. The ontology of the
mythic hero, by contrast, posits a prosaically unmixed condition.
His adventures develop him into the monocentric identity that by
definition remains "outside" the other and so finds no foreign substances stirring in his essence. This is the monolithic (i.e., "single-
stoned") unity of the Aristotelian substance or of the Thomist soul,
incapable of internal relations and multiplicity. Its internal undividedness—its version of in-dividuality—reflects its impermeability.
Such a self subsists free of all immanence of the world in one's own
being, indeed free of all becoming, for only by separating itself from
all feeling for the changing world does the classic Aristotelian-
Christian God elude change.

Fabulously complex, serpentine, stormy and profoundly fluid, a
dangerous and demonic deviant: does the gynomorphic dragon
portend an alternative to the monolithic ego? She combines in herself the cosmogonic elements, the traces of all that has been, the
infinite influx of the other, the others, the influent world into which
she herself flows freely, fiercely, and de-formingly. Deforming, that
is, of the formative principle according to which the boundary between inner and outer, self and other is absolute, and woman a
deformity.

To name Tiamat Mother again, to revere the Goddess in our own
Deep, to reclaim "the Old Hag" and her sister Gorgons as wisely
revolting "Hags," [108] involves the redescription of history and the
redefining of the forms of self. If the Athena in us is to remember
the mother whose severed head she wears, if we are to face the
maternal dragons in and outside of ourselves rather than "blame
our mothers" for our fear, we must face the ghosts of all these gods
and goddesses. Ghosts represent the way a killed past haunts the
present. As Alice Walker suggests, "Let us be intimate with / ances-
tral ghosts / and music / of the undead." [109] This mysterious music
intimates, perhaps even harmonizes, the oceanic force of Tiamat,
the rhythmic tides extending into depths beneath death, beneath
consciousness. There, if we do not dissolve into a slime of undiffer-

entiation, we realize that freedom in general, and women's freedom in particular, requires a deep and forward-looking memory, akin to Daly's reversal reversing "metamemory." If the separate ego of the patriarchal psyche defines itself by its perpetual act of dismembering the maternal monster, chopping to the prosaic beat of a repetitious self-indentity, consider Daly's summoning of woman's "Tidal Powers," released only as we name our Selves anew: "The rhythms of Naming deep Memory are quite unlike the tidy, tedious tick-tock of patriarchal clocks and watches. The rhythms of re-membering are Tidal." [110] Re-membering takes us (as the final chapter will develop) not only to a different time, but to a different sense of timing.

Tiamat/Tehom is herself the apotheosis of the Tidal, defamed as chaos ever again for her monstrously untidy creativity. The waiting, wifely women like Penelope, who in their tidy timelessness complement and so provide no alternative to the heroic ego, are only beginning to collaborate with sea monsters and gorgons. Yet the cosmic rhythm of weaving and unweaving (sustained by pre-Penelopean Muses) spins in its complex web a composite integrity no less fabulous than that of the mythic monster. Penelope freed of her trivial tidiness, the monster freed of her tidal destructiveness, join in a mix of metaphors that prophecies the mixed media of the postheroic personality.

The reader will remember that *monster* springs from the same root as *remember, remind, mind, Mnemosyne*. The monsters have indeed reminded us of the preheroic, prepatriarchal power of the goddess of wisdom and of her serpentine symbolism. But it is important to remember what sort of methodology of memory serves us best. Evidence remains piecemeal, ambiguous and largely nontextual for any truly egalitarian, let alone matriarchal, society preceding the Indo-European invasions. The matricentric imagery predates written testimony, and from the gynophobic themes of recorded myth we can only draw likely but uncertain inferences— often only by inversion—about the literal past. But whether or not the sort of implications we have been pursuing in this chapter are literally true *of* the past, they may be true *to* the past inasmuch as it belongs to our memory. Casey describes how "freedom to be oneself" remains indistinguishable from the phenomenon of re-membering, for *"we are what we remember ourselves to be."* Memory thus involves freedom not merely to "reconstruct" but to "reconstrue." [111]

The importance of myths that, when read in reverse, reverse the inertia of the myth of female impotence lies in their present—a present giving rise to a future. Their images are presentiments of possibility as metaphors whose embodiment lies always still ahead. Thus the primeval monster at once reminds and presages, lending an incongruous image out of which to read the face of the future. Discussing the importance for feminism of the Goddess as metaphor, Nelle Morton points to the revolutionary potential of the very medium of the metaphor as at once iconclastic and visionary. Indeed the suppressed Goddess seems to arise as metaphor of metaphors.[112] It seems that the metaphoric vehicle always derives from the immanent past, as a sort of tidal momentum that swells into the future. To find images empowering of a selfhood beyond that of the separative ego and its selfless complement, we inevitably journey through the deep past, through a mythic memory heavy with dream and charged with desire.

Re-membering means nothing if not re-connecting. And reconnection, as will gradually become apparent, requires a complex cohesiveness of relation and of self. This sort of memory concerns not only the act of mythic remembering, but the message remembered as well. The composite complexity of the monster seems—in conjunction with its feminine associations—to render it the deviant by the normative standard (the *norma normans non normata* of the masculine ego). An entire way of life based on connectivity seems to have been dismembered along with the Goddesses. Yet to remember it now entails no return, no regression to a hypothetical golden age of goddess worship or copulating cosmic couples. No past participation mystique will persuade us today. We are re-collecting our *selves*.

A self that feels itself to *be* rememberingly—rather than solubly or severingly—comes to be as an event of self-composition. We begin to suspect that its very cohesion emanates not from its simple unity but from its composite complexity. It need not thereby fall into fragments; indeed, the hero with his sword of unification-by-exclusion remains far more responsible for fragmentation—recall not only his divisive monotheisms but the self-division of his reflexive unity. A connective self self-composes in an act of transcendence, for it expresses a fundamental freedom to create itself out of the components of its world—not merely to rearrange the parts. But such transcendence in-gathers the "intimate ghosts," the rhythmic tides, the smoldering ashes of the immanent past. It welcomes in the other—not just one other, but the universe of the many; and yet it does not identify with any particular other or even the sum of all others. Connection is not identification. Nor is it approbation. This taking-in could be an angry and judging internalization of the other as well as a tender invitation. But in that case the anger expresses not blind rage but a certain intimacy, a movement from alienation to knowingness, a commitment to face up to the otherness of the other. It does not turn to stone in the face of its monsters, this intrinsically composite self, for it recognizes in their apparent chaos its own complexity. Their anguish deepens it. It refuses the simple centrism that kills the monstrous multiplicity. It mixes strangely in itself flesh and fire, spirit and stone, arising in a subtle metamorphosis of aqueous depths and breathy breadths.

When the warrior sets the terms of transcendence and human subjectivity, the normative self is masculine. And when the male defines the terms of gender identity, the female becomes the deviant. But today neither man nor woman nor world can afford the warrior model. Having proved itself an evil deformity, the monster in its demonic sense, it must no more demonstrate its world-destroying weaponry. Or rather, the monster whose memory we honor must let her portentous wisdom become ours, indeed *become us*. Her wisdom is after all, like Medusa, beautiful: most becoming. To unblock further her becoming, her second coming, we now turn to a psychological exploration of the genesis of the separative self over and against the possibility of an influent and connective self.

THREE

Oceanic Feelings
and the Rising Daughter

The derivation of religious needs from the infant's helplessness and the longing for the father aroused by it seems to be
incontrovertible. . . . I cannot think of any need in childhood
as strong as the need for a father's protection. Thus the part
played by the oceanic feeling, which might seek something
like the restoration of limitless narcissism, is ousted from a
place in the foreground.
—Sigmund Freud, *Civilization and Its Discontents*

Mother and daughter the whole of the day in unanimous hu-
    mour
Thereupon gladdened each other in heart and in mind very
    greatly,
Clinging together in love till their spirits abated their sor-
    rows.
—*Homeric Hymn to Demeter*, trans. Daryl Hine

WHEN AFTER DUE CONSIDERATION Freud drains the "oceanic
feeling" from his account of the origins of religion, does he reenact
on modern, psychological grounds the cosmogonic conquest of Tehom? In both Freudian and biblical mythologems, the father as-
cends to domestic and divine primacy while the mother not only
recedes into the dark chaos of primordial fluidity, but forfeits any
meaningful presence. In the Book of Genesis she—deprived by the

93

dictates of monotheism of all residual procreativity and personality—makes herself felt only in the grammatical femininity of the precreation ocean named Deep; analogously, in *Civilization and Its Discontents,* Freud relegates the infant's original experience with the mother to an impotent, anonymous background. Neither theologically nor psychoanalytically does any first woman, any goddess-mother, survive the patriarchal creation in word or theory. Freud's analysis of the stage of oceanic feeling omits any explicit reference to a mother, while the father emerges as the strong protector and true parent. It is as though she does not exist. Any overt defeat of the mother, such as we witnessed in the thinly veiled matricides of the last chapter, is obviated by her irrelevance. In *Civilization's* chapter 1 as in Genesis 1, "she" is no longer powerful enough even to appear as enemy or monster.

Freud replays in the name of a patriarchal atheism the postulate of patriarchal theism: that the male is the true author of life and that his protective powers alone answer to human vulnerability. The primal bond of infant and mother, preceding as it does any ego separation, is diagnosed as "limitless narcissism," much as the pre-creation Tehom appears as the "waste and void." We find on the one hand the chaos of an uncivilized id, an unformed personality for which, as the libido cathects only the self,[1] no object relation to a mother is possible; on the other, the chaos of an origin in which no mother goddess is possible, nor any complex of divine love-relations, since this monotheism requires a nature divested of all immanent spirit. In both cases the mother, having disappeared from the picture, seems to represent a primal threat to the integrity of ego or of creator: the threat of regression to "primary narcissism," like a regression to polytheism or goddess worship, which would signal an unhealthy or unholy dissolution. In the intertextuality of both the biblical and the Freudian texts, one must suspect a mechanism of denial by which the mother is latently represented even as she is manifestly omitted.

Several interlinked questions have already risen into view for this chapter's pursuit. What does the mother's disappearance have to do with the cultivation of a separative self? What does her subsequent reappearance in later psychoanalytic theory and in Jungian analytic psychology reveal concerning the nature of the self? How *is* any connective self to be an individual, free, that is, of the primary narcissism of subject-object (infant-mother) merger?

Feminists have long sounded the alarm against the patriarchalism of Freud and, less unilaterally, of Jung. Rather than simply reiterating a firmly established tradition of critique, our methodology must remain two-edged: cutting both with and against the theories themselves. Then the varieties of depth psychology, even or precisely in their sexism, can shed light on the sexist psychocultural patterns forming the separative and soluble self-cycle. Before turning to feminist theories of psychoanalysis, we may read both major theories of depth psychology, the Freudian and Jungian, as descriptive of personality structures shaped within and by patriarchal culture. So Juliet Mitchell, perhaps the most Freudian of feminists, states the basis of her strategy: "However it may have been used, psychoanalysis is not a recommendation *for* a patriarchal society, but an analysis *of* one."[2] Whether or not such a sanguine distinction between description and prescription finally holds up, she argues persuasively that feminism can ill afford to discard Freud's analysis of the unconscious dynamics (especially of the oedipus complex) by which patriarchal society so universally controls human selves.[3] As we shall see, a roughly parallel case can be made for Jung, a case both helped and complicated by Jung's own intermittent awareness that the dominance of the "masculine" at the level of culture and archetype must give way to a new synthesis. The fine essays of *Feminist Archetypal Theory* pursue such a revisionist Jungian strategy.[4]

For the present task it does not suffice to remember either historically, philosophically or mythologically: a certain psychological anamnesis, not unlike the psychoanalytic recollection of early childhood factors, must sustain any attempt to challenge the presupposition of the separative self. For if men are not by nature separative nor women essentially soluble, then we have by some means *become* so; and if we have become participants in this divisive dyad, then in principle we can become something else. But to free ourselves of the old complementarity, we must become psychosocially conscious of its causes as they operate deep within our selves, where we internalize vast, impersonal social patterns.

Shrunken Residues

To return to *Civilization and Its Discontents:* the "oceanic feeling," even though it is but a phrase coined by Romain Rolland in his letter to Freud to dispute the thesis of *The Future of an Illusion,* has gathered the momentum of a primary Freudian thought.

Freud does not dispute the existence of such a feeling in some normal people, but only as alongside what he calls "the narrower and more sharply demarcated ego-feeling of maturity, like a kind of counterpart to it."[5] It is of course this mature ego feeling that expresses for Freud the minimal aim of human development and contrasts markedly with the feeling "of an indissoluble bond, of being one with the external world as a whole." This indissoluble bondedness would then belong to the vestiges of earliest childhood, lingering only as an abnormal and regressive infantilism. "Normally, there is nothing of which we are more certain than the feeling of our self, of our own ego. This ego appears to us as something autonomous and unitary, marked off distinctly from everything else."[6] Here we have a straightforward statement of the experience of that sort of ego-self we have variously described as heroic, independent, reflexive, substantial, and continuously self-identical.

Freud did not invent the ideal of the separate ego: he merely lends it a new descriptive context and, significantly for our questions, shows that to exist at all it must in fact *develop,* for which it needs the support of cultural instigation. As he says elsewhere: "it is impossible to suppose that a unity comparable to the ego exists from the very start; the ego has to develop."[7] Freud's thesis certainly undermines any static, Cartesian dualism, in which the ego, however immature, would be metaphysically presupposed from the outset as the substantial human subject. Though for Freud the ego is there in germ from the start, in the id—which itself functions as a permanent substrate of personality—the dynamics of its development receive concerted attention. For without the proper conditions, the ego might not quite emerge from the womblike phase of oceanic feeling, that is, narcissistic symbiosis with the nurturing mother.

The ego's sense of its clear boundaries is belied by Freud's own theory of the id. Id signifies an impersonal and unconscious psychic depth that is neither ego nor completely separable from ego; its unruly impulses of desire, greed and aggression contaminate the entire personality. Internally, in relation to its own underside, the ego's autonomy cannot hold. But Freud distinguishes such inward leakage from the relation to the outer world, toward which "the ego seems to maintain clear and sharp lines of demarcation." Only pathology, he argues, accounts for those adult cases in which the boundaries between subject and object blur—but for a single exception: the state of being in love. "At the height of being in love the boundary between ego and object threatens to melt away. Against all the evidence of his senses, a man [sic] who is in love declares that 'I' and 'you' are one, and is prepared to behave as if it were a fact."[8] In other words, a man's passion for a woman, we may presume, recapitulates the ego's early merger with the mother.

This inference accords with Freud's earlier accounts of "normal" male heterosexuality as a successful transference of early love of the mother to an appropriate partner. The oedipal complex refers not to the infant's narcissism but to the object relation to the mother that only gradually becomes possible (only when the young boy shatters the complex can he identify with the father). Yet there is a libidinal continuity linking the earlier autoerotic and oral phases with the oedipal-phallic relation to the mother. If Freud's treatment of this continuity remains vague, it only echoes the same absence of the mother to which I originally pointed. Oral themes in general, and the role of the mother in particular, seem to be systematically underplayed in Freud's opus. As even a loyal Freudian states it: "Freud never fully appreciated the significance of the oral stage." Indeed, "only scattered references to the mother and the oral stage appeared in the analytic literature before World War II."[9] (Melanie Klein would be the first psychoanalyst to push the causes of neurosis and psychosis back to the earliest days of life and so to reopen the mother question.) To these themes we will return. But now let us simply note that it is no surprise that being in love should serve—as Freud rightly observes—as the single socially sanctioned exception to the normal (manly) state of ego autonomy. For the aim of the oedipal resolution is to enable heterosexual bonding to someone other than the mother and to establish it in such a way as to assure male dominance. I am for the moment assuming that the oedipal complex describes accurately enough not nature but an infrastructure of the social apparatus.

Thus the brief regression to oceanic feeling is culturally allowed, we might surmise, both to assure mating and yet to limit the dangers of boundary-loss to a brief romantic phase, after which "business as usual" will limit it even further, even to the male's moment of orgasm. Women, captivated by the amorous male in his temporary reversion to oceanic openness, may soon find themselves captives indeed, powerless to prevent the dry boundaries and the hardening inequalities of the relation as it settles into patriarchal marriage. Being in love means something quite different for women, for whom it does not seem to constitute so violent an exception to our "normal" states. We might further speculate that being in love functions as a sort of social safety valve for the excess pressure of oceanic feeling, by which that feeling is channeled, along with women, into the institutions of heterosexual marriages and affairs. Without such emotional controls, males might otherwise explore subversive, altered states of "normalcy" to which love would be a key rather than the exception.

Freud's intention here is to give an account of *any* alleged feeling of internal relatedness to the world, since it occurs in adults apart from heterosexual romance according to Rolland's account of religious experience. Freud represents the exemplary Western Man when he admits to finding such a feeling incomprehensible: "The idea of *men's* receiving an intimation of their connection with the world around them through an immediate feeling which is from the outset directed to that purpose sounds so strange and fits in so badly with the fabric of our psychology that one is justified in attempting to discover a psycho-analytic . . . explanation of such a feeling" (my emphasis).[10] Ad hominem judgments aside, this honest confession of a lack of all connective feeling is revealing. To find intimations of interconnection so mysterious, so misfitting, may indeed be "men's" problem and prerogative. Such a feeling contradicts Freud's psychology, we may presume, because it has been omitted from the ideals of the andocentric civilization to which his analysis is limited. Along with women, the mystics, poets and otherwise sensitive or "religious" personalities to whom Rolland points remain at the margins.

In characterizing the desirable, normal ego feeling, Freud establishes a sharp division between the inner and the outer that the infant must begin to accomplish at the breast. Motives of defense direct the process of differentiation from the start, enabling "one to defend oneself against sensations of unpleasure which one actually feels or with which one is threatened." The need to ward off unpleasure in accordance with the developing "reality principle"— rather than to seek pleasure—initiates the production of the separate self. This is a helpful account: "One comes to learn a procedure by which, through a deliberate direction of one's sensory activities and through suitable muscular action, one can differentiate between what is internal—what belongs to the ego—and what is external—what emanates from the outer world."[11] From its infant incipience, the ego is cast in the brawny macho image of the muscular man. Indeed Hillman has commented on this strand of Freud's developmental theory: "a consciousness that works in this mode defines reality as that which responds to muscle power."[12] He suggests, from his own post-Jungian perspective, that the archetype of the heroic warrior, in its Herculean manifestation, has here taken hold of Freud. One imagines the emerging individual as an infant Heracles strangling the serpents of unpleasure in his cradle. (Sent, we might add, by the Terrible Mother Hera for whom Heracles is ironically named, suggesting that the heroic ego needs this primal opposition to an evil mother.) With "suitable muscular action" (especially represented by anal expulsion), the project of separation seems to be vigorously launched well before the oedipal complex is in place. In this way we get a glimpse behind the established scenes of the subject-object dualism into the ontogenesis of separation. If in the Aristotelian parlance a substantial individual is one that is not "in" something else, Freud offers an anal-expulsive theory for the achievement of this independence: the ego learns to "project, i.e., to transfer outwards, all that becomes troublesome to him from within."[13] Freud, a fan of separation, not only acknowledges that separate selfhood is nonoriginal, but that it must be achieved by an active process of *exclusion*.

What precisely is transferred outward as troublesome? The entire immanent world, it would seem: "originally the ego includes everything, later it *separates off an external world from itself*" (my emphasis).[14] This state of all-inclusive expansiveness, or primary narcissism, will then be recaptured in the ecstasies of mysticism. In Freud's psychoanalytic explanation, religious or other states of unboundedness can only count as nostalgia for an infantile unconsciousness. Yet even from this reductionist vantage point, Freud indulges in an interesting skepticism—as though he somehow regrets the ineluctable course of civilized normalcy. "Our present ego-feeling is, therefore, only a shrunken residue of a much more inclusive—indeed, all-embracing—feeling which corresponded to a more intimate bond between the ego and the world about it."[15]

In other words, Freud here confesses the massive loss, indeed loss of self, enforced by this normalcy: we forfeit the intimate sense of interconnection with the world and a plenitude of vital feeling, only to gain an egocentered dualism of self and other. Indeed, his remark well characterizes the poverty of psychic separatism. Yet he believes in no alternative to the dessicated self-attenuation. Maturity, then, means drying up oceanic feeling.

But does maturity really require us to break the "intimate bond"? And if it survives, need it be as a pathological anomaly alongside "normal" ego feeling? Is it intrinsically narcissistic and an obstacle to differentiation? Need we content ourselves to live as "shrunken residues"?

The Patricidal Ego Ideal

Inasmuch as maturity is defined in terms of separation, all intimacy will conjure up maternity and dependency. We see through Freud's eyes how connectivity will threaten the "civilized" with a return to the merger and self-loss imputed to infantile narcissism. Let us for now hold in awareness the role of the prepersonal mother, symbolizing solubility itself: the oceanic feeling, by which we might recollect and reconnect our original selves, wells up out of a mother-child unity that is always to be individually outgrown and culturally disgraced. The adult ego stands *over* and *against* the world and so dissociates itself from the feeling of connection *with* the world. Within the framework of this andromorphic self, intimations of a pervasive intimacy taste of the dread and salty sea mother. To every woman, whether she chooses to mother or not, adheres the monstrous atmosphere of oceanic feeling; one might lose oneself in her; she had a mother as did the man, but unlike him, she identified with her, she can always become her mother. And so she may seem vaguely monstrous to herself.

The doctrinal psychoanalytic preference for the father, which according to Freud "incontrovertibly" overpowers any longing for the mother, inaugurates a further phase of the slaughter of Tiamat. This patricentricity is presented precisely as part of the project of separate selfhood. The primordial experience of woman—her self-experience and man's experience of her—summons within a culture of separatism an endless current of anxiety, for she symbolizes the lack or the loss of all separateness. Her tidal feeling threatens the tidy boundaries.[16] Yet is any ocean boundless? The boundaries of an ocean are its shores, shifting continuously and subtly, sometimes gently, sometimes tempestuously, partly predictably, never controllably. The metaphor suggests an altered notion of ego boundary.

Freud counts immediate connectedness as narcissism. But the self-objectifying capacity of the reflexive self, which the first chapter exposed in a kind of metaphysical narcissism, marks the normative Freudian ego. The case is complex: that such an ego turns its hostile oppositionalism against itself as well as its world is clear already as Freud dramatizes the ego's battle against the aqueous incursions of the id. Though he deposes the ego's illusion of its own simple, rational unity, his subject has to turn against itself, against its own depths. And though for Freud the ego is not clearly demarcated from its own unconscious, this unconscious itself seems to be clearly bounded, containing only the personal past and the instinctual drives of the individual. We confront the situation of a Freudian psyche, which contains (among other things) an ego essentially separate from its world but permeable toward the id from which it arose. Is the unconscious itself ontologically self-encapsulated and so functioning as a kind of primal underlying substance? This would only mean that the fundamental unit of separateness includes more than the ego.

At least in his more speculative writings on culture, however, Freud recognized the need for a less separate psyche—in order, ironically, to sustain his case for a universal father complex. *Totem and Taboo* presents his myth of the original father, in which a brutal patriarch castrates his sons and keeps the women for himself. When the sons rise up and kill the father, the murdered father is commemorated and worshiped in the form of the animal totem and then finally in the form of the monotheistic father God. An ambivalent mix of guilt and adulation then results from the desire at once to *be* and to *have* the father, expressed in eating him, the oral form of identification. Identification via incorporation expresses the ambivalence at the core of the oedipal complex: the son, wishing to be like the father, wants to take his place and so internalizes, that is, ingests him. In other words, the hostile competition between father and son for the love of the mother, which characterizes the complex in individuals, is projected back to the origins of civilization: "the beginnings of religion, ethics, society and art meet in the Oedipus complex." But to account for the persistence of ambivalence through countless generations, Freud posits the possibility of a "psyche of the mass." Thus the father complex can be traced through the variations of individual experience: "We let the sense of guilt for a deed survive for thousands of years, remaining effective in generations which could not have known anything of this deed." [17]

Apart from the matter of historical content, the hypothesis of a "mass psyche," of "a continuity in the psychic life of mankind [sic]," is revolutionary in its implications for understanding the structure of the psyche. It suggests a profound and inescapable bond between all humans; it punctures the self-encapsulation of the ego. But the mass psyche is a concept invoked only lightly by Freud. It links up with his occasional notion of "primal fantasy" and especially with his view of the interdependence of individual and social psychology, as developed in *Group Psychology and the Analysis of the Ego* (1921).[18] Indeed the id, at least in Freud's late theory, is not the simple biological mechanism churning up animalistic desires as the popular caricature has it, but is in fact a cumulative inheritance of collective human experience:

The experiences of the ego seem at first to be lost for inheritance; but, when they have been repeated often enough and with sufficient strength in many individuals in successive generations, they transform themselves, so to say, into experiences of the id, the impressions of which are preserved by heredity. Thus in the id . . . are harboured residues of the existences of countless egos.[19]

While the ego contributes its own experience to the continuum of psychic experience, it turns out that the ego itself emerges from a process of internalizing those persons who represent its ego ideals. As Mitchell summarizes the theory of this process, "the ego is thus formed by this setting up of objects inside itself. It is also an important method of identification, so that it can be said that the ego is created by identifications." [20]

These clues point toward a dynamic of interconnection by cumulative incorporation, both individually and historically. They stand in tension with Freud's assumption of separate ego feeling, but especially with the ego ideals of the culture whose unconscious he seeks to describe. Perhaps this is why Freud's rare hints of a mass psyche or group mind remain so meager, especially if compared to Jung's systematic concept of a "collective" or "transpersonal" unconscious. (Jung's concept cannot be attributed to Freudian inspiration; if anything, the reverse is more likely, as the collective unconscious already figures prominently in *Symbols of Transformation* [1912], which signaled Jung's definitive break with Freud.)[21] We will soon return to Jung and his version. In the light of our previous discussion of de Beauvoir's work, it is interesting to note that she (like Sartre) objects to any hypothesis of an unconscious. As Mitchell points out, de Beauvoir mistakenly attributes to Freud the term *collective unconscious*.[22] Mitchell takes pains to free Freud of any onus of Jungianism. But is de Beauvoir's conflation of the theories not consonant with her defense of a separative transcendence? "It is the concept of choice," de Beauvoir argues, "that psychoanalysis most vehemently rejects in the name of determinism and the 'collective unconscious.'"[23] This charge, which all depth psychology would deny, would hold good only if the choices of individual freedom are absolutely separable from shared history." But is this not the freedom of individualism? Certainly her fears find some justification in Freud's bioculturally closed system, with its obsessive return to the father complex—though this is only a particular use of the theory of the unconscious.

This takes us back to the matter of content: the whole of civilized history is said to be generated by the oedipal complex, originating in the murder of the primal father. Freud, basing himself on the theories of Darwin, Atkinson and particularly Robertson Smith on totemism (which he tenaciously adhered to in *Moses and Monotheism,* though knowing them to be considered by then ethnologically refuted), intended his mythic account quite literally. On the one hand we can only support the admission that civilization as we know it is based on an unresolved, and therefore neurotic, father complex: this underwrites a feminist interpretation of history. But with this disclosure comes the assumption that civilization per se is patriarchal. That is, the oedipal theory is to function as a universal principle applicable to all forms of culture. What could offer a finer mechanism for reading women permanently out of culture? Though Freud (especially in *The Future of an Illusion*) advocates the ideal of science (e.g., in the invocation of *logos* and *ananke*) as a rational atheism in which dependence on the father, with its neurotic ambivalence, is finally outgrown, he glorifies theological and familial paternity as the sine qua non of all civilized futures. Even apart from the question of prepatriarchal cultures, this basis for entry into the future seems as impossible on feminist as on religious grounds.

Mitchell more or less accepts Freud's view of history, for she will not distinguish civilization from written textuality—and certainly the authors of civilization as we know it have been male. (It would seem that such nonpatriarchal cultures as the Minoan do not quite count as civilization because they preferred the oral tradition for important matters—to be known "by heart." But this is a different issue.) Mitchell finds hope for the overthrow of patriarchy in an internal contradiction that (in capitalism) it has brought on itself: "It would seem that the specifically capitalist ideology of a supposedly natural nuclear family would be in harsh contradiction to the kinship structure as it is articulated in the oedipal complex, which in this instance is expressed within this nuclear family." [24] She analyzes the kinship structure, with the help of Lévi-Strauss, as the exogamous brother clan that for Freud superseded the father horde. However unconvincing is her attempt to validate Freud's account of history (though she acknowledges it as mythic) she has pointed to an important tension, the discrepancy between brother-clan and nuclear father-family. Internal contradictions admit of eventual overthrow.

Do not the terms in which Freud diagnoses the oedipal neurosis prejudice the case from the outset, however? The ego ideal transmitted from generation to generation is derived from the father: emancipation, based on a final internalization of the ideal, freeing one from illusion, requires patricentricity. The mother remains obscured. And though it is culturally true that she has been thus rendered invisible, amorphous, the mere object of the male subject's desire, we need not presume—despite Lacan—that the unconscious *is* the father's law. [25] In personal and collective psychology the mother plays at least as prominent a role in the inferred contents of the unconscious—doubtless all the more due to the denial of her power. In its very capacity to resist the ego and represent to it the undesired content of its repressions, why would the "social psyche" not at some level have gathered a momentous energy of matrimorphic experiences? Is the oceanic feeling that Freud denies finally a sort of distillate of this nonpatriarchal momentum, occasionally surging into awareness?

The Freudian insights we have considered display the irony of a collective psyche transmitting the paternal principle of separation: that is, an unconscious that implicitly relates all individuals to their most ancient ancestors, yet in so doing foists upon them a father-identified, monolithic ego, an ego inimical to depth relation. Indeed, we encounter again the explicit image of the heroic male. In *Group Psychology*, Freud (borrowing from Rank's work on hero myths) claims that the hero stays and takes the place of the father: "The hero was a man who by himself had slain the father—the father who still appeared in the myth as a totemic monster. Just as the father had been the boy's first ideal, so in the hero who aspires to the father's place the poet now created the first ego ideal." By virtue of the myth, which emphasizes the hero's aggressive individualism, "the individual emerges from group psychology." That is, the ego ideal, transmitted through group psychology, is as we have imagined that of the solitary, patriarchal hero. Then—and here is a sentiment oddly close to that of the previous chapter—"the lie of the heroic myth culminates in the deification of the hero," precisely as "Father God."[26]

Patricide is the primordial deed in the Freudian vision of history, and patricide finally eventuates in the death of God. For in Freud's reading Christ emerges as the hero who at once atones for the murder of the primal father, but who enacts the murder of his deified substitute: thus God the Father is replaced by God the Son, whose sacrament is a totemic rite of incorporation in the oral mode of the Eucharist. Freud himself seems only to be carrying out the ongoing project of deicide. This is not a work to challenge patriarchy per se, but all illusions of divine protection. A healthy call to maturity, perhaps, and a welcome contribution to the overthrow of God the Father. But we may not wish to smash all possible images of deity along with the patriarchal idol. The "shrunken residue" with which Freud had to content himself results from draining out all oceanic feeling. Perhaps the goddesses, gorgons and other images of non-patriarchal power in the cosmos will turn out to be inseparable from an oceanically widened experience of self. One thing is clear: the disappearance of the mother is exactly reflected in that of any mother goddess, both in culture and in Freud's analysis. And is not Freud's own emphasis upon patricide perhaps a form of latent matricide? For the Freudian patricide itself presupposes a prior, still more deeply repressed, matricide—a matricide reenacted at the level of theory when Freud privileges the father. Does this repressive preference not exemplify the real "lie of the heroic myth"?

Marduk at Mid-life

With the analytical psychology of C. G. Jung, we move from the patricentric prose of Freud into a system mother-centered in its content and mythic in its medium. It was Jung who introduced into the analytic literature the importance of the mother imago (Klein would later pioneer the field of early childhood relations with the literal mother). He also initiated the psychological use of the very concept of "self," through his preoccupation with "individuation" and "wholeness." Though individuation presupposes an ego defined by separation from the mother, the whole self at which individuation aims requires ultimate reconciliation, in terms of the Jungian imagery, with the slaughtered mother. His advocacy of self, rather than ego alone, is surely related to his matricentricism. Whereas the matricide is itself repressed in the Freudian scheme, it takes center stage in Jung's thought. Here we will find even Tiamat, named, still undergoing her cyclic sacrifice at the hands of Marduk, marking both the onset and the apex of Jung's career. But to what extent does Jung's theory construct itself with the weapons of Marduk out of the First Mother's carcass? Especially in the light of Jung's own double messages to women, this will prove no easy question to answer.

Symbols of Transformation,[27] first published in 1912, effected a definitive break with Freud, inaugurating Jung's original vision; it offers a mythologically opulent interpretation of the published fantasies of a Miss Miller. In the rich symbolism of her visions, Jung discovers the archetypal journey of the hero: the hero's dragon fight, the sacrifice of the dragon and finally the sacrifice of the hero to the mother, by which the hero returns to her womb and is reborn. From the outset Jung takes the dragon to be the mother. He reinterprets the psychoanalytic incest theory, speculating that the desire for reunion with the mother involves more than sexual instinct, indeed becomes symbolic of the return to the unconscious itself as the generatrix and annihilator of all merely subjective experience. Here we encounter the Mother not primarily as introject of the literal mother, but as archetypal pattern for all that is originative, bearing and birth giving, indeed for the cycles of birth, death and rebirth by which life renews itself at every level.

How does the maternal presence become such a Magna Mater? "The most important relationship of childhood, the relation to the mother, will be compensated by the mother archetype as soon as detachment from the childhood state is indicated." [28] Rather than being superceded by the oedipal father, the experience of the mother is transformed—not merely sublimated—into a psychic reality which manifests herself both as monster and as *mater spiritualis*. Traditionally she has appeared in collective symbols such as the fairy godmother, Mother Church, Mother Mary or Mother Nature, archaically as the multitude of Goddesses. But the archetypal mother remains the subject of ambivalence because the symbolic incest, which provides escape from maturation, remains a great temptation to the fledgling ego. "Whoever sunders himself from the mother longs to get back to the mother. This longing can easily turn into a consuming passion which threatens all that has been won. The mother then appears on the one hand as the supreme goal, and on the other as the most frightful danger—the 'Terrible Mother.'" [29] Then we encounter all the demonized manifestations, of which our monsters of chapter 2 are classic specimens. Jung lists embodiments of the Terrible Mother found elsewhere: "the witch, the dragon (or any devouring or entwining animal, such as a large fish or a serpent), the grave, deep water, death, nightmares and bogies (Empusa, Lilith, etc.)." [30] The sea monster manages to incorporate the best of all of these beasts in her fabulous syncretism. It is from Jung that we learn most definitively that the mythic matricide is an act of self-defense on the part of the heroic ego consciousness and that this matricide repeats itself endlessly in a culture centered around such an ego's consciousness. So it is that early in his career Jung finds in the narrative of Marduk's triumph over Tiamat "complete confirmation" of his surmise that "the fight with the 'nocturnal serpent' accordingly signifies conquest of the mother." [31]

In this sense Jung's theory of ego development originates in the ancient matricide. His theory supports our suspicion that the matricidal symbolism not only expresses but provokes the Western development of a separate and andromorphic ego. Symbols are never passive; they participate in that to which they point (cf. Paul Tillich). We note also that the hero figure in "Miss Miller's" fantasies is invariably a male, a fact that finds its dogmatic interpretation in

Neumann's designation of all ego development as metaphorically masculine. But for now let us linger with the images. Pointing to the parallels with the Old Testament dragon fights, Jung generalizes concerning the function of this conquest: "The world is created from the mother, i.e., with the libido that is withdrawn from her through the sacrifice, and through prevention of the regression that threatened to overcome the hero." [32] In other words, the ego-self is creating its reality, its life world, from the energy it derives from the archetypal mother. The hero sacrifices her in her sea monster form and so becomes heir to her life force, which he can use for his own dryer, daylight work of world making. The hero's glorious first task is to murder the mother and steal her power.

"It is easy to see what the battle with the sea-monster means: it is the attempt to free the ego-consciousness from the deadly grip of the unconscious." [33] "Deadly" presumably because it prevents the emergence of conscious individuality. Unconsciousness for Jung suggests an analogy, abstracted from early relations, to Freud's "boundless narcissism"—self-containment in a womblike infinity. He continues: "Unfortunately, however, this heroic deed has no lasting effects. Again and again the hero must renew the struggle, and always under the symbol of deliverance from the mother." [34]

But we might argue that the deeper misfortune lies in this need for the mother to serve as scapegoat for the hostility, opposition and disconnection by which the heroic ego develops. For this mythic drama inexorably plays itself out in the domain of literal relationships. Nothing motivates action in the real world as well as symbolism; the psychocultural scope of myth encompasses the socioeconomic interactions as well as the interpersonal and intrapsychic. Though Jung often evades these consequences, no theorist in the century more clearly demonstrates the elemental force of live images than he. "The psychological mechanism that transforms energy is the symbol." [35] In other words, symbolic, psychic matricide conspires with interpersonal and social misogyny.

While the hero figures in history, as in Jung's account, are almost invariably male, they appear as ego instigators for both male and female psyches; thus Jung is not in the least troubled by the fact that Miss Miller is fantasizing the development of her ego consciousness in masculine terms. We must wonder how such identification as Miss Miller's with the heroic matricide would affect a female sense of self. Is such male identification the prerequisite of any distinctive selfhood within a collective patriarchy? But we also continue to pose the question: Must either female or male identity shape itself in opposition to the mother?

Though Jung may not provide satisfactory answers to such questions, his descriptions of the psychological role of the fundamental matricide remain invaluable. While he steadfastly operates *within* the patriarchal myth, he also exposes it. In this we can read him like Freud. But Jung helps to uncover a deep structure of matriphobic strife underlying the civilizations of the world. The psyche according to Jung finds only short-lived satisfaction in the conquest of the Mother. The teleology of the psyche drives beyond the matricidal stage. For the hero who thus establishes his world at the expense of the mother, indeed creates it from stolen Goddess power (in Mary Daly's sense), must eventually repay the debt. The youthful sacrifice of the Mother eventuates in the hero's self-sacrifice *to* the Mother. The ego constituted by the illusion of its own autonomy vis-à-vis the Deep—its own unconscious depths—must now face the depth of the illusion.

Here we encounter the basis for Jung's theory of the mid-life transition. Indeed he pioneered the very notion of a mid-life crisis, as that point at which the demands of the larger psyche—the Self—hitherto repressed by the one-sided demands of societal existence, must finally be met. The "first half" of life tends to be preoccupied with issues of ego development and the establishment of a socially effective persona, involving, predictably, career and family for the male and the "biological task" of motherhood for the female. Jung did not invent the conventional situation; he does, however, observe that these social roles break down at mid-life. The psyche that clings to them undergoes breakdown, neurosis or a deadening inertia. The confrontations with one's inner others—the "shadow," (one's repressed, underdeveloped and so recalcitrant alter-ego)—and with anima and animus (the contrasexual aspects of one's own personality) become the doors to any further psychic liveliness. Jung's actual characterizations of the anima as the feminine soul in a male and the animus as the masculine spirit in a female are notoriously ridden with sexism. We encounter here the social stereotype masquerading as the eternal archetype (the anima as seductive, sensuous, intuitive, inspiring; the animus as rational, opinionated, focusing, spiritual). Yet even in the face of this infamous liability, we may acknowledge the historic value of a psychology that saw little hope for healthy well-being beyond mid-life for men or for women, unless traits and tasks conventionally reserved for the opposite sex are activated and assimilated by both. The theory early pointed toward a selfhood exceeding the sort of oppositional dyad we have seen in the separative and soluble selves. Their complementary dualism would spring from what Jung calls the "projection" of the anima and the animus: making the actual other into the image of a potentiality one has not owned for oneself and *as* oneself. Projection of the man's anima onto a woman causes her to bear the burden of those traits he ought to develop in and for himself, but has repressed because of their "femininity." For example, though he is in fact every bit as dependent, vulnerable or sexual as a woman, if he does not "rescue" such Andromeda traits in himself, he will try to keep the actual woman in a captive state of dependency upon him, her femininity at his disposal. By projection he expels unwelcome, female-associated traits from his own ego. Projection certainly collaborates with the exclusive mechanisms of the separative ego: to project is literally to exclude, to put outside oneself. (Something like the reverse is purported to be true of women, but the parallelism invariably breaks down, as women Jungian analysts such as Bolen and de Perera have demonstrated. Perhaps this is due partly to the fact that the terms of gender complementarity have themselves been set by men.)

At the metaphoric mid-life point, a Self infinitely larger than the earlier ego consciousness beckons. Jung's classic distinction of ego and Self moves his theory out of the lockstep of the warrior mythos. The hero must sacrifice his pretensions to the demands of the greater Self. The Self works upon ego consciousness through the heroic image of the journey, a journey that leads beyond warrior consciousness. But it lures us also through an indefinite variety of nonanthropomorphic symbols (such as animals, rocks and quaternities in dreams). It expresses the unlimited force field of the psyche's potential, unbalancing any smug equilibriums, demanding more work, more opening, more realization of whatever is other, disparate, repressed—the lost coins, the prodigal children. Confusingly, the Self is itself an archetype and so always represents the potential for actualization, but is not anything already actualized by and as myself: to identify one's ego with it is inflation. (Inflation in Jung also takes place in the uroboric infantile unity with mother and universe and so offers another parallel with Freud's primary narcissism.) Self includes but is not the same as "I." I arise from its depths, and emerge all the more enriched if I can hear its oneiric parables and heed its elusive impulses. The complex expanse of the Jungian Self seems quite the opposite of the shrunken residue, which we could describe as an ego denying its Self.

But if Jung's encompassing insights are to work for rather than against women we must face up to certain perils and pitfalls. It seeks to unfold the life development of males and females in terms of symmetrical if opposed schemes—each called from within to overcome the one-sided sex roles imposed by society. But the notions of the initial matricide and the ultimate sacrifice of the warrior ego are meant to characterize development for both sexes and so portray the ego in irremediably masculine terms. Furthermore, the entire scheme of the two halves misfits women: while often it is indeed at mid-life that we realize what has been missing, there has been lacking precisely the development of a firm enough ego, or focal self, and therefore the sacrifice of ego at this point appears not only irrelevant, but literally suicidal—self-killing. This androcentrism, concealed by the seductive rhetoric of complementary symmetry, underlies the appalling inequity of anima and animus functions that sometimes surfaces in Jung's thinking: "Just as a man brings forth his work as a complete creation out of his inner feminine nature, so the inner masculine side of a woman brings forth creative seeds which have the power to fertilize the feminine side of the man." [36] In other words, when the man gets in touch with his anima, his creativity flourishes; when a woman gets in touch with her animus, it inspires her man's anima, and *his* creativity flourishes! Woman's "wholeness" remains a means to man's end.

Exploitative imbalances within collective patriarchal culture receive a new lease on life through such justification. Like Freud, Jung here as elsewhere renders *descriptive* truths *normative*. While this scheme is mythically matrifocal, it remains psychologically androcentric: the heroic male subject emerges from the Mother, sacrifices her and creates his cosmos from her carcass in "the first half"; then again at mid-life he returns willy-nilly to her destructive/regenerative womb, from which he may or may not emerge reborn. But this mythopsychic journey seems to be a male prerogative, and those men who can best afford to undergo the transformation (even in the simple economic sense of good therapy) are often those who most forcefully enacted the matricidal sexism during the first half. Neither in the Jungian scheme nor in the culture it reflects do we find valued and comparably established possibilities for women in their "second half." On the contrary, the menopausal woman is so much without cultural support for her life changes that her solitude is usually too privative and too private to be transformative. And as her roles of maiden and mother fade, she finds herself devalued as crone—the wisdom of wise old men, not wise old women, is sought, when wisdom is sought at all.

My object at present, however, is less to repudiate Jung for his unregenerate sexism, or even for his explicit antifeminism,[37] than to discern why these biases rest comfortably upon a system that in so many ways—and so unlike Freud's—celebrates the "feminine" and seeks its symbolic restitution. Beyond matters of cultural stereotype, I believe this discrepancy has everything to do with the mythologem of matricide, especially when it is interpreted as fear of unconsciousness. But what are the terms of consciousness? A passage from a later work links the matricidal to the masculine in the formation of consciousness itself:

There is no consciousness without discrimination of opposites. This is the paternal principle, the Logos, which eternally struggles to extricate itself from the primal warmth
and primal darkness of the maternal womb; in a word, from
unconsciousness. Unconsciousness is the primal sin, evil itself, for the Logos. Therefore, its first creative act of liberation is matricide.[38]

This statement would seem altogether accurate if we add that it describes consciousness as it has emerged in the last 3,500 years under the sign of the paternal Logos. This historically bound consciousness experiences the unconscious and the first Mother as "evil." Logos consciousness has arisen quite directly from the chain of theological patriarchies extending from the *Enuma Elish,* to the Book of Genesis, and to the Gospel of John. This is consciousness conceived as opposition—consciousness on the model of the vanquishing hero, the light conquering the darkness. Consciousness is *over against* its object. It is a perpetual process of repulsion *from,* not unlike the expulsion that motivates the early Freudian ego. In other words, it is characterized in strictly negative terms, as extrication from the mother: one long matriphobic work of self-separation.

At least in the context of the masculine first half of life, Jung expresses no ambivalence toward this overtly patriarchal oppositionalism. In fact his own scheme draws such deep inspiration from the German mystical and Hegelian tradition of dialectical polarity that opposition becomes for him the inner dynamic of all growth and individuation: consider such polar pairs as ego and Self, persona and shadow, extravert and introvert, masculine and feminine. The matricide must always occur if there is to be conscious life, though he also celebrates the restitution of the Mother through the sacrifice of that ego created by the matricide. But how few of those male egos who achieve an early *superbia* of separation will in fact pass through the sacrificial initiation of mid-life to some genuinely altered consciousness! And of those who do, many will have contributed the tasks and outward energies of their "first half" to the continuing creation of Marduk's cosmos—a civilization founded on the reduction of female power to sexual subservience and domesticated maternity. Women today also can partake in the normative, first-half matricidal consciousness—only to lay themselves open to charges of "animus-possession." For men and women, do the rituals of ego-assertion/ego-sacrifice perhaps perpetuate the same old cycle?

Is some alternative to the separative model of ego-liberation, with its implicit misogyny, perhaps conceivable from the start? Friction, struggle, even opposition are no doubt part of the emergence of any differentiated awareness: in any event of knowing, *this* must be distinguished from *that*, *a* from *b*, I from you. But all modes of contrast are not played out in the grandiose theatre of opposition and union. Though, as Hillman argues, Jung's pairs of opposites cannot count as "either/or thinking . . . his pairs are antagonistic and complementary at the same time, but never contradictories"[39] Hillman also warns that Jung's "oppositionalism" holds Jungians captive to the deeply-entrenched divide-and-conquer motives of the heroic ego. With these various reservations up front, we nonetheless turn to Jung's theory of the collective unconscious. For it seems to offer a revolutionary, empirically based and psychologically elaborated ground for the nonseparative ego.

Open to All the World?

Sacrificing its own illusory claims to autonomy, the ego's task becomes that of reconnecting with the depth and breadth of life from which it had so early cut itself off. For the mother archetype symbolizes the ego's relation to its own deeper psyche, the transpersonal or collective unconscious. By its very nature, it belies the separate ego of the warrior-hero. This was also true of the Freudian id, a domain undermining the control and the pretenses of the conscious ego and in Freud's thought beginning to open into a social history shared by all persons. But the discovery and charting of a collective unconscious is Jung's greatest achievement. It suggests not only a permeability inward, toward one's own memories, drives and their repressions; it discloses a level where the dichotomies (though not the distinctions) between the personal and the collective, self and other, ego and world, my past and yours, the human and the divine, disintegrate.

Reintegration of the psyche on the basis of its own transpersonal scope requires the process Jung calls "individuation." Authentic individuality can be gained only when I experience myself as fundamentally connected to all of life: this is the wisdom of the Jungian outlook. An ego-transcending selfhood is massively relational, exposing the individuality of the separate ego as the sham of individualism and a fabrication of persona. "The collective unconscious is anything but an incapsulated personal system; it is sheer objectivity, as wide as the world and open to all the world." [40] This vision of a radical world–openness suggests the essence of a connective self. The subject encounters the world of others not just externally but also in itself, as part of its own life. Real parents, friends, foes, and trees certainly retain their status as external objects; they are freed as we retract our projections to be more exactly themselves for us. At the same time the idea of this "transpersonal psyche" arouses a sense for the delicate currents flowing from that depth where all things become part of each other. For good or for ill, human, perhaps even planetary history is stored up in a collective memory, crystallized in the form of archetypal patterns of infinitely repeated experience. These are for Jung no more than for Freud the preestablished symbols that rightly worry de Beauvoir; they do not become images until they interact with our concrete experience. The influence of life upon life is cumulative: we never begin from scratch, but with deep and difficult accumulations of past history. This helps explain why widely held myths (such as that of matricide) are so tenacious in their grip, operating like compulsions. Yet it also suggests a basis for hope. If it is true that in its depths our unconscious bottoms out, flooding into the world, as it floods into us, the influence is not unilateral: our conscious, individual and communal experiences and actions can and do make a difference, affecting—however gradually—the collective unconscious itself.

If in a few minds and souls the figure of Tiamat takes on a new, salutory life, for instance, she will begin to surge up in the collective consciousness as well. After a while a certain readiness for change can make itself felt, where before there had been only combat and resistance. Of course, any widespread changes can be explained strictly on more externalist, sociological or economic models, models which Jungians neglect all too easily in favor of inner–worldliness. However, does the very dichotomy between internal and external worlds or models not express the separative paradigm? We do well to give some credence to this theory of the transpersonal psyche precisely because it points beyond the inner-outer, private-public dualisms. It has a socially revolutionary potential that Jung himself, with his eternalist predelections, hardly explored.

There are spiritual undertones in any archetypally founded hope. The Mother is at once a primary content of the unconscious and a representation of its generativity. For example, the contemporary recrudescence of Tiamat greeted as promise, not threat, would raise oceanic feeling to the second power! If Freud's atheism seemed consonant with his patricidal priority, Jung's acknowledgment of the matricide and consequent attempt to reverse it reopen the reality of ultimate concern. The image regains the transparency of an icon. The archetypal perforations in the individual's life, through which collective life flows in and the individual input flows out, are at the same time windows to the sacred. While Jung's religious realism can serve to glorify privileged old patterns, to deify the cumulative past and to justify its conservative inertias, the alternative of dogmatic theism and dogmatic atheism merely close doors on the possible. Jung's concept of the Self as *imago dei* can unduly mystify psychology. Yet it can also root the human in a sacred Deep beneath consciousness, helping to heal the patriarchal dichotomy of God and World.

I mentioned at the beginning of this discussion that Tiamat appears at the end as well as the beginning of Jung's career. Here is the later text: "To challenge the unformed chaotic Tiamat world is in fact the primordial experience. . . . When man lays his hand to this work, he repeats, as the alchemists say, 'the creative work of God.' "[41] The matricidal opus is in a sense still implied here. Nevertheless, the notion of *challenging* the primordial Deep surely has different connotations from *killing* Her, suggesting the desire to rouse, face, and struggle with our depths. Indeed, the hint of a more reverent, less murderous approach to the Deep femaleness can be gleaned from Genesis 1: but only if the Tehom is acknowledged as no less divine than the Spirit, and only if woman also lays *her* hand to this task. Then perhaps the unconscious rituals of collective matricide can gradually become obsolete. But the collaboration of sexism and separatism, playing itself out even within systems that peer beyond the limits of paternalism, will continue until an alternative pattern for self-differentiation emerges. The matricidal style of male ego-differentiation during the first half of life costs the world and its women far too much to be endured. Indeed it even costs men's psyches more than they care to admit, causing them to use women and world as scapegoats.

Let me suggest that in a certain sense one finds the characteristics of the so-called second half of life already in the first half for women. Women (as Nancy Chodorow will soon explain) are far less likely to have eradicated the sense of connection to others, nature and self which men seek to regain in later life. Yet it would be ludicrous to infer—as the complementary logic of the scheme might imply—that therefore women should develop masculine, matricidal egos as our second-half chore of individuation. Of course such logic may seem a propos when women, having raised families or otherwise given themselves to purely relational tasks in their earlier life, go about developing professional skills or asserting newfound strengths—but why submit this process, itself delayed only by patriarchal social order, to the metaphors of masculine matriphobia? Would not this only pit women, Athena-style, against our deep Self?

If women sustain a more lucid connection with the unconscious from the outset, this makes us not less but more conscious. For what is it to become conscious but to make intentional connection with what has previously remained unconscious? We do not need to become "masculine" as we mature, but more focussed, more creative, more luminous just as women.

I am admitting a deep and ambivalent indebtedness to Jung for his discovery of the collective psyche and his acknowledgment of the primacy of matriphobia in this culture's unconscious: he offers vivid evidence that the ancient myths of matricidal heroics cannot be relegated to a distant past, but still shape personality today. His recollection of the dismembered Tiamat provokes a collective anamnesis. It begins, in spite of his own ambivalence, to convert the matriphobic amnesia evident, for instance, in his colleague Freud's work, into conscious admission of the power of the female. As we have seen, however, Jung does not restrict himself to a phenomenonological description of matricide but also exalts it as a symbolic necessity. Furthermore, the hero emerges as the paradigm for both the ego and the Self, confirming the suspicion that the Jungian perspective remains deeply androcentric. Despite its ego-transcending energies, its importance to so many women, and its fascination with the "feminine," his vision remains mired in the myth of the masculine warrior. Thus it can tend to counteract its own best intentions until patterns of non-antagonized consciousness can reshape it.

Perhaps efforts to dedramatize the struggle of opposites can only bear fruit if they challenge Jung's nearly remainderless translation of motherhood into the Magna Mater. Literal mothers must receive their due. Individual mothers of course are not held responsible for their children's adult personalities in Jung's scheme, and in this way it provides relief from all mother-blaming misogynism. "Why risk saying too much," pleads Jung, "about that human being who was our mother, the accidental carrier of that great experience which includes herself and myself and all mankind, and indeed the whole of created nature, the experience of life whose children we are?" [42] The problem with such radical deliteralizing is that it degrades mothers from the other side, not by blaming them but by ignoring them. If their role is "accidental," compared to the—we may presume—essential archetype, not only is the endless psychic and physical work of maternal nurture denigrated to the rank of the merely external; the old Aristotelian dualism of substance and accident, with its implicit separatism, has come back into play. Relations in this view, like bodies, are merely accidental.

For our purposes, however, we will need to rejoin the discussion of the maternal monster with that of actual mothers. After all, archetypes are cumulatively compounded of the endless reiteration of such an actual human experience as mothering and being mothered. While any literal mother enacts this collective experience in her child, her contribution is not thereby trivial and accidental! Such reduction of human experience to archetype gravely diminishes the import of human relations and oddly belies the "openness to all the world" of the shared psyche.

Validating women's experience, validating Tiamat and validating the liveliest sense of the collective unconscious requires a full-fledged exploration of the role of relations. This begins in early childhood, with the very first relation—in our culture, a relation to the mother or mother substitute. We cannot symbolize away either the tragic or the graceful realities of this actual relation, especially within a culture that makes motherhood at once a sacred duty and a low self-subjugation to the Father. We must at this point seek insight into the influences of actual early relations on gender development and the initial sense of self as separate, or otherwise. We have seen both Freud and Jung identifying human development with separation from the maternal, a similarity all the more telling against the background of their radical divergences. Now we turn to a conversation with certain contemporary, largely feminist, perspectives emerging from a reformed psychoanalytic base. Recognizing male dominance as a social structure of oppression as well as a psychological complex, they can provide us with critical pieces in the puzzle of human development, and together yield a possible answer to our fundamental question: How do separation and sexism collaborate in the structuring of our selves? Now we shall address more concretely the question of why male dominance roosts with such tenacity among the universals of our culture.

Mom the Mermaid

Dorothy Dinnerstein analyzes the sources and the effects of the primordial ambivalence toward the female. Her richly layered work, *The Mermaid and the Minotaur*, takes its cue from Melanie Klein's classic essay "On Envy." Woman invariably appears, according to Dinnerstein's astute thesis,[43] as an encompassing, semihuman presence, evoking in us all, ever after, the desires, needs, frustrations, and humiliations of the infant. The father, by contrast, offers relief from this vague and inevitable power; he appears on the scene late, clean and idealized in his detachment, free of the onus of the nursery and offering the child the saving possibilities of objectivity and autonomy. Consequently both men and women value the male more highly, resulting in men loathing women and women loathing themselves. Under the circumstances female complicity with patriarchy seems inevitable! Yet at the same time the mother in this culture offers a special nurturant for individuality, "a magic richness." Women, because they identify with mothers, retain inner access to "the magic non-self" that the mother represented for the infant.[44] Men by contrast rarely find this magic in themselves, and so depend upon women to re-mother them.

Dinnerstein locates the ultimate cause of the situation quite concretely in the childcare arrangements that the human race has maintained throughout history. As long as women remain the primary caretakers in the early years, the same sexist conditions will replicate themselves. Only the equal participation of men in early child-rearing can alleviate the situation. Her thesis is not as simplistic as it might at first sound. For Dinnerstein, like Klein, believes that the first parental presences will always appear to threaten as well as to support the autonomy of the emerging ego-individuality. (Klein's "bad breast" theory is in the background.) To the infant in a typical situation of primary female parenting, the mother is a "global, inchoate and all-embracing presence before she is a person, a discrete finite human individual with a subjectivity of her own."[45] The contempt of men for women and of women for themselves is brewed in this nursery atmosphere of nondifferentiation and maternal omnipresence. "The earliest roots of antagonism to women lie in the period before the infant has any clear idea where the self ends and the outside world begins, or any way of knowing that the mother is a separately sentient being." Inevitably, the first parental presence will be the promising/threatening background to true selfhood. For us the mother has been "that from which the self must be carved out."[46]

In Dinnerstein's image of the global, maternal, semisentient surround we may again fancy young Marduk carving his world from the monstrous carcass of the First Mother. *The Mermaid and the Minotaur* takes its title from the realm of the semihuman, the monstrous, the infant fantasy. Though the author offers little exegesis of these images, the mermaid certainly evokes the seductive danger of the fishy underside of female fluidity to the Odyssean ego.

Fathers, Dinnerstein believes, can on principle (like the Minotaur, we may suppose) exude this atmosphere of the presubjective. All it would take is full male involvement in earliest childcare. But because women dominate in infancy, "unqualified human personhood can be sealed off from the contaminating atmosphere of infant fantasy and defined as male."[47] Injustice consists in letting the mother bear the major brunt of the later emotional rebellion (rebellion against the father seems sharper and swifter, less bloody and hurtful—as we saw in the images of *Enuma Elish*). If then both parents are in future to absorb fairly equal portions of the ambivalence and alienation directed at them by the growing child, Dinnerstein demonstrates that full male participation is necessary. Males then would also gain access to the magical nurturant in themselves and be less dependent upon women for affective refreshment. The psychosocial picture would be different indeed if men and women found parents of both genders equally nurturing and equally threatening from the outset.

While I cannot disagree with Dinnerstein's basic project, I am disturbed by two fundamental assumptions. First, she presupposes that completely equal early contributions are possible (even without resorting to test-tube babies, etc.). Certainly equal affective and practical involvement of male and female parent figures is imaginable and desirable. But is it yet evident that even under the most liberated of circumstances, men *can* make a precisely equal initial impact on children? Prenatal bonding and breast-feeding may work a certain inevitable imbalance in favor of maternal influence. If the literal equality of early influence is the only key to liberation, the door may not open.

Second, Dinnerstein does not question the ideal of ego separation. Here she stands consciously with Freud and de Beauvoir. The fully autonomous and discrete subject, for whom the dividing line between self and world is clear, remains for her the undoubted condition and even the aim of maturity and freedom. Not that she abandons us to the state of a dessicated residuum. Rather, the internalized magical promise and danger of the original Other is internalized, releasing marvelous adventures of self-refreshment and overcoming projective dependency upon the opposite sex. But the psychoanalytic and existential ideals of the separately sentient individual sit heavy on her vision. Indeed, this criticism is related to the previous one. For if connectivity is not felt to have an intrinsic value at least equal to that of independence, then the biological surplus of nurture that may come from women in the first months of life will always undermine the feminist project. That is, women's mothering, even under firmly egalitarian conditions, would continue to present a radical psychosocial liability for women in general. It would continue to result in an irredeemable surd of subautonomy in daughters, and of later matriphobia and so misogyny in both sons and daughters. And certainly single or Lesbian mothers would be doomed to produce misogynist children.

If, however, individuality were no longer opposed to relationship, the extra edge of early maternal presence need not work out to women's disadvantage. Indeed, our historically unbroken association with the ways of relation might then offer, far from a constricting demand, a welcome wisdom. This resource, with its very ancient roots, will never spread wide without precisely the sort of transformation Dinnerstein advocates—implying such solid economic and social changes as work conditions permitting both male and female participation in childcare. But in the meantime our memories of mothers who had no wider world and larger purposes than motherhood, memories lacking the early copresence of tender male parenting, will continue to surround everything female with an aura of the sub-subjective, the monstrous.

Perhaps this wisdom of women must be sought already, in the face of all ambivalence, at the roots of empathetic connection. Indeed, this wisdom may stem from a place within the psyche where the "global, inchoate and all-embracing presence" of all that is *not* my ego continues to belong. Dinnerstein exposes the emotional obstacles to any deep reconnection with the mother and so with any woman. Yet as she sees no realism in the less clearly bounded interaction it recalls, she can of course only advocate female achievement of a discrete ego. We still learn from her to emulate traditional masculine autonomy.

We must turn to Carol Gilligan, and especially to Nancy Chodorow, for a related account of gender development from early childhood, but one that finds positive potential in the *daughter's* particularity. Gilligan's sociological study, to which we turn only briefly, echoes Chodorow's much weightier psychoanalytic account of psychosocial gender structures. Through their readily paired work, a radically new insight into the female predelection for connection enters feminist theory.

Separation Vs. Attachment

Carol Gilligan's *In a Different Voice* burst upon the women's studies scene with resounding éclat: its empirical grounding reopened on firmly feminist footing the rocky question of sexual difference.[48] As her work has already received widespread attention, we need only underline the relevance of its main thesis to our general query concerning sexism and separation. Gilligan argues that psychological theorists have in general equated the process of separation with the process of maturation. They identify development itself with separation, and attachments appear as developmental impediments.[49] She shows how this equation is derived from normal male experience: "Implicitly adopting the male life as the norm, they have tried to fashion women out of a male cloth. It all goes back, of course, to Adam and Eve—a story which shows, among other things, that if you make a woman out of a man, you are bound to get into trouble."[50] Her case is pitched against Kohlberg's theory of moral development, but she demonstrates comparable "trouble" elsewhere, as in the theories of Freud and Erickson. Based on a long-range interview process parallel to Kohlberg's, her research corroborates the present project's argument.

Gilligan demonstrates that the celebration of autonomous, separate selfhood, as a value abstracted from and superior to relationship, only answers to male experience. Then female experience, in which issues of differentiation are inextricably bound up with issues of relationship, appears deviant and implicitly inferior. As we heard Aristotle argue, man is the norm for the species, from which woman, like any monster, diverges. In Freud's theory of female castration and penis envy, to which we will return, precisely the same structure is recapitulated: females are defined by a deforming lack. Gilligan has gathered good evidence that it is precisely women's tendency to value connection as the essential context of our identity that has traditionally (i.e., in patriarchal culture and psychology) marked us as inferior. As we have been suspecting, woman's purported monstrosity, her deviation from the norm, springs from her connectivity.

Gilligan here articulates her hypothesis of gender difference: "Since masculinity is defined through separation while femininity is defined through attachment, male gender identity is threatened by intimacy while female gender identity is threatened by separation. Thus males tend to have difficulty with relationships, while females tend to have problems with individuation." [51] As a description of the conventional dyad, her account hits the mark. Yet one does not quite know by whom masculinity and femininity are so "defined": androcentric theorists, her own theory, culture, or nature? Indeed, Gilligan's balanced approach, leading her to couch the problem in terms of a diametrical opposition of strengths and vulnerabilities, might suggest a misleading gender symmetry. Yet her thesis in fact rests upon the deep asymmetry in the perspectives of male psychologists, reflecting the assumptions of a male-dominated culture.

Her claim is not that women should or do acquiesce in a merely relational sort of personality, caught up in self-sacrificial care for others to the exclusion of their own self-development. But she shows that as women mature, they begin to exercise a responsibility to self, analogous to their responsibilities for others, thus gradually easing the dependency expressed in the fear of separation. Though women may cease to depend upon particular relationships, their basic commitment to relationship seems rarely in her study to be unseated by commitment to self and work. Rather, women gradually cultivate caring relationship *to* self and work. Men undergo in her view an opposite but complementary process. Initially they show a tendency to associate intimacy with violence. But they can come to realize that integrity may include genuine intimacy and care without loss of self (and career). The basis of her optimism about male development remains less persuasive. This is partly because she does not analyze the process by which males might transcend the sense of fundamental separateness: the reasons why they should undergo such self-transformation remain much more mysterious in her account than the parallel but opposite motives for women.

While admirably irenic, such complementariness minimizes the historical tension. The problem with this desire for balance shows its face in her too facile conclusion, where she proposes a dialectical synthesis based on "the integrity of two disparate modes of experience that are in the end connected." [52] Not that this hope is unfounded—certainly connection abides! But how can we evoke separate but equal integrities moving toward a synthesis, in which man and woman get the best of both worlds, when the very terms of the opposition have been posed by patriarchy from the start? And might not such a synthesis water down the possibilities of woman's peculiar contribution, resulting in an innocuous compromise? Also it might not fortify the assumption that men must *begin* with disconnection.

Certainly Gilligan's work (like any account of gender differences) runs the risk of giving inadvertent support to the old tradition of sexual complementarity. The popular accessibility of her book seems to exacerbate the danger that her own definitions of males as autonomous and females as attached will be misunderstood as declaring two essentially complementary natures. Then—however unfairly—the theory can be homologized to the stereotypical oppositions of masculine and feminine essences, which we repudiate in Jungian psychologies. This familiar risk is in itself no reason to avoid the issue of difference. The alternative, to reduce all difference to biology and/or conditioning, begs the important question: What are our resources for a postpatriarchal self and world? Gilligan is courageous to raise the issue of difference so boldly, pointing us in what I believe is very much the right direction.

The risk of misconstruing Gilligan's analysis is allayed when one consistently reads her work against its own background in the post-Freudian developmental analysis of Nancy Chodorow, to whom we now turn our attention.

The Preoedipal Surprise

Chodorow's *The Reproduction of Mothering: Psychoanalysis and the Sociology of Gender* may be offered as linchpin for any feminist analysis of female relational and male separative self–structures.[53] With her revised standard version of psychoanalysis, she revisits the preoedipal phase so hastily passed over by Freudian theory. From the radically dissimilar effects on male and female children of this early period of intimacy with the mother, she derives an important new interpretation of the causes of sexism and the psychosocial mechanism by which it reproduces itself in both females and males. Chodorow's starkly ingenuous starting point is simply: "Women mother."[54] And she proceeds to ask why. Why, beyond childbearing and lactation, do women normally assume the role of primary caretaker, while men remain distant and yet dominant in the family unit?

Like Dinnerstein and Gilligan, she recognizes that the question cannot be answered by mere biological or behavioral explanations: more than instinctual drive or social role conditioning is involved. She builds her theory on Freud's own late admission that the oedipal complex does not operate symmetrically in boys and girls. As we will see, he came to realize that the preoedipal period plays a role so much longer and more important in the lives of females that it challenges the very doctrine of a universal oedipal complex. But Chodorow also draws inspiration from the psychoanalytic movement known as object-relations theory. This theory rose to prominence in Britain during the 1930s and 1940s and is especially associated with the names of Fairbairn, Guntrip, Balint, and, of growing importance today, Winnicott. While Freud emphatically distinguished drives from biology, his attention focused primarily upon sexuality, and "object-choices" (interpersonal relationships) remained in the background until his essay "On Narcissism" (1914). But the British school moved psychoanalysis firmly into the realm of the interpersonal. Separation anxiety rather than fear of castration was now understood as the original form of anxiety. The delicate dynamics of the child-parent (generally mother) relationship, seen to be reciprocal from the start, take the center stage. The infant is from birth a self capable of relation and therefore motivated by more than mere needs and drives.

In Chodorow's account of why those interpersonal dynamics issue in patriarchal sex roles, the nuclear family emerges as the villain of the piece. Trapped since the seventeenth century in a self-encapsulation dictated by capitalism and technology, the modern family is the social institution that mediates the ideological superstructures of society to the most intimate infrastructures of the personality. Within the patriarchal family unit (which is socially still normative if in fact increasingly rare), the psychodynamics have assured that in general women will "mother," men will remain dominant, and persons within heterosexual couples will—asymmetrically—depend upon each other for an intimacy that is doomed to disappoint. Why? "Because women are themselves mothered by women, they grow up with the relational capacities and needs, and psychological definition of self-in-relationship, which commits them to mothering. Men, because they are mothered by women, do not." [55] The argument might sound circular: women mother because their mothers were women. But Chodorow is exposing the vicious circularity of the family system itself, as it plays itself out regardless of the intentions of individual parents. The very structure of a family in which women are primary caretakers preprograms daughters to identify with their mothers, with whom they also relate intimately; they consequently experience self-identity as intrinsically relational, but become entangled in emotional obstacles to self-differentiation. Sons, by contrast, experience themselves as not-female, as opposite to the mother with whom they first identified, and therefore as separate. Their affective and relational capacities are nipped in the bud. The mother herself feels the boy as sexually other, the girl as same, and by her manner communicates her feeling.

In the absence of close male caretakers, the boy, treated as opposite by his primary parent, internalizes this negative otherness as his basic sense of self: he is not-mother. The father is usually too absent to provide an alternative intimacy. Here we see evidence of the oppositional, separative impulse in a new light: the male child has no more, indeed much less, choice in this matter than the mother. Both are trapped within the psychodynamics of an institutionally predetermined situation. Does the notion of the male as Other contradict de Beauvoir's analysis of man as the subject who renders woman the Other? *Au contraire.* We might speculate that the male, caught in this unsought opposition, later turns woman into the Other because he has always already known himself as *her* Other: he is perhaps caught in a vicious circle of his own, in an alienation that takes on the hues of defense and vengeance against all women. Whereas if the female child, having known herself from the beginning as the *same* as her mother, offers so little resistance to her later objectification as men's sexual other, it may be because her relatively unstifled emotional life sugarcoats the fact of her inferior status. Yet it is precisely her affective expressiveness that, under the circumstances of overidentification with the mother, will hinder her emergence as a distinctive self.

Prescinding temporarily from such speculation, let us reconsider these divergent personality structures. What are their causes? Freud, we said, admitted late that girls seem to linger much longer than boys in the intimate identification with the mother characteristic of the preoedipal period (the period inaugurated in oceanic feeling). "The pre-Oedipus phase in women gains an importance which we have not attributed to it hitherto," he ruefully acknowledges. "Girls remain in it for an indeterminate length of time; they demolish it late and, even so, incompletely."[56] Freud interprets this phase as phallic even in girls because, from the point of view of his heterosexism, the intimate attachment to the mother as primary love object can only be masculine in nature. Hence his interpretation of the clitoris as a small, "castrated" penis. (For Freudian theory the phallic phase supervenes upon the pregenital oral and anal phases as the final moment of the preoedipal period, though he held to no strict sequence.) Here we encounter Freud's theory of female castration, the point at which girls relinquish their "masculine attachment" to their mothers and "[the daughter] acknowledges the fact of her castration, and with it, too, the superiority of the male and her own inferiority; but she rebels against this unwelcome state of affairs."[57]

One may find oneself unwilling to read such classically misogynist lines as merely descriptive accounts of the results of culture. Certainly they have metaphorical resonance with the feminine sense of powerlessness. Certainly we have often heard talented women wish they were male—not for the bodily but for the cultural benefits of possessing a male member. Yet Freud never doubts that castration is the proper description of female bodiliness. But whether he advocates or merely analyzes the humiliating female acknowledgment of "inferiority," Freud brings a long tradition of phallic triumphalism into twentieth-century discourse. We noted its Aristotelian roots; Thomas Aquinas, who develops the Aristotelian substantialism, prefigures Freud when he argues that "woman is defective and misbegotten."[58] Freud makes the classical case plausible to nonmetaphysical modernity. The only acceptable outcome in his version, which unlike its classical antecedents knows of the feminist alternatives, is heterosexual marriage and motherhood. Woman reaches these goals by the "circuitous" path along which "she takes her father as her object" and repudiates her mother as degraded, lacking the penis and having deprived the daughter of one. An impressive series of women, from analysts such as Deutsch, Horney and Lampl–de Groot, feminists from de Beauvoir through Betty Friedan and Kate Millet, and recently feminist psychoanalyst Luce Irigaray, have already countered his theory effectively (as though continuing the daughter's "rebellion"). From otherwise widely varying perspectives, they seem to share the view—roughly put—that while penis envy and the sense of castration may well emerge in the fantasies and dreams of some women, they represent a secondary symbolism. Envy of masculinity simply shows the depth at which females very young perceive and resent the familial and cultural disempowerment of the women with whom they identify.

The value of the theory of castration for Chodorow lies not in any literalist reading of young girls' desire. Rather, it lies in the asymmetry of the interpersonal situation at the point of crisis symbolized by the castration. For females, this is the point of transition in which the daughter must shift from her original mother-love to father-love—if, that is, she is to embark in the "normal" course of heterosexual development. But as Mitchell summarizes it, "where the castration complex shatters the boy's Oedipus complex, it inaugurates the girl's, as in despair and in despite she turns from the mother to the father." [59] The longer preoedipal period in women, leading to a late and inconclusive transition to the father as love object, is of great importance to Chodorow. For here will lie not only the roots of—in Freud's words—the girl's "sense of inferiority," [60] but the basis of her empathetic tendencies as well. The girl's late equivalent to the oedipal complex will involve her in a desire for the father not only as love object, but as escape from the too tight symbiosis with the mother. Here lies the catch: anger at her mother's impotence may lead her into an alliance with the father, idealized in his distance and social power. But it is precisely this idealization of the traditional father that will result in the ways of passive femininity and in the desire to have a baby later by a father figure, which leads to the "reproduction of mothering." Here she too easily picks up the thread of her earlier identification with the mother, but now as primarily man-centered.

According to both Freud and Chodorow, the male child, like the female, begins with the mother figure as primary love object; but soon matters psychic proceed very differently. As the son simultaneously hates and admires the father as rival for her attention, patricidal wishes are formed. But becoming aware of the lack of a penis in women arouses in him the terror of his own vulnerability: if she lost it, so could he. "One thing that is left over in men from the influence of the Oedipus complex," continues Freud, "is a certain amount of disparagement in their attitude towards women, whom they regard as being castrated." [61] As Dinnerstein also testified, both males and females emerge from this period denigrating women. But while the process of differentiation from (in Freud's terms, repudiation of) the mother is gradual and convoluted in the female, in the male child the transition is abrupt. The father symbolically seems to threaten him with the dread act of castration. "In boys . . . the complex is not simply repressed, it is literally smashed to pieces by the shock of threatened castration."[62] Though motivated by defensive fear, a sense of deep loss and threat, the boy wins the supremely compensatory patrimony: identification with the father and with his dignified and dominant role. Misogyny is thus assured its transgenerational perpetuity.

A comment of Freud's as he analyzes the extended preoedipal period in woman seems inadvertently prophetic: "Our insight into this early, pre-Oedipus, phase in girls comes to us as a surprise, like the discovery, in another field, of the Minoan-Mycenaan civilization behind the civilization of Greece."[63] How interesting to find him, in his surprise at the asymmetry, admitting that there has been nonpatriarchal "civilization." In our own mythological excursion we have felt the pulsings of that pre-Hellenic power, as its images seep through the overlays of patriarchal narrative and theory. And does not the male's "smashing to pieces" of the complex, that is, of the bond with the mother, suggest precisely that matricidal violence we have witnessed in the killing of monsters? Yet how far from the bewildered little boy lie the images of the free-willing hero.

Differentiation and Complexity

How then does Chodorow use the preoedipal hypothesis as the basis of a feminist project? We saw with her that the young boy has no choice but to define himself in negative terms, as *not* a woman. To this oppositional tendency, reinforced by the father's absence and the mother's collusion, is added the precipitous break with his primary love object, the mother. He is left with a sense of himself as separate. "Boys are more likely to have been pushed out of the preoedipal relationship, and to have had to curtail their primary love and sense of empathic tie with their mother. A boy . . . has been required to engage in a more emphatic individuation and a more defensive firming of experienced ego boundaries."[64] The simple fact of the omnipotent presence of the mother in the early phases and the boy's exclusion from his intimacy with her at the very point he experiences the intrusion of the distant father will in other words ensure the ongoing recrudescence of the separative masculinity. The boy is willy-nilly encouraged—even by the mother—to participate in the heroic myth of matricide.

And what are little girls made of? Chodorow appreciates Freud's discovery of their longer preoedipal period, but rather than diagnosing with him a regrettable identity-confusion that will result in a greater narcissism and a lesser sense of objectivity and justice, she spies a significantly two-sided situation. Because "mothers tend to experience their daughters as more like, and continuous with, themselves," girls will indeed find themselves more preoccupied with issues of separation and differentiation, precisely because they have become too deeply mired in relation. But the situation is not without its potentially saving graces: "Girls emerge from this period with a basis for 'empathy' built into their primary definition of self in a way that boys do not. Girls emerge with a stronger basis for experiencing another's needs or feelings as one's own."[65] Through original empathy with the mother figure, the daughter may be gifted with an active empathetic sense. Yet she is at the same time prepared to confuse another's desires with her own—and so indeed to become prey to self-loss and "second sex" status. The supposed need to be needed, the readiness to sacrifice talent, time, energy and finally self to others, especially to family—that need upon which the patriarchal nuclear family depends—is nourished in this process of gender formation. Feeling herself the same as her mother, she is positively defined; but she is not encouraged to be different from her mother—difference is the boy's privilege. Here lies a root of the self-denying stability of the Penelopean wife, indeed of the dooms of devotion under the dictates of masculine definition. But although woman becomes the Other for man, she is not primordially defined in terms of opposition:

Girls do not define themselves in terms of the denial of preoedipal relational modes to the same extent as do boys. Therefore regression to these same modes tends not to feel as much a basic threat to their ego. . . . *Girls come to experience themselves as less differentiated than boys, as more continuous with and related to the external object-world.*[66]

While boys must define themselves in opposition to the first other, the mother, girls find themselves in a psychic continuum of attachment and identification. But if the mother's caretaking is rarely shared by other—including male—primary figures, the mother-daughter bond may work to asphyxiate the daughter's sense of self. The mother, coming from comparable bonding with her mother, had few chances to actualize her own potential in the larger world and may seek her own life in her identification with her daughter. She may innocently expect from the daughter (more than from the son, whose otherness wins him respect) an uninterrupted intimacy of like interests and aims, a perpetual availability for emotional empathy and for friendship, and a certain guilt-prone stasis, which all too easily collaborates with society at large to drain the daughter of her creative powers.

Chodorow underemphasizes the work of social and ideological structures beyond the family in requiring, exploiting and institutionalizing that sexism to which the family structure already tends. She is in this still far less confined to the private sphere than Jung, whose obfuscation of all real relations and social patterns as "accidental" tends toward cultural conservatism. And unlike Freud, who tended to acquiesce in the discontents of civilization, Chodorow mobilizes the revolutionary potential of psychoanalytic theory for social critique. That is, she not only sees through Freud's particular misogyny but consistently undermines the patriarchal family unit by exposing its contingency. Its causes appear in her analysis as powerful, but by no means natural or necessary.

By the same token, however, if these object-relational forces are real, implanted—independent of culpability on the part of individual parents—by the sociology of the family unit, feminism can hardly afford to turn a blind eye to them. For even as feminists we sometimes must work beyond a distressing depth of rage in ourselves against our mothers. While we may consciously realize that our mothers are themselves victims and not to be blamed for the oppressive effects of the nuclear family, we do need to recognize the relational occasions of the oppression. Otherwise, if we too blithely skip over the intimate familial causes to focus on the larger system, we are more vulnerable to either a male-identified, matricidal Athena behavior pattern or a regression to the undifferentiating influence of the bond: decapitation or capitulation (and often some of both). The regressive tendency will most likely be lived out in sexual intimacy with a male, who then readily defines the indefinite feminine counterpart. Freud recognized that while the woman may seem to have married a father, it may instead be unresolved conflict with the mother that shapes her relation to the heterosexual partner.[67]

The image of woman can in other words bifurcate within woman's psyche into the patriarchal mother-daughter dyad of dragon mother and helpless maiden. Daughterly diffuseness and monstrous maternity then flow from the same preoedipal source, two precipitates of a single solubility. This ominous operation of oceanic feeling in daughters (i.e., all women) threatens to abort selfhood in inappropriate merger. While the threat may have little to do with the mother's objective attributes, it arouses in women an ambivalence toward the mother and, by unconscious inference, toward all women. As Dinnerstein has shown, this female misogyny inevitably returns, by a feedback loop that guarantees female complicity, in the form of female self-loathing. Thus while we may fear and fight frantically our own mother-modeled dissolution in the needs and terms of others, we often seem pitted against ourselves as well as our mothers' image. In the attempt to break out of the endless cycle of relational demands that steals from us our libido for creativity, work, decision and assertion, we are tempted to recapitulate the masculine oedipal gestures. The cleanness of masculine separation, in the vacuum of alternative models for maturation, exercises an undoubted appeal. For a woman, as Chodorow argues, generally enters into a later, more gradual, more conscious and therefore more agonizing struggle to become an individual and not her mother's clone. Here in this struggle, the needed and liberating differentiation can be confused with the radical separation of psychic matricide. Yet for a woman, matricide is always partially suicide. But equally so is a narcissistic, self-dissolving empathy.

On what psychological basis, then, can we possibly acclaim or even validate female connectivity? Through Chodorow's lens, we are observing the way the less rigid ego boundaries of females result in a less individuated personality structure. Softer boundaries naturally tempt the self to diffuseness, passivity, resentful dependency even upon dependents, and a lowered level of energy available for focused cultural work. Yet surely this solubility represents the status quo for women only within the institutions of patriarchy. But must fluid ego boundaries automatically lessen the possibilities of differentiation? Is rigidity synonymous with individuality? If we seek to argue that it is not, we are first confronted by the question of history: If a patriarchal situation sustains the psychic basis of connec-tivity in women, how can we abstract such a gender difference from the institution that engenders it? Why should we try to redeem this form of femininity, much less romanticize it?

I believe nonetheless there is a way to claim, precisely in the light of this history, that such an empathic self-structure can generate strength rather than surrender. Let us return to the personality dis-tinctions that according to Chodorow result from the asymmetries of the oedipal stage. Here she does not make value judgments. But her descriptive account of gender differences within patriarchal family conditions implies an important shift from the androcentric bias of the classical Freudian account:

From the retention of preoedipal attachments to their
mother, growing girls come to define and experience themselves as continuous with others; their experience of self
contains more flexible or permeable ego boundaries. Boys
come to define themselves as more separate and distinct,
with a greater sense of rigid ego boundaries and differentiation. The basic feminine sense of self is connected to the
world, the basic masculine sense of self is separate.[68]

Certainly this describes the patriarchal dyads: women are thus pre-pared for the role of mother and nurturer, and men for the role of warrior or worker in alienated and nonrelational settings. Chodo-row rightly describes the typical female personality structure as un-derdifferentiated, that is, lacking both an adequate sense of unique selfhood and an ability to distinguish the feelings, needs and desires of one's self from those of others. At this point in history something like this seems empirically true to the countless generations of un-equal opportunity for self-development. But even granting that the opportunities for education, articulation and meaningful work now proliferate for women, the question remains: Where do we go from here? Will the separative values of domination and division be over-come, or merely better distributed? An expanding range of external choices (for first world women of the white middle class) will not suffice to bring about a postpatriarchal culture.

It is not clear that the female sense of connection with the world must be overcome in favor of the rigid boundaries upon which all worldly power has so far been predicated. True, relatedness has in fact functioned in tandem with nondifferentiation and self-surren-der. *But need differentiation imply separation? Need connection im-ply merger?* Or can a richly differentiated self after all evolve on the basis of connection, never outgrowing its permeable ego bounda-ries.

I find a problem in Chodorow's way of opposing feminine con-nection and individual differentiation. It lies in the relationship of *differentiation* and *complexity*, which ought to be corollary con-cepts: the more complexity, the more differentiation, and vice versa. In contrast to the "simpler oedipal situation and more direct affec-tive relationships" of boys, girls, according to Chodorow, "enter adulthood with a complex layering of affective ties and a rich, on-going inner object world."[69] While complexity of inner and outer relations is not synonymous with self-differentiation, the one surely provides the only basis for the other. What gives rise to *difference* if not the complicating process of intrapsychic and interpersonal interaction? What else would qualitatively distinguish one self from another? The simpler, the less intricate, a self is, the more like every other it remains. Sameness and simplicity work together. (There is also the sense of simplicity as a serene integration of complexity: This is another matter altogether.) A simpler self will be numerically distinct, but not particularly distinctive. Moreover, the shears of separation can cut a cleaner figure around a less complex self, and so Chodorow's implicit association of simplicity with masculinity is a propos. But if, as she well argues, females emerge with more affective and relational complexity than do males from patriarchal childhood, females may be already more differentiated than she sus-pects. Perhaps after all women may self-affirmingly begin with what we already are. Connection may provide the germs for a *different* concept of differentiation, beyond the culture of father as differen-tiator, mother as that from which one differentiates.

How do women come to possess what Chodorow calls their "complex layering," their "rich, ongoing inner object world"? Again, the critical circumstance lies in the fact that women mother. As we have heard, both men and women experience and retain the mother as a primary love object, but pass into very different endo-psychic consellations: men "shatter" the bond to the mother, and as it will later reappear as the basis for heterosexuality, their sexual identity will be bound up with a strong denial of the preoedipal reality.[70] Women only gradually repress the bond and manage to incorporate the father into the oedipal situation as a more or less equal object of affection. Thus men's psyche becomes dyadic in structure (self—female other), while women's becomes triadic (self—mother—male other). The original bond to the exclusive mother makes later male-to-male intimacy of any sort threatening to men since the father first made himself known as competitor. By contrast, women are notably more capable of emotional closeness with both men and women, either as lesbians or heterosexuals. (The creative example of lesbian relations within the women's movement helps release for all women the depth-charge of this original mother-daughter continuum.)[71] And perhaps male homosexuality will help to reopen the door usually closed on emotional intimacy between men.

Emotionally frustrated by the limited range of relations permitted by traditional circumstances and by the male partner's own education in denial of affect, woman in the patriarchal unit recreates the original triform intimacy in the primary way available to her: she mothers. Thus according to Chodorow, mothering "reproduces" itself. Because there is so often a desperation, or lack, motivating the urge to mother, the naturally empathetic bond between mother and child may be supercharged with the mother's own ambivalence and need. Her emotional undernourishment will promote a double dependency: the mother will feed off the child, who has no choice but to nourish itself from her. The maternal empathy is then a "pseudoempathy."

It is crucial to distinguish between real and false empathy. The latter is "based on maternal projection rather than any real perception or understanding of their infant's needs."[72] In cases of pseudoempathy mothers keep "daughters from forming their own identity."[73] Real empathy can only encourage the daughter's individualization—and is often actualized in mother-daughter relations. But real empathy, a connection not based on self-deprivation and frustration, will surely be hard for a woman to sustain amidst the psychic and social forces that deny her what she needs for her own sense of worth. So of course mothering will often function narcissistically to fill in the void.

The triadic—or multiple, for once they get beyond one and two, relations multiply—structure of women's psyche can indeed be used to replicate the status quo. But let us note that though the multiple nature of female selfhood can and has served to capture us in our own web of relations, it cannot be proved that such a structure of self emerges only within a patriarchal situation. The male sense of separation may often be sealed by the patriarchal-oedipal resolution. But the female failure to comply with these terms, to dissolve the early bond and with it all sense of intimate connection to the world, is in no comparable way a product of patriarchy. Not connection itself, but the derivative problems of (a) insufficient differentiation from the mother, (b) the accompanying female self-devaluation, and (c) the subsequent affective and cultural deprivation that reproduces the entire cycle again, can accurately be derived from a state of male dominance.

The ongoing experience of relatedness cannot be attributed to patriarchal structures. Both male and female children enter life deeply connecting with the available parent(s). Relatedness is the a priori. Disempathy and separation, not connection, are what must be explained. The particular permutations, interruptions and distortions of the relational continuum, whether it spreads to include an ever widening network of relations or is kept tightly confined— these take us beyond the original connectivity. Here society and its often inadvertent agent, the family, will as Chodorow so well shows, rehearse us in those interplays of self and other, of female and male, which will later seem all too natural.

The Labyrinthine Way

I want to claim that the female connection to mother and world preserves the oceanic feeling of an empathic continuum initially common to both sexes. This fluid bondedness need not, in its movement from the primary maternal bond to inclusion of other figures be seen as in itself sexist, even if the specific relations and objects it includes have been in fact male-defined. This empathic continuum may contain its own self-transforming principle of differentiation. The oceanic currents of deep assimilation, of identification and internalization, of resistance and of intimacy, may all turn out to be natural modes of gradual individuation. Contrary to the dictates of the shrunken residue, *one becomes more and different by taking in more of what is different.*

This brings us back to a problem critical for feminist analysis: that of the basis for claims of gender-specific personality types.

When Chodorow asserts that "the basic feminine sense of self is connected to the world, the basic masculine sense of self is separate," she comes dangerously close to apologizing for the very system she challenges. For if such differences are regarded as "natural," which talk of "basics" surely if unintentionally does imply, then after all men have an excuse for their need to dominate and women have no recourse but to mother. But let me claim—on the basis of our engagement with Chodorow—that no such natural difference obtains. Separation is clearly inflicted on young boys by their fathers' distance, by their mothers' treatment of them as Other, and by the social habits of manhood. It involves a traumatic break and a severe repression of early intimacy with the mother. The self-structure of separation is a patriarchal artifice. If, however, our above claim is true, connection is not so much forced upon females as simply left to turn in on itself in the isolation within the narrow range of relations traditionally open to women. The web is not originally a trap.

If separation is a form of imposed selfhood, we may assume that the male child is also originally a relational being, feeling at first connected to the world every bit as intimately as the young girl. At a certain point in his development the lack of an intimate paternal presence throws the boy into the beginnings of his woman-negating self-definition (where "be a man" means "do not be like a girl"). This is the same point at which the girl's too exclusive identification with the mother begins to be problematic for her as well. Connection to the other, then, along with its accompanying complexity of internal relations, does not define an essence of femininity any more than separation defines masculinity. Chodorow's distinction holds good within the sociohistorical circumstances in which we find ourselves. His-story has glorified the heroic warrior as the one who conquers the complex beast of women's many-faced connections. Few men live up to the heroic ideal, though most identify with some form of it. A small number oppose it from a philosophical, mystical, poetic or political vantage point. But unless they own up to the sexism at work in the defensively discrete ego, these more relational males will not prevail against the power drive inherent in their own modes of separation.

A lust for power over the other, the enemy, the woman, and the world is deeply entrenched in the patriarchal male (and derivatively in the female) psyche. It conceals an unconscious fear of the mother, in her monstrous ability to overpower the infant ego. Power *over* the other then makes up for the lost sense of relation *with* the other. Dominance, whether of rude or subtle variety, somehow compensates for the fundamental castration of connection *to* these others. If castration symbolizes a primordial male fear, is it because men feel *already* cut off? (*Castrum* originally refers to a walled fortification, a place separated, cut off from the world for self-defense.)

Can a trust in noncoercive influence again take the place of domination, a sense of depth and engagement replace the masculine defense? If the play of interlinked possibilities empowers all its participants, can it render the patriarchal ploys for gaining power-over-the-other obsolescent? If only the pleasure and pain of this play can be *felt*. George Eliot attributes precisely such a sensitivity to the character Ladislaw in *Middlemarch* when she observes that "he was a creature who entered into everyone's feelings and could take the pressure of their thought instead of urging his own with iron resistance."[74] Never mind that this male is a romantic fiction and that the actual connectivity belongs to the perspective of a great woman writer. The possibility Eliot envisions is real.

Where is the hope for such change, however, given the massive history of these impersonal, personality-shaping forces? Chodorow lifts up the ironic sociological fact that in this century, in which women's legal rights are finally being established, the gap between the domestic and the economic spheres has only widened and the insularity of the nuclear family has increased. We may infer that this modern worsening of the situation that causes sexism could subtly cancel out the accomplishments of feminism. On the other hand, the increasing participation of women in the economic sphere is at the same time undermining the nuclear family. But when the mother is thrown into the desperate situation of being at once sole caretaker and working-class breadwinner, it is simply not clear whether the old maternal omnipotence is overcome.

Like Dinnerstein, Chodorow invests her optimism in the transformation already underway of the familial gestalt, but (unlike her) esteems the connected sense of self in the ensuing personalities:

Children could be dependent from the outset on people of both genders and establish an individuated sense of self in relation to both. In this way, masculinity would not become tied to denial of dependence and devaluation of women.

Feminine personality would be less preoccupied with individuation, and children would not develop fears of *maternal* omnipotence and expectations of *women's* unique self-sacrificing qualities. This would reduce men's needs to guard their masculinity and their control of social and cultural spheres which treat and define women as secondary and powerless, and would help women to develop the autonomy which too much embeddedness in relationship has often taken from them.[75]

Different from Dinnerstein, Chodorow's view of this equality, because it acknowledges women's history with relationship, does not seem to depend upon an absolute equality of early parental contributions: the issue is full involvement on the part of female and male parent-figures in what traditionally was "mothering." Then there is reason to think, Chodorow reassures us, that gender identity would simply break down. She envisions—and I think not cheaply—the best of both worlds—more self-differentiation for women, more affective connection for men. The sexually derived sense of self would indeed change, but in the direction of more, of multiple possibilities, and not of even fewer (as the "unisex" version of androgyny, for instance, implies).

We learn from Dinnerstein and Chodorow how psychoanalysis can unveil the gender politics of the family operative at the deepest levels of our selfhood and of our ambivalence toward mothers. From Chodorow we gained what Dinnerstein could no more offer than Freud: an assessment of female connectivity as neither an aberration nor a misfortune but as a difference with liabilities and strengths. Chodorow, like Gilligan, discerns in it both an obstacle to self-development and a legitimate alternative to the masculine norm. But in Gilligan's and Chodorow's work we do not yet discover how to validate a feminine psychic structure that has been functioning to valorize male dominance. While Chodorow's sociological descriptions remain convincing, we challenged her opposition of differentiation and fluidity. It may hold true of the patriarchal dyad of separative and soluble selfhood. But it fails to situate in the "feminine" fluidity any germ of an alternative model of self-differentiation—any model not implicitly mother-opposed and therefore archetypally matricidal. So I have been arguing that the germ is there indeed, buried not so deeply in women as in men, in the preoedipal phase—and not because patriarchal cultures plant it there but because they cannot uproot it.

Indeed, the patriarchal arrangement depends upon the stunting of connectivity into the state of the dependent nurturer, the mother from need and not from choice. To cease to be nurturing or otherwise relational beings may seem to women an inviting form of dissent. But even if separate selfhood were a genuinely desirable state of being to *be* in, such male-emulous egocentricity will come too late, too angrily, and too awkwardly to women for political effectiveness, let alone creativity. So I suggest for pragmatic as well as normative reasons, that we instead affirm the empathic continuum from which we emerge (men originally, women continuously).

The connective selfhood of the preoedipal period, despite the threat of an undifferentiated narcissism, must and can be cultivated into maturity rather than stifled and superseded. Then the complexity of our inner and outer interactions remains no longer a labyrinth of self-loss, which the heroic ego, like Theseus, recognizes as a deadly monster lair for himself. Even Theseus learned that Ariadne holds the thread. Within the fathers' epoch, women's self-transformation must lead the way—not *out* of complexity—but *within* the labyrinthine way of a connective ego. (Labyrinths were originally ritual floor designs upon which the priestess danced the myths of the mother Goddess.)[76] A mature, centering and self-affirming sense of relation endangers the way of separation and control most profoundly. But if woman's complexity is the sine qua non of human connexity, can we get there without succumbing to the narcissism and inauthenticity that so contaminate the early bond to the mother?

There are many twists to the psychoanalytic maze of gender and self that we cannot here explore. But we can briefly mention three psychoanalysts who are working neither as feminists nor on gender-issues, but whose thoughts on selfhood and narcissism will add helpful guidelines to the present project.

Narcissism and the True Self

Heinz Kohut is the founder of an American movement called self-psychology. He and his followers consider it a faithful transformation of classical psychoanalysis, albeit rejected by orthodox Freudians. In his emphasis on self rather than ego, Kohut's work bears a resemblance to that of Jung, and also diverges from the postwar focus on interpersonal theory and object relations. Returning to the question of narcissism, which Freud had obscurely opened, he discerns "two separate and largely independent developmental lines: one which leads from autoeroticism via narcissism to object love; another which leads from autoeroticism via narcissism to higher forms and transformations of narcissism." [77] However unpromising is Kohut's attempt to separate interpersonal from self-development, there is something of great interest here. For we began this chapter with a consideration of Freud's dismissal of the oceanic feeling as "endless narcissism." As it is the anonymous mother who goes down the drain along with the infant state, our ears perk up at a different treatment of this original continuum of self and mother/environment.

If, as Kohut argues, primary narcissism is a state not fully translated into "object love," then perhaps the clean separation of subject and object is not the only aim of health. That narcissism is to be transformed rather than simply superseded may support the present advocacy of a maturational continuity with preoedipality. Kohut analyzes five human capacities as transformations of narcissism: creativity, empathy, transience, humor and wisdom. To create, to feel for another, to face death, to laugh and to integrate our multifarious experience—these are modes of connection to our worlds which spring not from dependency and need but from a self strong and resilient in itself. But Kohut's own isolation of these capacities from relation—though underlining the importance of an adequate feeling of self—may finally impede any attempt to redefine the self as relational. Nonetheless it offers an interesting corrective to object-relations theories, inasmuch as they presuppose an ego as present from birth, [78] or overburden the mother with responsibility for the child's personality.

But a more object-relational theory seems crucial to me for understanding the dangers and promises of the narcissistic phase precisely in terms of interaction. For the association of the mother and hence of all women with the lingering narcissism (transformed or not) is not only shaped by early relations, but formative of all future ones.

Recently the Swiss psychoanalyst Alice Miller has with her accessible wisdom brought the personal and social issues of narcissistic self-formation to a wider public. She shares with Chodorow a deep reliance on object-relations theory and also draws upon Kohut's analysis of narcissism. She teaches that adult narcissistic disturbance is pervasive in our culture. Its symptoms are an inadequate sense of self, which leaves people exposed to perpetual anxiety or guilt, and often the feeling of a failure "to live up to some ideal image and measure they feel they must adhere to." Though the narcissistically disturbed often succeed in their undertakings, "behind all this lurks depression, the feeling of emptiness and self-alienation, and a sense that their life has no meaning."[79] The cause of such suffering lies in childhood, where the child's legitimate and healthy "narcissistic needs—for respect, echoing, understanding, sympathy, and mirroring"—were not fulfilled by the parents. But the parents were unable to meet these needs of their child because they themselves had been narcissistically deprived in childhood. Such a childhood produces parents who depend for their own "narcissistic equilibrium" on their children "behaving, or acting, in a particular way." The child soon learns to not to feel those emotions—like "jealousy, envy, anger, loneliness, impotence or anxiety"—that the parents deem unacceptable.[80] The child's empathetic skills are therefore turned fully to sensing and then becoming what the parents need. The parent—and of course until recently this has almost always meant a mother figure—demands but does not provide empathy. "Each mother can only react empathetically to the extent that she has become free of her own childhood, and she is forced to react without empathy to the extent that, denying the vicissitudes of her early life, she wears invisible chains."[81]

These "invisible chains," which will bind the child in the pattern of emotional unreality, shed new light on old doctrines like the law of karma or the transgenerational transmission of "original sin." As a result of the parents' insatiable hunger for mother-love, a false facade soon replaces the child's "true self," that is, the ability to experience all authentic feelings as one's own. Having disowned the less admirable parts of the self, the child will grow up still hungry for narcissistic gratification, that is unconditional love, from a mythic mother, who can never be found—and so will turn his or her own children, by a bizarre reversal, into that longed-for mother. In other words, such parents unconsciously demand from their children the nonjudgmental regard they did not receive from their own parents. Thus the "false," compliant self transmits itself inexorably to the next generation.

The language of "true" and "false" self is borrowed from the work of D. W. Winnicott, for whom the development of the true self is dependent on what he calls the "good enough mother"[82]—a concept affording welcome relief from the mythical demand placed on women by the ideal of the "good mother" (which we find in Klein's work)—or especially the cultural stereotype of the "perfect mother." The good enough mother mirrors the infant back to itself with the real empathy that allows it to be itself, to see and feel itself. In the trust thus engendered, a "potential space" comes to be that is derived at once from connection and differentiation and is the source of creativity. The space is irreducible to either intrapsychic reality or an outer object world. Interestingly, he identifies it with the ability to have "experience": "I have located this important area of *experience* in the potential space between the individual and the environment, that which initially both joins and separates the baby and the mother when the mother's love, displayed . . . as human reliability, does in fact give the baby a sense of trust."[83]

Winnicott is much occupied with the dynamics of separation, given the tenacity of the original infant-parent matrix. His idea of "transitional objects" (like Teddy Bears or blankets) means to account for the gradual transition away from dependence on the mother. "The good-enough mother . . . starts off with an almost complete adaptation to her infant's needs, and as time proceeds she adapts less and less completely, gradually, according to the infant's growing ability to deal with her failure."[84] By this "failure," the mother slowly grants the infant (and herself, we might add) a sense of freedom, precisely by frustrating the child in its dependency. We may surmise that a narcissistically disturbed mother will no more be able to let go at the right moment than she was able to provide the initial empathic condition of trust. From Winnicott we learn that all creativity, which refers to all creative living in a "space" not determinable by the subject-object dichotomy, depends upon the adequate interplay of "relation" and "separation" in the early phases of life. Yet by separation Winnicott means something different from the sort of self-encapsulation of the ego I have linked with patriarchal masculinity. For creativity and culture mean the access (of the "true self") to the "intermediate zone." Though in a sense his project, like that of all object-relations analysts, lies in investigating and assisting an adequate "separation" of the ego from the mother, he offers a speculation intriguing for our purposes:

> It could be said that with human beings *there can be no separation, only a threat of separation;* and the threat is maximally or minimally traumatic according to the experience of the first separatings.

How, one may ask, does separation of subject and object, of baby and mother, seem in fact to happen, and to happen with profit to all concerned . . . ? And this in spite of the *impossibility of separation?* (The paradox must be tolerated.) (my emphasis)[85]

I am not convinced, however, that we must stop at the paradox; for if instead of separation we speak of differentiation, or distinctness, no conceptual conflict remains at this point. Winnicott points us to the possibility that only in the play between subject and object, in which there is neither separation nor fusion, does "experience" take place. Such play is the prerogative of a self true to its feelings; many (how many?) people in some sense then do not "experience." This parallels Miller's reading of the narcissistic disturbance in parenting: "what is missing above all is the framework within which the child could experience his feelings and emotions." [86]

Neither Miller nor Winnicott analyze the issues of narcissistic disturbance and false self in terms of the politics of gender. Rita Nakashima Brock has made an excellent suggestion for integrating Miller's analysis with Chodorow. Chodorow has shown us the causes of a feminine self inadequately differentiated and prone to manipulation and dependency and of a masculine ego rigidly defined and tempted to misogynist power tactics. Brock suggests that these patriarchal options represent two poles of the false self.[87] The one lacks enough sense of self, the other enough sense of relation, to experience their own experience, to feel their own feelings.

Furthermore, object relations analyses focus on the mother's parenting. They can claim the advantage over much of the psychoanalytic literature of rendering the mother visible, acknowledging her importance and avoiding any misleading symmetries regarding oedipal relations (as Freud's earlier work, and the attempt by young Jung to formulate an "Electra complex," produce). Miller even notes that in her writing, "mother" refers to "the person closest to the child during the first years of life. This need not be the biological mother nor even a woman." [88] Dinnerstein and Chodorow have delineated, however, the momentous cultural consequences of the fact that this person has generally been a woman. But does this mean that when we apply Miller's and Winnicott's theses, the patriarchal, distant father manages not only to avoid the intense ambivalence directed toward the primary, female parent, but to get off the psychoanalytic hook altogether? Does his failure to function as a primary parent actually release him from responsibility for causing narcissistic disturbance? Is he exonerated by absenteeism? Tracing the consequences of the mother's narcissistic insecurities can readily implicate us in the misogyny of mother blaming, unmitigated by the explanatory sociology that grounds Chodorow's generalizations. It need not, I believe. For though the patriarchal father's absence may invite his idealization by the child, the very lack of emotional presence and the failure of empathy, which disqualify him as a primary parent, also mark him as a narcissistically disturbed and profoundly disturbing influence. If he were literally absent, as is rarely the case, this effect would be less evident. His is more often a confusing absence-in-presence. But given the early need of the male child for a father figure and the formative role of such a figure in the female's relationship to all subsequent males, the extent of the father's false selfhood will leave ineradicable marks. But marks of absence, made with too little emotional vitality, will be hard indeed to trace later. I would imagine that the death of God the Father has less to do with guilt and supersession than with the cumulative unreality of the idealized father. But theology aside, this lack of emotional presence will cripple men in their sense of themselves as male, leading by compensation to preposterous power plays. In addition to external constraints, women will suffer injury in relation to the internalized male, to what Jung calls animus. Furthermore, it will contribute to a difficulty for women in sensing the concrete *reality* of men—a dilemma hardly abetted by men's own damped-down feeling.

But the narcissistic wound endured in relation to the mother, inasmuch as she is herself living out of a false self, will remain bright and gory in comparison to that inflicted by the father—especially for women, who as Chodorow showed do not define themselves by denial of preoedipal modes. This is where a feminist social framework for Miller's thought becomes crucial. In a culture that systematically inhibits female self-esteem and implants psychic mechanisms for feminine self-sabotage, mothers are all too likely to pass on their crippled self-feeling to their children, and especially to those who most resemble them, their daughters. Thus the intimate problem of narcissistic disturbance, which Miller herself sees as the most formidable social problem, indeed as the root of violence,[89] cannot be understood outside of the politics of gender.

The buoyant communal experimenting of the sixties may have ended, but so has the hegemony of the traditional family. Despite the current conservative backlash, the massive social facts of economic pressure and divorce keep the working mother or the two-career family an ever-growing necessity; lesbian mothers continue to work out viable structures; and feminist consciousness sustains the hope of varieties of community beyond any self-encapsulated coupling. Willy-nilly, we continue to experiment.

Becoming As a Child

But neither individuals nor the human race can afford simply to wait upon the advent of better-parented generations. Even the social and economic adjustments that would make alternative child-care situations possible are unlikely to take place unless the desired end already makes itself somehow felt. But is immediate change really possible among traditionally woman-mothered persons? Are we spinning our feminist wheels after all? History cannot be shucked, either by individuals or peoples. "The past is not a husk yet change goes on," answers Adrienne Rich.[90] Change *is* already taking place and takes place in the present even as we project possible futures in which adults will look back on an irrepressible childhood.

Let us step—with one foot—free of the literalism to which sociological or psychoanalytic theory is prone. The child we remember, the child we anticipate—that child we bear and rear in us *now*. The child within, even ailing, repressed and fearful, carries not only the personal past but the possible future. Women and men can return—now—to reclaim and transform the "preoedipal phase" and so retrace their steps to maturation. (Formal therapy may or may not facilitate this journey.) As to retracing steps, however: in the case of Hansel and Gretel, the trail of seeds left in the woods does not survive the hungry birds. The journey is always unpredictable. The child is my particular childhood; but it is also akin to an archetype, not as a static symbolism but as a collective pattern both in need of redemption and necessary for redemption. "The child," writes Jung, "is all that is abandoned and exposed and at the same time divinely powerful; the insignificant, dubious beginning, and the triumphal end." [91]

The child still—even now—trembles with wonder at the world it feels so closely. We would feel the wonder if we did not fear it. Or rather, do we mistake the wonder for fear? The child's intimation of immediate connection with the world does not return her to the womb. Oceanic feeling can permeate and moisten without drowning. But between our reactive and oppositional cycles of dry separations and soggy dissolutions, how can we reclaim without regression the fluid boundaries of the child? Perhaps the first step, or plunge, happens by letting ourselves feel how we are already there; by trusting that we already are distinctive in and through our connections; that we are already being empowered in our very permeability; that something in us is never cut off, never lost. We can feel the oceanic feelings surging through us, this moment ebbing and flowing, not threatening.

Nonetheless, to receive this child-hood takes more than just its recognition. Miller shows that because we may have partly killed or buried the real past child early in life, its rebirth requires mourning the lost child. To move to Jungian symbolization prematurely, skipping over this griefwork, may indeed abort the rejuvenescence, actual and archetypal, of the child. [92] "Avoiding this mourning means that one remains at bottom the one who is despised. For I have to despise everything in myself that is not wonderful, good, and clever. Thus I perpetuate intrapsychially the loneliness of childhood: I despise weakness, impotence, uncertainty—in short, the child in myself and in others." [93] That inner child, who incarnates the energy of the "true self," is—however maimed—still there for us. Winnicott implies that the true self is indestructible as a potentiality: "One has to allow for the possibility that there cannot be a complete destruction of a human individual's capacity for creative living and that, even in the most extreme case of compliance or the establishment of a false personality, hidden away somewhere there exists a secret life that is satisfactory because of its being creative or original to that human being. Its unsatisfactoriness must be measured in terms of its being hidden, its lack of enrichment through living experience."[94] Certain parables of Jesus spring to mind here—the lost sheep, the prodigal child, the light under the barrel, the mustard seed—images of something small and precious, easily overlooked, that must be found at any cost, and without which the value of life is negligible.

The child is always already there in us—however lost she or he seems to us, however neglected, undernourished and left behind in a repressed state of preoedipality. Yet it is from the child that the crucial new possibilities are born. *The author's dream while writing these paragraphs: a very young girl, about a year and a half, is about to give birth. My mother and I are frightened for her, for the pain and shock and danger. But then I just explain to her that she is about to have a baby of her own. She responds with precocious understanding and with delight, and we are reassured, confident she will make it through.* The child who gives birth: from the archetypal child always already alive in us, our new selves are, however painfully, being born. The three generations of women constellate to create something new. If only we communicate with this child— reassure the dream source and so ourselves by sharing with her our consciousness of her and of her pregnancy. The archetype of the child is reached through the real childhood, and the real child is brought to present pregnancy through the archetype. A hideously premature birth? Or one long overdue? Does the child often become the mother because the ego of the woman left something essential back in the yet connective world of childhood? Something we can yet return to, or catch up with, by assisting in this birth?

Being what we have always been becoming: does not this initiate a less defensive consciousness, one that swims with Tiamat, challenging her and being challenged? Here is another oneiric report, from an undergraduate suffering the problems of getting free of her mother's power over her—she dreamt frequently of being eaten by a shark. Then she shared the dream and became conscious of its message, of its image of her problem of differentiation from the mother and of the devouring unconsciousness to which this inability to claim her individuality was leaving her prey. Later, she dreamed of swimming freely with the shark, holding its fin and enjoying the exhilaration of the deep water passage. She reported a major breakthrough that day in communication with her mother.

She did not triumph heroically by killing the shark. She faced up to her matriphobia and her mother, and the shark-mother now faced her in the wondrous con-fluency of indepth connection. Baby-mothers, shark-mothers, daughters getting born and giving birth, daughters no longer devoured but going deep-sea swimming with the monster-mother: let us heed our real relations, let us hear our dream revelations, trusting that another Wisdom, strange and steady, is even now awaiting our attention.

"To pay careful attention"—Jung often points out this original definition of the word *religion,* interpreting it as a careful observation, a heedful obedience, of the stream of awareness. And as we will explore later, *re-ligio* means etymologically "I bind together again," that is, "I reconnect." Carefully heeding the connectivity that is already here, as new connections take shape: only so can we appreciate both the Jungian account of the collective unconscious and Chodorow's analysis of preoedipal relations. But how can we hold together two such disparate accounts of the psyche with its separations and connections?

Jung, when he remembers the Mother, points toward a gyno-morphic, inwardly transmitted and transpersonally shared memory as a basis for rejoining us with our deeper Self. We learn much more from Chodorow about both the formative—and gynocentric—nature of early relations and about the way we internalize these object relations as the basis for our own female or male sense of self. Nevertheless, in order to use Chodorow's theory to affirm the value of connectivity and the historical fact of its female transmission, I believe we can draw upon the Jungian reservoir of collective experience as an inclusive, transpersonal context.

If the notion of a relational self, derived from an empathic continuum experienced by females more commonly and consciously than by males, is to be anything more than the result of the patriarchal family structure, a theory of the interrelatedness of all subjective life is needed. The collective unconscious provides such an objective or transpersonal basis of interconnection. As a metaphoric matrix from which all subjective individualization proceeds, it unveils an important picture of the *fundamental* character of relatedness. With it we can assert all the more vigorously that this relatedness that we struggle to redeem in our experience as women is more than an ambivalent and historically determined by-product of our identification with our mothers. Rather, we may claim that early identification with our mothers, perilous as it will remain under patriarchal circumstances, affords women who choose to become conscious of themselves a privileged access to what has remained, collectively, unconscious: the interweaving of all life in each individual. Thus for Jung the very experience of relationship to psychic life beyond our ego, the openness to what precedes and to what follows our ego consciousness, "has projected itself into the archetype of the child," which expresses a "wholeness." "Wholeness, empirically speaking, is . . . of immeasurable extent, older and younger than consciousness and enfolding it in time and space." In this sense the child symbolizes "both beginning and end, an initial and a terminal creature."[95]

The Resurrection of the Daughter

The idea of a collective or transpersonal psyche, joined with the post-Freudian account of gender differentiation, establishes an oceanic interfusion of all life, not only in the female, but as the basis of all consciousness. Here we can positively resituate that "global, inchoate and all-embracing presence" which Dinnerstein found only in the infant's fallacy. It is the intimate connection not just to the infant's mother, in whom it was first embodied, but to all that has been other: this global presence is the immanent world.

Nor need we always choose between the psychoanalytic recollection of childhood and the Jungian way of primordial images. As we saw, Freud recognized the transhistorical and collective basis of his id, as well as the constitution of each personality through identifications and incorporations that are essentially symbolizations. For Winnicott, the "transitional object" is always a symbol (as of the breast or mother), so symbolization of relation allows differentiation from the outset. To encounter symbols as in some sense archetypal only reminds us that these processes of individual development are, in infinitely varied forms, universal issues, that they are irreducible to any literal origin, and that they are sacred, dangerous and accessible *now.*

At the same time, Chodorow's revisionist Freudian perspective, insisting as it does on the social causes and effects of real interpersonal relations, offers an essential corrective to Jung. For without some such feminist analysis the concept of the collective unconscious will be sabotaged by Jung's own androcentrism, where the separative impulse carries the day and dreamily keeps connection a private and so paradoxically separate matter of the individual's individuation. Not that we can do without the dream, the myth, the dark fringes of thought and feeling. When psychology begins to bring the unconscious into consciousness, it opens a new place to look for what had been lost. But then it is imperative that the notion of the unconscious not be trapped within an insular individuality—a danger to both Freud and Jung. The matricidal break with the literal or symbolic mother, by which such isolate selfhood comes to be, remains psychologically compelling only in a culture in which maternity itself is an isolating trap for women. It is neither an instinctual nor an eternal necessity.

Early in this chapter, Freud's psychology of religion showed itself allied on the one hand with psychological matricide by omission and on the other with a theological patricide. Feminism may tacitly approve the death of God the Father, to which Freud's analysis contributes as energetically as Nietzsche's. But we may not conclude our discussion without noting the connection between psychological misogyny and atheism. Judith van Herik's *Freud on Femininity and Faith* argues that Freud discerned similar mental structures in femininity and Christian "illusion." She concludes that "the message emerges that renunciation of illusion will mean renunciation of the feminine attitude to the divine father as well as of the normal masculine attitude to him, in favor of scientific resignation to a postpaternal universe."[96] "The human ideal (which is the masculine ideal)" ends the rule of the Father only to ensure the rule of the sons.[97] But the "feminine," passive attitude of illusory dependence upon the father is not the only possible contribution of religion. Daughters transforming the so-called narcissism of the relation to the mother may find themselves empowered and not drowned by the subtle religiosity of oceanic feeling, learning to differentiate themselves in and through an intimate bond with the universe. Thus the symbol of the Mother Goddess reemerges today, not as an illusory projection of an external omnipotence, upon which creatures unilaterally depend, but as a life force, indeed as a libido, internal to everything.

Here Jung's work, which can be described in its entirety as psychology of religion, remains promising. If Freud heralds the death of the Father, Jung celebrates—from the vantage point of the

Child—the apotheosis of the Mother. Despite the damage wrought by his "eternal feminine," there is an implicit connection (suggested in Chapter 2) between affirmation of the image of woman and affirmation of any divine imago. If each archetype can present a face of the sacred, is this because the collective unconscious ushers into consciousness an open universe of intricate interwovenness? For the sacred irreducibility of our interconnections rightly suggests itself—our Self—in multiform images. Feminist theology does not require any restriction to female images of the divine. However, our humanity may not come into its own without metaphors of our divinity.

Accordingly, let us invoke that unique ancient alternative to the psychomyths of matricide, divine sons and monster-mothers—the tale of Demeter and her daughter Persephone. Being a daughter, not a mother, is what all women share with our mothers and all other women. Here the mother's grieving rage ultimately effects the resurrection of the maiden from the underworld, where according to the classical version, she had been held captive by Hades after he raped and abducted, that is, married her. Contra Freud's advocacy of the protective father, it is a tale of protection not by the father but by the mother. Instead of the image of father and son as the solely salvific duo, an image of Mother and Daughter bestows its saving grace. How extraordinary to find a woman's power, indeed her anger, celebrated as effective and soteriological, so far from monstrous that even patriarchal Athens sought its initiations in her Eleusinian mysteries for over two thousand years. Demeter's anti-Olympian action, her threat to leave the earth permanently barren (and so deprive the Olympians of human offerings) if her daughter were not freed from Hades, has won adoration rather than vilification. Somehow the mother-daughter dyad, even or precisely in a culture of high dualism and rampant phallic narcissism,[98] communicated to both men and women the redeeming power of reconnection. Connection can triumph—then in a mystery, now in history?—over the deadening force of a rapacious separation. If the mother-daughter bond has the mysterious power to pluck life out of death, it is also true that the mythic compromise (Persephone must return to Hades for one-third of every year) shows that complete redemption from the fathers' dominance is impossible within the world they rule. Yet the compromise also suggests that relation—even to the most dysrelational males—is not ultimately broken. The ethic of connection is painfully consistent as it works itself out in all relations, even the relation to separation itself.

We have learned from Chodorow that the bond between mother and daughter tends to communicate a permeable and empathic selfhood. For largely distorted reasons and under oppressive circumstances, it is women who still usually mother. But nonetheless if brought into consciousness, the mother-daughter relation can be redemptive for all: it can convey, if saved from its patriarchal bondage, an altered state otherwise buried away with its preoedipal residue in the psychic underworld.[100]

Demeter and Persephone, at the ritualized moment of the daughter's resurrection, together give birth to the special son, Triptolemus. Together they teach him. Does he symbolize a pre- or postpartriarchal maleness, luminous as he carries his sheaf of golden wheat out to the world? The two open into three, and either the mother is giving birth to both or both mother and daughter are giving birth simultaneously, since the daughter herself becomes a symbolic mother—the scanty evidence from the mystery drama cannot be sorted out on this point. Either way, the threesome corresponds to the psychoanalytic discovery of the triadic structure of women's psyche. In this myth, however, the place of the patriarchal father is taken by the beloved son, the new male.

The daughter's transformation, depicted in bas-reliefs of her rising joyously from the netherworld like a plant bursting from the soil, carries for all who would participate in it the secret of a selfhood that does not flourish by increasing separation but by the power of relation. The original continuum with the mother (symbolic and literal) need not be matricidally ruptured; rather, in the myth it survives violation to include all of human civilization, the surrounding green world of agriculture, joining nature and culture, and the spiritual world in which the divine is dependent upon the offerings of humans.

What would it be like if the original continuum from which we all emerge, call it preoedipal, narcissistic, oceanic or empathic, were neither shattered nor repressed, but extended and transformed? If maturation meant the gradual differentiation and modulation of the empathic continuum? We would know ourselves neither bound to parent figures nor severed from them. Freedom and creativity, humor, wisdom and individuality would evolve not in dissociation from parents but in a widening net of relations in which parents

would remain significant presences, real and symbolic. If symbols—
or better, metaphors—transform, their deliteralizing force can be
encouraged rather than stifled along with the imagination of the
child. A widening play of image and relationship will create both a
more spacious world and a bigger self, never lacking in the "transitional objects" that liberate us from dependency. A state of interdependence, intrapsychically and panculturally, requires a field of
infinitely diversifying and endlessly overlapping energies, male and
female. Connection without constriction: this is a mystery the rising
girl-child may be able to teach us.

The Selves of Psyche

Psyche's journey toward eros and immortality is a journey into the dark side of our mind. . . . For the part of the mind that is dark to us in this culture, that is sleeping in us, that we name 'unconscious', is the knowledge that we are inseparable from all other beings in the universe. Intimations of this have reached us.
—Susan Griffin, *Pornography and Silence*

Each actual entity is a locus for the universe.
—Alfred North Whitehead, *Process and Reality*

It is the insistence on the *connections,* the demand to synthesize, the refusal to be narrowed into desiring less than everything—that is so much the form of metaphysical feminism.
—Robin Morgan, *Going Too Far*

OUR INSEPARABILITY FROM all other beings in the universe—how can we anchor this knowledge in consciousness and our consciousness in this knowledge? Despite the habit of damming them out as oceanic feelings, "intimations" have indeed reached us.[1] We have just examined some interpersonal and transpersonal models of our fundamental interrelatedness. But something more is needed. If we are to insist on the connections, on the intrinsic, that is, essential, connectivity of self, we need a greater theoretical width than psychology permits. Archaic as it may seem, we shall have to get metaphysical. Or rather, we shall own up to being in a certain sense already metaphysical, already steeped in intuitions of what is really real—of something shared by all realities inasmuch as they *are* real. But why leap beyond particular selves to what selves have in common with everything else—especially when we are trying to avoid the pretentious claims of androcentric abstraction? Let me repeat: we do anyway, always, already. Everyone participates, however vaguely, in some conceptual network that relates one experience to the next. It is precisely a matter of connection. For the *meta* of metaphysics can mean "with" as well as "beyond," (and so with and not "beyond the physical") the sense of a perspective that moves *beyond* any isolated being into its interlinkage *with* all others. We may find ourselves refreshed by a less sociopsychological, indeed less anthropocentric excursion into the notion of self.

To explicate the metaphysics in which we are already implicated has us collaborate in the first mythic labor of Psyche, in her pursuit of Eros. It is a matter of sorting the endless seed pile of experience into a few categories. Though at first Psyche's task seemed foredoomed to failure, infinite patience is after all not required: remember that the ants came to Psyche's aid. As the female psyche does not heroically shun help on its journey, we will find ourselves especially helped in this chapter by the thought of Alfred North Whitehead.

In the old Roman allegory of Psyche, it is the desire for Eros—indeed the love of love—that motivates the quest. Psyche, refusing to love Eros blindly any more, to merge unconsciously in a narcissistic night union with a lover she has never *seen,* is subjected to the worst punishment: separation. Behaving just like a patriarchal male, Eros flees her need to know him. But having refused a soluble unconsciousness, she now refuses an inflicted separation. Even in Apuleius' misogynist narrative, we see her overturning the terms and setting out on a journey. She will have Eros—the very principle of connection—on new and equal terms. Soul cannot thrive in either separation or unconsciousness—it must reclaim its Eros: that is, it must love with open eyes, laying conscious, selective, responsible claim to its relatedness. Our connections, whether or not enhanced by our consciousness of them, constitute a metaphysical force-field: after all, Eros was originally the bisexual principle of world-creation.[2] We will again encounter the cosmic Eros in Whitehead's thought, as the "divine element in the universe" luring all things toward each other and so toward self-realization. In her stubborn quest, Psyche practices "the refusal to be narrowed into desiring less than everything." Eros is a name for that unlimited desire, the desire that drives beyond the fixed bounds of all separations.

Cosmic Tapestries

Feminist sensibility affirms the quest for connection—not as a mere wish, but a driving desire to realize what is real. Realization means both becoming conscious of the real and making it actual, and so exercises both cognitive and transformative power. But in what sense can feminist theory be metaphysical? Certainly not in the sense of some pseudo-objectivity or technical construction that pretends to totalize truth while subordinating and transcending the physical (and always implicitly the female).[3] Steeped in the awareness of contingent forces—of family, institution, emotion, body—feminism cannot and does not view reality sub specie aeternitatis; when the subject makes its own vantage point absolute, it merely absolves itself of reality and so surely disqualifies itself as an expert. If the subject has cut itself off from reality, it will have nothing to tell us. As to constructing models meant to correspond literally or univocally with reality, which has been the project of traditional metaphysics, feminism is a work of deconstruction. Indeed deconstructionist philosophy, especially as assimilated by Luce Irigaray, has helped extirpate the "phallocentric" outgrowths of metaphysical tradition. Derrida initiated the deconstruction, or disclosure, of all forms of metaphysical—or "ontotheological"—totalization. So the feminist eros for Everything cannot construct any fixed and final totality; totalitarian thinking would follow. Whitehead, even *as* metaphysician, would insist that "Philosophy can never hope finally to formulate these metaphysical first principles. . . . Words and phrases must be stretched towards a generality foreign to their ordinary usage; . . . they remain metaphors mutely appealing for an intuitive leap."[4] In spite of its tradition, metaphysics need not remove itself from the crude irreversibility of history and the din of praxis. "Metaphysics is nothing but the description of the generalities which apply to all the details of practice."[5]

Feminist theory, like all theory, is *theoria,* "seeing," that is, vision; through seeing (and hearing and feeling) relations, we begin to apprehend them in everything and to sense the relation of one thing with everything else. But as we can never have a direct experience of Everything all at once, but only of some particular things, this seeing peers into the invisible: this is the poignancy of Psyche's transgression and the function of metaphoric generalization. Only "an intuitive leap" can carry the desire for "nothing less than everything": we move through particular relations between particular things to glimpse the unseen interrelatedness of all things—and always back again to the particular. The intuitive trust in interralatedness seems to function as the first principle of much feminist reflection. But metaphysics is not limited to self-conscious theory. For example, take the words of comic heroine and lesbian mother Arden Benbow (in a fairly serious moment): "Things are connected, you know. Human events are all linked by a brilliant network of feelings, beliefs, ideas that wink on and off like Christmas tree lights." [6] Or from "Bridging," by Marge Piercy, we hear another evocation of the metaphysics of connection:

A clear umbilicus
goes out invisibly between,
thread we spin fluid and finer than hair
but strong enough to hang a bridge on. [7]

The brilliance of a network, the strength of a web—both women evoke the power of a fundamental vision. Though they are not working as theorists, the "ideas" winking on and off, the "invisibly" discernible bridge, both suggest an indirectly accessible dimension. They elicit the generality of first principles through the very particularity of their images.

This emerging feminist vision requires something like metaphysical sensibility, because such vision drives beyond the sphere of the interpersonal, seeking a broader context in which all relations may be reassessed. It is not just a matter of person-to-person relations but of a panrelational whole. "Gender, race, global politics, family structure, economics, the environment, childhood, aging—all reveal their interconnectedness as we move around the holograph," [8] declares Robin Morgan in The Anatomy of Freedom, announcing the deep affinities she will explore between the politics of feminism and the metaphors from the new physics. Holography generates a model of reality as an interconnected holon, a whole refracted in the particularity of each of its parts. "The internal workings of the human body or of an atomic particle," continues Morgan, "of spiritual faith and scientific fact, of aesthetics and astrophysics, disclose themselves as interwoven expressions of one dynamic whole." The global extension of the intuition of connection at once implicates feminism in metaphysical breadth and ramifies in an insistent praxis. Morgan well dramatizes the scope of our vision, work and hope:

Feminism is, at this moment and on this planet, the DNA/ RNA call for survival and for the next step in evolution— and even beyond that feminism is, in its metaphysical and metafeminist dynamic, the helix of hope that we humans have for communication with whatever lies before us in the vast, witty mystery of the universe.[9]

A vision of the world—a worldview—is not just a matter of *what* we see but of *how* we see it. If feminism sees connections where they have not been seen before, it is through insistence upon a congruence of theory at once with method and with sociopolitical practice. To see connections, we must see connectively. That is, we see connections in and by making them. Inspired and angered and energized by the relations we feel, we weave the web further by making the connection conscious. Thinking relationally about relatedness embroiders new designs into the tapestry of relation.

But very quickly our minds are again crippled by the mechanisms of separation and bondage. The Hag—to borrow Daly's hagiographic term of honor for the third member of the Goddess triad, the wise old Crone—cannot help waxing metaphysical, presiding as she does over the moon's mysteries.[10] The Crone, who specializes in the darkening moon, has become expert in invisibilities. This does not mean we should wait until the final third of life to philosophize, to trace the internal relations of things. Have not most women felt from an early age somehow too old for our years, as though there was something we already knew, something embarrassingly weighty and *old*, something that had nothing to do with school, something that was like knowing Everything? Though beat down as proud and bound back as unfeminine, the Hag is always already with us—though we may bring her into her own in our actual aging processes, as we become able to spin more mythically honest, more ruggedly encompassing visions.

So far, however, we have our metaphysics mainly from old cronies, masculine usurpers of the rights of the Crone. The wise old man archetype—or is it really the hero?—has managed to turn the wise old woman into little more than his withered and nagging support system. (If there have been a few truly wise men, their style need not dominate ours, nor their ideas overpower our own germinating insights.) The Hag especially knows that knowing things are connected becomes a trivial insight, unless we know this knowledge *connectingly*. As a kind of knowledge that obviates blind belief and transcends strict cognition, it is gnosis,[11] transformative knowledge. Gnosis, Daly reminds us, is to make connections in a dissociative world, and counts as a subversive activity:

The mindbinders and those who remain mindbound do not see the patterns of the cosmic tapestries, nor do they hear the labyrinthine symphony. For their thinking has been crippled and tied to linear tracks. . . . Since they do not understand that creativity means seeing the interconnectedness between seemingly disparate phenomena, the mindbound accuse Hags of 'lumping things together.' Their perception is a complete reversal.[12]

Daly thus performs her characteristic, methodological reversal and so exposes an important binary opposition: between the creative activity of interconnection and the crippling action of mindbinding (she alludes here to the image of Chinese footbinding). Binding can either mean connection or bondage. Patriarchy, she suggests, reverses these meanings so that what is in fact mind bondage appears to the "mindbound" to constitute the process of meaningful thought—as in traditional theological-metaphysical totalization. Creative connectivity then appears as chaos and confinement, as an undifferentiated heap, a constrictive—maternally monstrous—mix of matters.

The Metaphysics of Several Selves

As we cultivate theoretical support for the Hag's affirmation of global connectivity, we seek specifically to bring this affirmation home to our *self*-understanding. Abstract interrelatedness only means anything when it becomes physically and soulfully almost tangible: when we understand our *selves* to be loci of unlimited relation. For it is a self conceived as separate that has after all projected its grid of fragmentation upon the world. Theory has laid out an extended series of argumentative alternatives—but all within an androcentric continuum. Something else is happening when women reconsider—precisely as misfits to the norms of subjectivity—the very concept of self. To move beyond the tradition of the deficient female leaves all previous standards insufficient. Let me restate the working methodology: we are not asking to be admitted to the going norm, which would accordingly be poked and stretched a bit; nor are we content to formulate concepts only of women's selfhood; but rather, as women we are envisioning anew what it means to be a self. This is not to step out of our skins, to subordinate gender-specific concerns to supposedly transcendent, humanistic ones, but rather to spin a meaning of self out of our femaleness, without reducing it to anything exclusively "feminine". This move has been supported by the psychoanalysis of women's relational sense, if qualified by my claim that women may have a special access to the mysterious missing link for the radical reformulation of what a self is.

Yet the previous chapter's work with psychoanalysis leaves us with as many questions as answers. We could not gain from within a theory such as Chodorow's adequate warrant for a connective self. The feminine associations with relational empathy remain confined to the social circumstances of patriarchy. Within the terms of her analysis, Chodorow can only oppose "masculine" ego differentiation to "feminine" connectedness. But we are searching for some path of differentiation *in* relation. This would permit women to remain faithful to the complex inner and outer connectivity that we may sense as integral to our selves, while liberating ourselves from the accompanying modes of dependency and self-suppression. It would challenge males to modes of relatedness that require not the sacrifice of their maleness but of their ego rigidities and corollary manipulation of women. But then differentiation—becoming uniquely ourselves—must not be cast in the category of separation. It requires a reformulation of the concept of self—too abstract a task for Chodorow's more sociological project. She rightly neither promises nor delivers any such construction. Yet even making an odd couple of Jung and Chodorow could not produce the relational self. For Jung's "Self," though resonant with universal interrelatedness, remains too dualistically pitted against the ego. The requirement that the ego sacrifice itself to the Self, derived from the religious symbolism of the hero's death, compensates (as does classical theology) the *hybris* of the rigidly autonomous masculine ego. But the prideful opposition of ego versus either God or Self—as *imago dei*—has been institutionalized by theology (which makes it original sin) or by Jungians (who make it necessary for differentiation). As we have observed, this particular dualism of ego and God-image, merely perpetuates the patriarchal cycle. Moreover, since Jung lacked an adequate metaphysical alternative to any self-other dualisms, his hypothesis of the transpersonal or collective unconscious does not easily translate into a dynamic and immediate process of relation.

Not just the metaphysics but the common sense of the West is weighed down by the presupposition that to be a single individual is to be an enduring, self-identical substance, essentially independent from others (except God, with whom matters simply reverse themselves). Subjectivity is read off this categorical grid as a reflexive, self-objectifying instance of a oneness over and against the many. And so to reimagine the self, we are willy-nilly involved in the old metaphysical dilemma of the One and the Many. Recall how the "opaque blade" of the undivided ego, caught in its oppositions to the Others, ricochets back upon itself in the idea of reflexive self-knowledge: the one, defined in terms of dyadic oppositions, ends up divided against itself. So normative selfhood has been preoccupied with a game of one and two, echoed in the constructions of monism and dualism. "Whence the mystery that woman represents in a culture claiming to count everything, to number everything by units, to inventory everything as individualities. *She is neither one nor two.*" [13] Thus Luce Irigaray deconstructs the scheme: she eludes it. She has us refuse to stand up and be counted. In the economics of separation, woman has counted for little. Now, she may in her own irony remain uncountable, and so unaccountable to the patriarchs of simple unity. Indeed how can one *count* selves that, in Susan Griffin's words, "are inseparable from all other beings in the universe." By what calculus? Yet after all, *self* functions in our language as a count noun.[14] Selves are supposed to be identifiable as more or less consistent unities enduring through their histories and clearly marked off from each other in space. What else is possible? Would something else even be desirable? If we stop counting ourselves as unit individuals, will we not lose ourselves? Here Irigaray offers a crucial intuition: "Woman always remains several, but she is kept from dispersion because the other is already within her." [15]

Several yet not dispersed: this apparent paradox will guide our query. For with Chodorow we encounter women's complex psychic harmony—our multiplicity of inner and outer relations—still ensnaring us in diffusion, distraction, devotion. Then simplicity and separation can monopolize differentiated selfhood. But can I not be multiple without dispersion? Might such composite selfhood not finally allow our relatedness to bear its fruit? "Kept from dispersion because the other is already within her": Irigaray plays upon the "autoerotically familiar" metaphor of the lips of the vulva, which are at once joined, distinct, and related—different but not separate. If we consciously claim our participation in all things, or the way the Other is a part of ourselves, we may indeed be protected from dissolution by connection. The logic for our metaphysical exploration is clear enough: If I take the many into myself, then am I not many? Still, some intuition of an integral oneness, of a continuity of identity, may return: but in the light of the "brilliant network," this will be no simple or literal oneness. Moving through a history of theological and philosophical thought on the oneness of the self, let us pursue the question: What kind of integrity accrues to a self in whom the many take part?

Tumultuous Varieties

We have observed that the theory of the separate self begins with Aristotle's reflection on the nature of any individual being as a substance—that is, as what cannot be "in" another or immanent to another, what is therefore self-subsistent and independent. We noted the indirect linkage of sexism with the substantialism of Aristotle's scheme. But with Aristotle this substantial individuality is never quite a "self," nor even identified with psyche: soul in some mysterious sense still evades the category of substance. In the *De Anima* there seems to be only *one* soul, or animating form, in the universe, which informs the multitude of many bodies. The sense of self as one's *own* and as subjective interiority only enters theoretical discourse through the Christian itinerary of the journeying soul first publicized by Augustine. But as Augustine takes his conceptual base from the Platonic tradition (for which ideas, not individuals, have the character of substance), we will find in Augustine the emergence of a subjectivity tending toward the conditions of separation but not yet substantial. The synthesis of the emerging Christian individualism with Greek substantialism awaits Thomas Aquinas.

Even as we hold out for a self uncountable in the inventory of simple unities, we can nonetheless feel in Augustine the anguish of the self-divided Western will seeking its unity of self: "Behold, my life is but a distraction and Thy right hand upheld me, in my Lord the Son of Man, the Mediator betwixt Thee, The One, and us many, many also through our manifold distraction amid many things, that by Him I may . . . be recollected, . . . to follow the One." [16] Augustine's term for *distraction* (*distrahere*) puns with its other meaning of "tearing apart," or "dividing." In the passionate complexity of this passage, the first auto-bio-grapher of the Western world is indeed a "self-life-writer," writing out the life of the self. In its agonies of self-dividedness, its yearning for unity, this self dramatizes the fragmentation of the self-reflexive state. "Distraction" names well the loss of focus and the dissipation of will symptomatic of any underdifferentiated state of being. Augustine seeks "recollection"— to be re-membered, put back together, as one, in the One. Certainly this soul is not content with the dichotomous divisions marking off a discrete individual. The quest for the One expresses the drive to transcend fragmentation. It searches for the lost parts of itself, the split-off elements of personality: in Jung's terms, the ego seeks its Self; in Winnicott's, the false personality structure recalls its true self. In the light of psychoanalytic theory, it seems only natural that Augustine desires "recollection" in its dual sense of memory and integration. Much that he seeks in God, he may have lost in childhood. Indeed, we could speculate about the mediatorial power of the "Son" image for Christianity in general. Aside from its manifest deification of a human male and its latent patricide (to which Freud as a Jew had special cause to be sensitive), let us consider that the symbol of a "Son" picks out a particular phase of maleness: that of the child. Does the persuasive force of the Christ image in the patriarchal world have something to do with its appeal to the violated preoedipal boy, the lost child? Does "the Son" mediate between the absent Father and the human male so well because a deep recollection of childhood promises to redeem the lost sense of connection? In his inconsolable if ambivalent yearning for the Father (inevitable in the patriarchal situation of distant fathers), Augustine seeks his own wholeness. But Augustine, as we know, was literally reconciled with his mother Monica by coming to Christ—an intimate bond that suggests "an incomplete oedipal resolution" in the first place. But (as the previous chapter would argue) this is all to the good and might account for the residual "oceanic feeling" that both plagues and attracts this man. I mean no reductionism here—the younger Augustine, like many mystics, is in touch with a numinous affect that authentically opens him to his own nonseparate selfhood. And the Son image might to some degree work unconsciously—archetypally—on the dilemmas produced by the early personal history as a patriarchal son.[17]

But separation prevails as the solution to distraction. The recollecting force that begins to work in him is severely cut off from its own indirectly psychoanalytic potential: he immediately eschews any remembering of the past at all! The passage continues: "that by Him I may . . . be recollected . . . to follow the One, *forgetting what is behind,* and not distended but extended, not to things which shall be and shall pass away" (my emphasis). His sense of oneness—which remains always ahead, a desire and not yet an experience—is to be bought at a price. Augustine dissociates himself in one fell swoop from "the many," from "what is behind," that is, his past, and from "things which shall be," the finite future. "I have been severed amid times . . . and my thoughts, even the inmost bowels of my soul, are rent and mangled with tumultuous varieties, until I flow together into Thee, purified and molten by the fire of Thy love."[18] The erotically hot metaphor of liquid fire, bringing an end to separation in eschatological fusion, might tempt one to hope with the empassioned confessor for an ultimate experience of oneness. But he cannot distinguish between the fragmentation wrought by the separative ego and the complex plurality that is arguably the only real alternative to fragmentation. He can choose only between "tumultuous varieties" and "the One." As we shall see, such abhorrence of multiplicity belongs not accidentally with the antitemporalism of a certain basic disgust with the concrete particular. Christianity readily assimilated, and indeed amplified in its asceticism, the classical antipathy to the finite and to the many. Systemically if not systematically conjoined with these phobias is the devaluation of the female. The Christian ascetic seeks oneness not with the many but with the Father.

The Father's own oneness has classically been defined in terms of a simple unity, free of all diversity, of all multiplicity; if, as theology before and after Augustine has consistently argued, the oneness of the Creator is not simple, it would be compound (complex) and thus tainted with the nature of the Creation.[19] The Absolutely Other remains supremely separate from his own products. The Christian doctrine of divine simplicity purifies and reinforces the radical monotheism of the biblical tradition, purging the deity, as chapter 1 argued, of all mutability, affect and reciprocity with the world. For the metaphysics of substance is only fully instantiated in God, the wholly independent One. But what of the Three-in-One?

The postbiblical image of the trinity seems to arise quite spontaneously, almost as though to compensate for the momentum of monolithic thinking. It cannot—as is often done—be exhaustively explained in terms of the abstract christological need to account for the relation of the incarnate "Son of God" to the "Father." For in the idea (developed above all by Athanasius and Augustine) of three persons who share one essence, each person distinct in identity and functions yet inseparable from the others, the basis for an alternative metaphysic symbolically suggests itself: a metaphysic of internally related individuals, pointing toward the radically social and interdependent character of all individuality. Augustine in his later and belabored tome *De Trinitates* in fact lifts up the underdeveloped Aristotelian category of "relation," distinguishing it clearly from that of "accident," so he can apply it to the divine persons. Here at least, relation is not accidental, not external, but *of the essence*—since at least these three persons in relation are one "in essence." That is, each person's individuality entails being indivisible from the others, rather than indivisible as a separate self: "as they are indivisible so they work indivisibly," says Augustine.[20] But what goes wrong? What sabotages this oddly promising revelation of personhood as interpersonal connection? The answer will appear on two different levels of duplicity whose collaboration becomes increasingly apparent, the first in the idea of the substantial oneness of the one-in-three, the second in that of the begetting-power of a threefold masculinity.

Metaphysically, Augustine subsumes the symbol of the triune God under the category of substance, and specifically that of the *immutable* substance. Though he attempts to mitigate the undifferentiated oneness of substance with the notion of relation, the changelessness of God intrudes. To follow his own logic: "But in God nothing is said to be according to accident, because in Him *nothing is changeable;* and yet everything that is said, is not said according to substance. For it is said *in relation to something,* as the Father *in relation to* the Son" (my emphasis).[21] In other words, the particular personhood of the "Father," and the "Son" and the "Spirit" are constituted by their relations to each other. If everything "is not said according to substance" it may be because substance, in its monolithic independence, cannot tell the tales of interdependent persons. But by preserving the changelessness of God, Augustine seals the Godhead as a whole into its own independent substance, closed to any internal becoming or external influence: "He who is God is the only unchangeable substance."[22]

We must not get dragged down in the formal tedium of this wedding of Greek substantialism with Christian dogmatism. Something of great symbolic import is going on here: the repression of an insight that might have undermined the conceptual essence of patriarchy. Thus it is instructive to note the bizarre contortions to which Christian metaphysics submits the dogma of the Trinity in order to curb the relational implications of its Personhood. For instance, attempting to describe the Holy Spirit's function as the unity of the Father and Son, or the love between the "Begetter" and the "Begotten," Augustine ends up literally hypostatizing love itself as "a substance." This clumsy objectification of love, making the very principle of relation into a "person," might seem to dignify love by deifying it—acknowledging the transcendent power of relation. But because this metaphysic cannot ultimately brook relation, it seems to remove it by deifying and reifying it. The Spirit, as Third Person, always seems the odd one out (or odd man out, as we shall see). By making the divine spirit of love into a separate substance, both relatedness and divinity are sealed off in their independence from the world.

The triune symbolism seems of its own accord to intimate an interdependence at the heart of reality. So the mere reassertion of divine oneness would not have proved a strong enough prophylactic against the interdependence of God and world. The fathers of the church rightly perceive that a *complex* unity would admit process and change into the Godhead. So trinitarian speculation performs endless metaphysical convolutions on the theme of how God, though a trinity, is not complex but "simple." "For nothing simple is changeable, but every creature is changeable." [23] God remains not only three-in-one (a legitimate paradox) but at the same time *simply* one (a willful contradiction?): "Neither, since He is a Trinity, is he therefore to be thought triple (triplex). Otherwise the Father alone, or the Son alone, will be less than the Father and Son together." [24] And does not such unity of persons preclude any genuine relation, in which two are indeed *more* than one, because each person does indeed augment the experience of the other? Thus the divine simplicity not only explicitly absolves the Absolute from relation to his world, which can never affect him; it also latently absolves him from any real relation to his own selves, that is, from an internal complexity based on real interrelation.

In the *Confessions,* we heard Augustine aspiring to this oneness purged of all change and all particularity, seeking to free himself of all relations but to God, who symbolizes the supreme Separateness. *De Trinitate* expresses the spirit of divine-human love this way: "we ourselves are one by His gift, and one Spirit with Him, because our soul cleaves to Him so as to follow Him." [25] Again—we need not deny the intuition that integrity comes only in love, nor even that love implies transcendence (or "God"). But Agape, Christian love, means the gift of the superior to the abject dependent. The language of "cleaving" intentionally plays on the traditional male-female dyad. [26] Again we sense that humanity is the passive "feminine" other for the divine masculinity. And any tenderness in the love discourse, which might weaken authority, must be quickly dispelled. He continues: "And it is good for us to cleave to God, since He will destroy every man who is estranged from Him." That puts the case clearly: love, for a patriarchal metaphysic incapable of connection, boils down to fear of destruction. No wonder the "love" ethic of Christianity has so readily resulted in the violent suppression of Jews, women, witches, pagans and differently-minded Christians.

Moreover, love of others must be unilaterally channeled through the fearful love of God: community is not intrinsically sacred. Only vertical relation of transcendence is sanctified. We noted in the last chapter an inverted psychoanalytic analogue: for Freud and Jung, the boundaries melt downward, toward the unconscious—the horizontal possibilities are minimally validated. In neither classic theological nor psychological ego-transcendence does the ego transcend itself toward the other, the neighbor. Despite the relational potential of primitive Christian metaphors, such as the Body in which "we are members one of another," or the Johannine vine and branches, and despite the indistinguishability of love of God and love of neighbor in Jesus' teachings, let alone the background of Hebrew focus on community, no persuasive doctrine of community, of interpersonal or global creaturely love, could grow amidst the teachings of the Church Fathers.

This brings us to another dimension of trinitarian "paradox": that of its triple-faced masculinity. In light of Chodorow's psychoanalytic disclosure of the relative "simplicity" of the (patriarchal) male psyche (cf. chap. 3), the projection of simple oneness as the consummate father-son relation should not surprise us. Nor should the sense of self-contradiction: for Chodorow showed that within the traditional absent-father family, it is the *female* psyche that is triadic in structure. Why then an all-male trinity? Does this God want the triune inclusiveness of the feminine experience without its emotional complexity? Is "God" the male who within patriarchy can—almost—have his cake and eat it too—have separative masculine omnipotence along with feminine relatedness? Of course, this is "bad faith" and does not quite come off, leaving the trinity a peculiar, rationalistic albatross of a doctrine.

But what an amazing coup to raise up not just one but three masculine faces of God. (The Hebrew Yahweh had at least the excuse of a stricter monotheism; that is, one deity must arguably be one sex or the other). As Mary Daly comments, "This naming of 'the three Divine Persons' is the paradigmatic model of the pseudogeneric term *person,* excluding all female mythic presence, denying female reality in the cosmos." [27]

The trinitarian meaning of *person* does historically precede its use as a generic term for human selves. In other words the sacredness of personhood in our culture derives from an all-male imagery. Thus men of God, in the image of the three-man God they have erected, could systematically eliminate the sacredness of women. The artificial substantialization of love into a "Person" perhaps results inevitably from the cosmic exclusion of female presence. The Goddess, she with the original procreative power, has been superseded by a Father begetting a Son eternally; a female is used only once, as merely human vessel. Love, become sterile and threatening, leaves scholastic contrivance to produce the doctrine of triune relation, while women are desacralized and degraded for the very power of their relatedness.

In fact, the trinity in its masculine self-enclosure accurately reflects the self-objectifying, self-mirroring narcissism we tracked earlier as this God's own original sin of incurvature. We had already attributed the transcendent self-encapsulation of the deity to the inflation of the male ego. Daly exposes trinitarian all-maleness in a delicious spoof:

This triune god is one act of eternal self-absorption/self-love. The term *person* is derived from the Latin *persona* meaning actor's mask, or character in a play. "The Processions of Divine Persons" is the most sensational one-act play of the centuries, the original *Love Story,* performed by the Supreme All Male Cast. Here we have the epitome of male bonding. . . . It is "sublime" (and therefore disguised) erotic male homosexual *mythos,* the perfect all-male marriage, the ideal all-male family, the best boys' club, the model monastery, the supreme Men's Association, the mold for all varieties of male monogender mating. To the timid objections voiced by Christian women, the classic answer has been: "You're included under the Holy Spirit. He's feminine." [28]

Daly refers here to the "Spirit's" grammatically feminine gender (both in the Hebrew *ruah* and the Greek *pneuma*), to which theologians have lately pointed, hoping to assimilate women who are beginning to question the politics of divine gender. But feminist theology has indeed unearthed a real, if meagre, iconographic tradition of a female Third Person.[29]

Given the female associations of the Spirit, we can understand why the Spirit is sometimes identified as Love itself. The female subject has culturally embodied the shunned value of relation. But eventually the homogenized masculinity carries the day, leaving what is female and what is relational together in the dark. The pristine self-absorption of the all-male absolute inevitably aborts the deeper possibilities of its own relatedness. Unlike Daly, I often sense within patriarchal traditions certain initially redemptive possibilities arising only to be immediately co-opted. In a symbol such as the trinity there may be an unheard, stifled voice of revelation, inviting a non-patriarchal pluralism. If so, the power of patriarchal presupposition to puncture even those transforming possibilities that occasionally erupt within its own terms seems then all the more virulent.

Daly's own method of re-reversal can account for whatever counter-phallicism operates within phallocentric symbol systems. Here, for example, "the irony involved in this invitation to assimilation can be better appreciated if we are aware of the Triple Goddess in early mythology." [30] She invokes the archaic, prepatriarchal background of Triple Goddesses (including the earliest forms of Athena), whom the invading Bronze Age patriarchs overthrew by raping, marrying and, in the Hebrew and Christian traditions, completely replacing by men—finally even in the original triplicity of female imagery. Some Christian theologians recognize that the doctrine of the trinity can be a "source of distortion" and an "artificial game," [31] but fail to relate the problem to patriarchy. Its triunity, originally manifesting a goddess and still preserved in the triadic personality structure of women, was subjected to artificial masculinization—that sex change operation long required of all symbols of sacred presence. Men are consequently almost feminized by the overwhelming masculinity of a God who is himself originally female!

Where is any *reality* in this? The category of "substance" must represent a concerted ploy to hold on via abstraction to the *Really Real*, when all feeling for it is fading. We see once again that the bad faith of androcentric imagery "works indivisibly" with the metaphysics of separate selfhood. Idols of control take the place of cosmic connectivity. Unveiling omnipresence as in fact omni-absence, Daly writes that "the ubiquity of false naming masks the ominous absence which is the essence of the patriarchal god. It confers upon him infinite worth in the rarefied realm of Reversal Religion's value system." [32] The Father's absence results in that "death of God"—Nietzschean, Freudian, Marxian, or merely apathetic— for which the patricidal dynamics operating within the matricidal infrastructure had long prepared. Echoing the absence of the pre-oedipal father, which gives rise to the psychology of separation,

Western theology subsumed the possibility of multiple interrelation under the simplicity of separation. But sacredness becomes unreality in separation from its world.

Selves create themselves in the images of their gods and goddesses, whose images in turn have been created by those selves. So naturally the concept of the substantial unity of the self only gradually imitates the substantial oneness of the Christian God. In his *Confessions,* before he locked himself into the doctrinal tensions represented by *De Trinitates,* Augustine did lift individuality into passion and prominence. And despite his later doctrines of God, soul is still for him more Neoplatonic than Aristotelian, barely involved in the formal separation of substance. Though from the beginning his insights were caught in the implicit sexism of separative thinking and in the explicit sexism of his day, his journeying might have led to a deepening of the experience of self. But we already recognize in the solitary spirituality of his journey a sublimated form of masculine individualism: thus the ideal of the spiritual hero emerges.

The Rise and Fall of Substance

Augustine seems to have prepared the Western ground at once for a deepened appreciation of individuality and for the increasing individualism of Christian thought and piety. It can be argued that the conjunction of his confessional soul with medieval Aristotelianism begets the fully substantial individual we encounter a millenium later in Thomas Aquinas's soul-body compound. The Angelic Doctor seems to have been spared even the temptations of "tumultuous varieties." Here we pick up the trail of the substance-predicate way of thinking where we left it off (cf. chap. 2) in Aristotle. Let us follow it through very briefly.

While the magnificent metaphysics of the Thomist vision does in a sense forge connections between all creatures of the cosmos, it also represents the triumph of substantialism. In this scheme things are either "accidents" or "substances." Thomas depicts the relations between entities, as "accidental," that is, external, to their essences. Aquinas does at moments glimpse another possibility. Not unexpectedly, we find that in his attempt to come to terms with the

three-in-oneness of the trinity, which always troubled substance categories, he formulates the notion of "subsistent relations." [33] Following Aristotle, however, he defines the basic metaphysical unit as
"the subject, i.e., a particular substance." [34] And substance has two
main characteristics: "The first is that it is capable of separate existence, for an accident is not separated from a substance, but a
substance can be separated from an accident. The second is that
substance is a determinate particular thing." [35] "Being separable and
being a particular thing" belong together: to be an individual is to
be separable—to be able to "exist by itself." Separability, or independence—not being "in" something else in Aristotle's sense—
quietly lodges itself in Christian metaphysics. But only God (or perhaps an angel) is a simple substance, because God has no body. But
"being a particular thing belongs chiefly to the composite." That is,
individual beings are by and large holistic syntheses of matter and
form, or in the case of human beings, of body and soul. The substantial form of humanness, the rational soul, is itself for Aquinas
(unlike Aristotle) a substance: it remains essentially self-identical,
undergoing external, "accidental" changes, but (except in the rare
cases of "substantial change") sustaining the underlying unity of a
dominant subject. While he has overcome the Neoplatonic separation of soul from body, Aquinas—at least on paper—lacks the mystical capacity to experience one's individual ego boundaries melting
in ecstatic union with the deity. The natural separates, in the clean
independence of its laws, from the supernatural. Moreover, the connections between beings consist solely in the shared identity of the
universals, the forms, that they embody as individual members of
species: no horizontal, worldly confluencies here.

The great virtue of the Aristotelian tradition lies in this appreciation of concrete, complex embodiment—an advantage that Aquinas linked with the biblical stress on resurrection of the *body* in
contrast to an Orphic-Platonic immortality of the soul alone. So
while selfhood inheres in a separate soul-body compound, it retains
(or regains) a certain internal complexity.

The eternal simplicity of the unmoved mover stands as the ideal,
however. Indeed, in unfolding God's activity of self-contemplation,
the logic of the simple substance sheds a telltale light on matters of
narcissistic self-encapsulation: "the first mover's act of understanding, which is of himself, is eternal and always in the same state.
Therefore the thing understood by the intellect of the first mover is

not composite."[36] In other words, the first mover knows only himself and so knows nothing composite; conversely he remains eternally the same—unmoved—precisely because he does not "understand" composite things. Ergo, God does not understand the things of the world! Because the known always influences the knower, because intelligibility after all entails the subject's participation in the object, this God—the supreme subject—cannot even know the world he has created. Thus is his simplicity preserved—by an eternal act of reflexivity. This unfathomably separate Being could only be concocted by the yearning of the patriarchal ego to be free of complexity and of change, of relation, and of needing to know the irksome other.

As modernity takes its rise a couple of centuries later with Descartes, the unity of body and soul established auspiciously by Aristotle and Aquinas splits into two substances: into *res extensa,* the "extended thing," which is the material body, and *res cogitans,* the "thinking thing," which he identifies with the soul, defined as essentially rational. If matter is extended in space, soul now lacks extension and so is reduced, we might say, not just to a point but to pointlessness. Meditating in chilly isolation by his stove, Descartes found convincing proof of his own existence only in the fact that he could think about whether he existed: he *was* thinking, therefore he *was.* His ability to ask hard questions must be celebrated. But if, perchance, existence is a cosmically communal affair, it is no wonder he lost touch with it. He now defines substance as *"that which needs nothing but itself in order to exist,"*[37] a suggestion of Aristotle. As Descartes identifies the thinking thing with the strictly reflexive self, we encounter for the first time in conceptual history the fully substantial self—the self-objectified self, autonomous and so fundamentally separate from everything, beginning with its own body. But Descartes himself must introduce God in order even to connect moments of the history of the same ego. So Descartes admits that only God, as a third kind of substance, can really meet the criterion of absolute independence. This divine substance therefore sustains the mind and the body and the missing relation between them by an act of new creation that must occur every moment. The hint of a more dynamic interdependence flashes by but vanishes in the bizarre materialization of relation supplied by the much-mocked pineal gland. The definition of substance basic to his own dualist vision is simply never reconciled with his doctrine of

God: bodies and minds subsist independently—but not quite! We have here the classic instance adduced by Whitehead of "incoherence," as "the arbitrary disconnection of first principles."[38] This systemic incoherence inhering in the cogitations of such a redoubtable substance as Descartes' mind only confirms how deeply rooted is the assumption that reality consists of separate things. He questions his own existence rather than the presupposition of substance.

Leibniz and Spinoza continue in the new tradition of philosophical rationalism. Yet both perceive the incoherence of their master's scheme. Leibniz tries to redeem rationalism by the grand pluralism of monadology, which turns every individual into a dynamic microcosm reflecting the whole. But the reflection happens in the private interior of the "windowless monad." Its relations to other monads are all internal. Yet they are incapable of essentially altering the composition of the individual, for the relations are preprogrammed in the monad's essence. Monads are devoid of real or caused relations to each other.

Spinoza goes the contrary route. Rather than multiplying reality into an infinite plurality of separate monads, he dissolves it into a single substance. God, world and human subjectivity become one reality. Within the pantheistic vision, there is no fragmentation. Individuals are "modes" of the one substance. Yet the substance-predicate thinking persists, and in a one-substance system the monism of the Absolute ultimately devours its predicates. Unity, rather than interrelating multiplicity, prevails. As Hegel interpreted Spinoza, his position was not tantamount to atheism as his early critics maintained, but to the denial of the reality of the world, to acosmism. Without the other to whom one relates, no world exists.

It was left to the British empiricists to challenge and gradually dismember the presupposition of substance. Hume (building on the deconstruction work of Locke and Berkeley) finally questions the coherence of any invisible and unchanging substance underlying predicates of relation and change. He is the one who applies this critique to the most cherished bastion of traditional metaphysics, the idea of the substantial self (or soul), which thereby crumbles into a "bundle of impressions." But we find no true alternative yet emerging from the rubble of philosophical rationalism. Having effectively devastated the simple unity of the substantial model, Hume can find no basis for personal identity, indeed for any *self* at all. Here is *his* confession: "Did our perceptions either inhere in something simple and individual, or did the mind perceive some real connexion among them, there would be no difficulty in the case. For my part I must plead the privilege of a sceptic, and confess, that this difficulty is too hard for my understanding." [39] Because he cannot find anything resembling a traditional substance in which to lodge the perceptions, he finds no grounds for any perceiving self. "I never can perceive this self without some one or more perceptions; nor can I ever perceive any thing but the perceptions." From this he infers that "Tis the composition of these, therefore, which forms the self." This notion of a self composed of its perceptions seems promising indeed: a compositive rather than a substantial self. This would allow for a complex cohesiveness of experience. It provides additional support for Hume's general thesis that philosophers have overestimated the powers of rationality. "If perceptions are distinct existences, they form a whole only by being connected together. But no connexions are ever discoverable by human understanding. We only *feel* a connexion or determination of the thought, to pass from one object to another." [40] But the compositive hypothesis does not convince him. Why? Because quite literally he cannot validate his feelings, which would persuade him of the reality of connection between the perceptions themselves, and between his perceptions and the thing perceived. Hume walks right up to a ground for a new postsubstantial view of self in conjunction with his critique of the rational basis of empiricism. He sees perspicuously that such a self would be a matter of connectivity rather than simple unity and that rational understanding would have to bow to feeling if the connections between simple and clear perceptions are themselves to be perceived. But connections are themselves invisible, inaudible—not objects of sense-perception or discursive reason. Moreover, an epistemology of feeling would seem to Hume a contradiction in terms.

The elusive feeling of connection that Hume apprehends but disregards will prove most important to our own theoretical task: only knowing through feeling may awaken those intimations "sleeping in us," in "the part of the mind that is dark to us in this culture." [41] Hume feels the connections but cannot think them. Earlier we encountered Freud confessing himself unable to feel such connections, but trying—on the basis of a friend's account of them—to think them. Perhaps the very fact that these "intimations of immediate connection with the world" were inaccessible to Freud and so deemed regressive accounts for *his* lack of any concept of self besides that of ego.

We have moved from the simple unity sought by Augustine to the heap of disparate perceptions left by Hume. Neither divulges the role of interconnection: the former does not need it; the latter cannot see it.

Self as Stream, Self as Society

It would be up to William James, with his unique combination of psychological and philosophical creativity, to lift the notion of relation into conceptual prominence. He praises Humean empiricism for clearing out the rationalist cobwebs of substance. Yet he counters the doctrine of discrete sensations held in common by Hume and Kant: "No one," argues James, "ever had a simple sensation by itself." [42] Our impressions are from the start inseparable from each other, expressing the patterns of a "figured consciousness." [43] Hence James's axiom that impressions fall *"simultaneously on a mind* WHICH HAS NOT YET EXPERIENCED THEM SEPARATELY (his emphasis)." [44] This principle is essential to the "radical empiricism" James opposes to Humean empiricism as well as to Kantian idealism and the earlier traditions of substantialism. If for Hume reality parsed into discrete sensations, for Kant it had grounded itself in the autonomous subject. For neither form of separatism could the relations between subjective sensations or between subjects and objects take on a reality of their own. The ghost of independent substance still haunts them. In a revolutionary move, James credits relations with full ontological and epistemological status. "The relations that connect experiences must themselves be experienced relations, and any kind of relation experienced must be accounted as 'real' as anything else in the system." [45]

James is able to legitimize relatedness precisely because he turns to the *experience* of relation. And for him experience consists most fundamentally of "feeling"—that sole access to relation, which Hume could not rationally valorize. James proceeds to construct an entire epistemology of such feeling-experience:

If we start with the supposition that there is only one primal stuff or material in the world, a stuff of which everything is composed, and if we call that stuff 'pure experience,' then knowing can easily be explained as a particular sort of relation towards one another into which portions of pure experience enter.[46]

The relational flux of "pure experience" replaces the discreteness of substance, sensation or subject. "Knowing," as one particular kind of experienced relation, no longer requires the controlling objectification of an other by a subject. For no separate subject exists to precede its objects: "The relation itself of knowing is a part of pure experience; one of its 'terms' becomes the subject or bearer of the knowledge, the knower, the other becomes the object known."[47]

Like a ballet in which out of a great whirl sometimes two figures emerge for a pas de deux of subject and object, experience is the spontaneous choreography of relations, where no spectator stands still and apart from the dance. Certainly women, sensing that knowledge is a form of feeling, and that rationality removed from relation perpetrates the worst irrationalities, will feel a kinship to this scheme. Moreover, we may be reminded of object-relations theory's retrieval of experience as something that the narcissistically disturbed, in their self-enclosure, in some sense do not *have*. It has been repressed in the abrogation of primary affect. The Jamesian project has distinctly therapeutic dimensions.

In this view, the self cannot retain any static unity: it is never simply *one*. Neither can it maintain a dualistic opposition to the other, nor make itself reflexively its own object: reality is not *two*. The looser unity of experience as feeling replaces the Cartesian soul. A new view of personality begins to emerge as James recurs to a predualistic moment in all experience, a moment not of undifferentiated unity so much as of patterned wholeness. That is, he proposes the idea of the "stream of consciousness." A person is not a single, enduring subject that underlies the flux of its experience. A person is more like a series of momentary experiences connected by the transitions he calls "conjunctive relations."

These transitions, or links, rather than any fixed identity, account for our sense of personal continuity through time. One moment claims the previous moment as its own: "Each pulse of cognitive consciousness . . . dies away and is replaced by another. The other, among the things it knows, knows its own predecessor, and finding it 'warm' . . . greets it, saying: 'Thou art *mine,* and part of the same self with me.'"[48] The emergent moment of consciousness thus appropriates the previous one; the self thus cumulatively builds itself up, knowing its previous moments as its own not through self-objectification or self-identity but through a quality of "warmth and intimacy."

Certainly there are problems with James's theory. He refuses any notion of an unconscious, preferring instead to speak of a "fringe of consciousness" not normally attended to. But without a full-bodied concept of the unconscious, we may not arrive at a persuasive alternative to substantialist presuppositions that account for personal identity through time. For an ebbing and flowing "stream of consciousness" will be hard-pressed to traverse moments of complete unconsciousness. Furthermore, James puts forth no adequate concept of the interdependence of different "streams," which would exhibit the reciprocity of their influence upon each other. He also sometimes reduces experience to biology—as when he identifies "the stream of thinking" chiefly with "the stream of my breathing."[49] Perhaps because he lacks concepts either of the unconscious or of mutual immanence, he must lean too heavily on raw physiology to provide stability amidst the flux. Yet his work as a physiologist nonetheless served him well as a philosopher. He points the way beyond idealism, dualism or materialism. The body is no more cast out of our subjectivity. On the contrary, "the body is the storm center, the origin of co-ordinates, the constant place of stress in all that experience-train."[50] And James's insistence on pluralism in the experience of selfhood, and finally in the cosmos, replaces the fixed unity of separate subjects with a shifting interplay of perspectives.

Twentieth-century reflection on the self intermittently sounds a fresh theme: that of the social nature of the self. Compounded of a new sociological and psychological awareness, the idea that the self is intrinsically social recasts the relation of the individual to society: Individuality emerges through a process of interaction between the organism and the environment. It was especially George Herbert Mead, one of the major figures in American pragmatist philosophy and a student of William James and Josiah Royce, who first thematized the social self. Mead's thought is rooted in the impact of Darwinism on nineteenth-century ideas. The keynotes of organism and evolution shape his discussion of self and universe as processes rather than fixed essences. Self and its consciousness emerge from the communication between organisms, and organism and environment thus reciprocally influence each other's development. Yet his so-called social behaviorism directly challenges the vulgarities of most scientific behaviorism. Mead never attenuates self to a mere function of its society, to a mechanism of response to stimuli.[51] Rather, Mead distinguishes between the I and the me, at any moment of the self's process:

The attitudes of the others constitute the organized 'me,' and then one reacts toward that as an 'I' . . . the 'I' gives the sense of freedom, of initiative. The 'me' represents a definite organization of the community there in our own attitudes, and calling for a response. . . . The self is essentially a social process going on with these two distinguishable phases.[52]

In other words, the me means not just myself as object, but the objectified presence of the others as part of myself. Mead acknowledges the similarity to Freud's superego, yet intends a more permeable, ongoing communication with a larger community. By contrast, the I guarantees at every moment the possibility of dissent from the internalized other. I am neither separate from nor a slave of the community. The I is the creative and unique response to the me. Both phases of the self together comprise its sociality—for through the spontaneity of the I, new influences enter the community. Unfortunately, Mead seems to bind his theory of self to the Cartesian assumption of reflexivity: "the self, as that which can be an object to itself, is essentially a social structure."[53] Because *self* is grammatically reflexive, he presumes that it represents "that which can be both subject and object." But he does not lock his theory into any strict sense of reflexivity. The I and me phases of self may be understood respectively as subject and object phases: the whole self is not an object to itself. Then we at once reclaim a certain open, reflecting motion, as indeed implied by the very term *self*, without plunging back into the self-mirroring metaphysical narcissism of a fixed substance.

In theology the influence of Mead's thought was notably absorbed by H. Richard Niebuhr (Reinhold's brother), who saw the affinity of the social self (as in Mead, and Harry Stack Sullivan) with Martin Buber's prophetically inspired communion of the I and the Thou.[54] In both the biblical tradition and social behaviorism, human identity emerges in dialogue with the other, apart from which I would not be who I am. Niebuhr welds these traditions into his Christian ethics of "responsibility" as the creative response to the other with whom I am in an ultimately boundless community of reciprocal accountability. Interestingly his definition of ethical responsibility as relational response anticipates the concept of responsibility with which Carol Gilligan characterizes the typically female ethical response as distinguished from emphases upon rights or rules (emphases that Niebuhr criticizes). But rather than amplifying the idea of the social self with a theological dimension, Niebuhr's evocation of God suddenly unravels the promising fabric of his thought. Legitimately aware of the dangers of dispersion in the multitude of influences to which the social self is open, Niebuhr recoils into "radical monotheism." "I am one in my many-ness in myself and so responsible as self, as I face the One action in the action of the many upon me." [55] Only my relation to the single One establishes my unity in the flux. God is conceived as a unilateral force of unity, upon whom I can only be "absolutely dependent." Thus Niebuhr's monotheism defeats his own pluralism: "The moral problem of the *one in the many* on its subjective side is the problem of the one self given to the I and required of it in all the pluralism of its being." [56] This is a oneness amidst but over and against the many, somehow apart from the many. That is, he construes the multiplicity more as threat and temptation than as an ambiguous plenum of relations: "In our personal and social manifoldness we have been left with a small seed of integrity, a haunting sense of unity and of universal responsibility." [57] While certainly one may appreciate Niebuhr's desire for an integral in-gathering that stands firm against dispersion, plurality itself is finally, as in Augustine, demonized: "in my sin I am a polytheist or polydemonist surrounded by, and reacting to, principalities and powers that rule in various domains." [58] Women know well the temptation to succumb to the principalities and powers of patriarchy. But we sense also that precisely such assertion of a one against the cosmic many is an androcentric principle, if not a principality! Philosophically and theologically, a radical monism or monotheism too easily tempts us away from a truly multiple integrity. The problem for Niebuhr, as for other relationally promising thinkers, may stem from the cultural absence of an adequate interpretive framework, a metaphysical basis for the relation of the one and the many. We now turn to the thought of Whitehead, whose metaphysics owes much to the influence of Mead and especially James.

Feeling the Many

Whitehead's magnum opus, *Process and Reality* (1929), could well be titled *Process and Relation*. It is all about "the becoming, the being, and the relatedness of 'actual entities.'"[59] Also called "actual occasions," these actual entities are for this "philosophy of organism" "the final real things of which the world is made up."[60] Readers may substitute "I" for "actual entity"; but any individual being is such a one, be it charmed quark or deity. Actual entities take the place once filled by substances, or by the concept of the individual. Process thought spins an entire cosmology from the relations of each of these entities to all other entities. Whitehead conceives these individuals as microcosms: like the Leibnizian monad, each is a microworld, reflecting the entire world in its own constitution. "But it differs from Leibniz's in that his [Leibniz's] monads change. In the organic theory, they merely *become*."[61] Actual entities do not change: does process philosophy present us with a static atomism? On the contrary: the very notion of a subject *changing* underlines, paradoxically, a static doctrine of substance. That is, for an individual entity literally to change, it remains the same subject, underlying its own changes; if the subject thus endures through its changes, it remains essentially the same. The consequence is that all changes are merely external or accidental. Moreover, the influences of the world, of other actual entities, are then external as well. We find ourselves close to the root of a common sense substantialism that inadvertently renders relations between actual individuals external. They cannot flow in and out of each other if they consist of abiding, presiding subjects.

Whitehead substitutes for change the idea of becoming: actual entities are events, not substances. How does an actual entity become? "Each monadic creature," answers Whitehead "is a mode of *the process of 'feeling' the world, of housing the world in one unit of complex feeling*."[62] In other words, the actual individual realities of the universe issue from their feelings; they do not precede or strictly speaking "have" these feelings. To become is to *feel* one's way into being. Process philosophy, here inspired by James, is an entire metaphysic of feeling.

Feeling in this metaphysical sense cannot be reduced to emotion, if the latter refers to affective states that are characteristically human. Unlike James, or almost any professional philosopher before him, Whitehead attributes feeling by analogy to every actual individual being in the universe, be it a molecule of oxygen, a giraffe, you or a deity. As a technical term, feeling directly opposes the entire tradition of philosophical rationalism as well as scientific mechanism. As we ascertained from Hume's skepticism, validation of feeling is what it would take to replace substantial with connective selves. Whitehead takes precisely this theoretical step: feelings *are* the direct connections between actual occasions of experience. "An actual entity has a perfectly definite bond with each item in the universe." [63] The feeling, or "positive prehension," *is* that bond. It is not just a matter of feeling the relations, but of feelings *as* relations. "Each actual entity is a throb of experience including the actual world within its scope. It is a process of 'feeling' the many data, so as to absorb them into the unity of one individual 'satisfaction.'" [64]

The particular individual is then a pulse of experience in which the world is *brought in* by feeling. Brought into what? For the feeler does not exist before the feelings. To feel the world means to emerge from feeling the world. These feelings make me what I am. That is, individuals actualize themselves—become actual—by feeling or refusing to feel ("negative prehension") everything else out there in the objective world. And to feel the world means literally to bring it in, to give it a home, to let its objective manyness turn into a new subjective oneness. A new theory of one and many, of subject and object, is here taking shape. Feeling is defined as "the basic generic operation of passing from the objectivity of the data to the subjectivity of the actual entity in question." [65] The initial feelings reach out and make the things *there* into realities *here;* a more complex synthesis of feelings effects the phases by which the actual entity becomes fully concrete. Through this process of "concrescence," the subject emerges from the world of others. Or in Mead's psychology, the I from the we. This idea of the emergent subject constitutes a metaphysical revolution, for it reverses the traditional precedence of a dominant subject over the objects that it controls as its province—as its predicates. By feeling, indeed by feeling the feelings of my world, which includes my personal past, my subjective experience comes into being. Whitehead is making a startling claim: I *am* this "throb of experience"; I *am* the complex unity of feeling that rises up at this moment in response to my feelings of the plural world.

Through the prism of process thought we witness a primal empathy that founds reality. This vision infinitely augments the psychological truth of an empathic continuum. *Em-pathos* means literally "in-feeling." Feeling the world into myself, feeling my way into the world, feeling the world in me, feeling myself in the world: all these meanings unfurl from the idea of radical relatedness, here called positive prehension, which we have already encountered as the doctrine of internal relations. The idea of internal relations originally arose within the monistic context of absolute idealism, according to which all relations are internal to the Absolute (whether conceived as substance, idea or pantheistic One). But Whitehead refuses any monistic One: for him (indeed as for Leibniz) the universe as a totality is essentially plural. It becomes one only in each of the many *ones,* the complex compositions of feeling that are the actual entities. Internal relatedness means that everything in some sense is *really* part of me, however dimly felt. *"Every actual entity is present in every other actual entity"* (my emphasis).[66] I cannot exist without in some sense taking part in you, in the child I once was, in the breeze stirring the down on my arm, in the child starving far away, in the flashing round of the spiral nebula. The actual entity "takes account" of every item in its universe: it gathers an instantaneous cosmic congregation. And inasmuch as I *feel* what I take account of, I may *own* it—I make the world my own world, and so create myself. Of course, I can fail to feel, I can exclude— yet negative prehensions, like repression, leave their mark as well. This idea of the internal relatedness of all things draws considerable support from the impossibility of locating a completely closed physical system smaller than the universe—which itself poses only a hypothetical limit.

The account-taking of prehensions, positive or negative, need not be conscious. I might not know you as I write this, yet nonetheless you influence me, however faint the pulse of you in me. In fact at the primordial level of relation, amid the simple, originative feelings that inaugurate this moment's experience, no consciousness is possible. Whitehead, like depth psychologists, distinguishes consciousness from feeling or awareness. The raw connections to the universe of objective others are felt, but remain by definition nonconscious. For consciousness only supervenes in this scheme as a late "phase" (these phases are not a matter of linear temporal sequence) in the self-creation of the momentary subject, a phase based on the complex contrasts between different feelings. Consciousness arises from the friction of contrasts between this and that, yes and no, the real and the possible. But opposition is only one kind of contrast.

Selves are unconscious and sometimes also conscious acts of self-composition, composing themselves of their relations. Relation in the process scheme holds everything together. Like James's conjunctive relations, feelings fuse actual entities at their edges. But the entities do not merge; rather they e-merge as novel and distinctive events from their "togetherness." The individuality of the actual entity is utterly unique: the precipitate of its becoming is as irrepeatable as that entity's spatio-temporal vantage point. (Only I exist at precisely this place, this time, this here and now.)

Whitehead's first principle is "creativity," whereby "the many become one, and are increased by one." [67] Thus relational composition answers the question of the one and the many. The whole point of the universe is to generate increasingly complex individual experiences: but such novel uniqueness can only take place through increasing intricacy and breadth of community.

Is the Whiteheadian oneness susceptible to deconstructive charges of monolithic foreclosure? If oneness per se is objectionable, if all notions of unity violate our severalness, then Whitehead's is no exception. However, if the exclusivity, the simplicity and the imperialism of unification are its real liabilities, then in process thought's insistence upon a complex unity we may have a conceptual alternative to either monism or fragmentation. A oneness compounded of the many, in which the many are taken in intact, joined but not dissolved even within the "real internal constitution" of the individual, suggests an integrity of the multiple. A lighter oneness, one that can never be metaphysically rigidified. Perhaps this provisional oneness does not contradict Irigaray's advocacy of woman's non-unity. It may be what we need: a one that is always intrinsically several—it cannot rid itself of the many that compose it. And it is not one over and against the others, but among them, and including them.

The metaphor of the actual occasion has replaced the idea of substance with that of composition: I am not a separate and enduring substance but an event in which the universe composes itself. This is true of everything real. "Neither physical nature nor life can be understood unless we fuse them together as essential factors in the compositions of 'really real' things whose inter-connections and individual characters constitute the universe." [68] Interconnection and individuality seem to coexist without contradiction, indeed to enhance each other. The more diversity I take in, the more I feelingly connect—and the roomier is my individual character. [69] But such compositive subjectivity, involving a subject who emerges *from* its objects, surely unhinges any traditional notion of a subject. Can one in fact speak of a subject any more? Whitehead proposes instead a "superject":

Descartes . . . conceives the thinker as creating the occasional thought. The philosophy of organism inverts the order. . . . The thinker is the final end whereby there is the thought. In this inversion we have the final contrast between a philosophy of substance and a philosophy of organism. The operations of an organism are directed towards the organism as a 'superject,' and are not directed from the organism as a 'subject.' [70]

The *sub* of *subject* refers to the sub-sistence of the traditional substantial subject, that is, to the way it underlies its attributes and relations, and so remains independent of them, while they are dependent upon it. The *super* of *superject* denotes the opposite: the way the actual occasion arises *from*, supervening *upon,* its world. When I continue to use the term *subject,* it will be with its superjective—which we might also call transsubjective—character in mind. Like the psychoanalytic discovery of the disconcerting unconscious depths beneath the ego individuality, the subject-superject arises from the endless breadth of its connections to the world.

These connections link each being at once to its own past and to the world or, more precisely, to the *past* world. For recall that this subject does not precede its own experiences but arises *from* its relations: the actual entity *becomes* but does not change. It is a momentary event. But what then becomes of the actual entity?

It perishes. Like Augustine's "things which shall be and shall pass away," each actual entity comes to be, achieves the satisfaction of its own composition, and passes away. Whitehead is not speaking of a life span, however, but of a moment. In a twinkling, we are and then are no longer—at least *not as the same subject.* The subject does not endure, does not change, and so can never preside over its universe. However, this momentary subject does not vanish into thin air, but achieves an "objective immortality" (which has nothing to do with a literal after-life) by which it now becomes an object for the world of supervening occasions. Here the transsubjective dimension becomes especially poignant: the subject's immediate feeling fills the present, but—is even then—condensing into a sort of objective content. As this objective datum, it will influence every future occasion. "The creativity of the world is the throbbing emotion of the past hurling itself into a new transcendent fact." [71]

As it perishes into the future, the individual occasion does not sacrifice the content of feeling that formed its own experience. Nor does the past become a passive datum, an inert given. [72] Rather, the past flows forcefully into its own immediate successors, who must take account of it, who will willy-nilly receive its imprint. I will empathically feel my *own* immediate past, its feelings perhaps of heat, tension, sorrow, exhaustion, curiosity—its perceptions and thoughts. And I will also be feeling the objective data of my world, in the emotions, colors, smells, densities and insights that constitute its multifarious impact. But it is technically the *past* I can feel, and know, although the past be the moment just preceding. The pure present has not yet become and has not made itself available as data for my becoming.

My present self may think "I feel angry." But the anger to which it refers is that of the immediate past—which will influence but need not totally determine the subsequent moments of experience. I *am* not this anger when I can name it. This is why the knower cannot know itself: it can have as the object of its knowing only a previous occasion, an antecedent self. Strict reflexivity is impossible. The self cannot literally know itself. The sword truly cannot cut itself. The knower and the known are not one. How this notion of a momentary event-individual, the subject-superject arising from its continuum of felt relations can be a basis for concepts of self and person we will discuss in the subsequent section. But now let us pause and draw certain central Whiteheadian themes through the feminist perspective of our general inquiry.

Far-flung Connections

Moon marked and touched by sun
my magic is unwritten
but when the sea turns back
it will leave my shape behind.[73]

Audre Lorde conjures, in this poem called "A Woman Speaks," a mystery of interconnection; the sea has felt the woman, the woman has felt the sea, both have felt moon and sun. In the rhythmic process of the tides, the woman's shape is left behind, almost like the serpent's skin sloughed for rebirth. Amidst all this positive prehension, she points to the trail of her own objective immortality—the world creativity throbbing in her past, absorbed by the sea and now become part of its past, communicated upon the sands. In the atmosphere of metamorphosis, the woman herself is elusive, has become, is always becoming, an other. She can never be known externally, objectively, but only through the traces of her influence: "and if you would know me / look into the entrails of Uranus / where the restless oceans pound." [74] A Goddess? A woman's Self? Both? Brewing the alchemical transmutation of vision required to "know" her—she who is no simple One, but extends throughout the universe—Lorde lets us actually *feel* our cosmological connections.

Perhaps to know any person one must search the planets. And perhaps any woman knows that to know any being, one must know its universe. As Whitehead so compellingly argues, to know any entity at all is to know its relations, feelingly, within its social environment. And no one will ever know it in its sheer, becoming present: in its immediacy, it can no more be objectified by others than by itself. It is always already an other, leaving its shape behind. If women often exhibit a natural sympathy with forms of process thought, this is psychologically no surprise. Young girls experience themselves as connected rather than separate (because, we saw, of prolonged identification with the first parent). If we place this psychosocial generalization in the context of process metaphysics, we can say the following: the connected, permeable ego ascribed to female children fits the description of an actual entity, that is, what is really actual, much more nearly than does the rigid and clearly delineated male ego. We do not wish to draw the inference (tempting as it may seem) that normal postoedipal males are therefore less real. However, they are quite literally less *in touch* with reality insofar as they are less prone to feel it. Put differently, the historical circumstances of male development and socialization foist upon men a massive structure of defense against positive prehensions of their world, against the fact of internal relations with all that is other. We analyzed the male effort to exclude the world from the parameters of self, while emphasizing continuity with his own conscious past and future. Has the impossible project of self-objectification come to overshadow subjective immediacy?

As we have seen, the relation to all subsequent others is first rehearsed in relation to the mother. But then this first matrix will be recapitulated as the inchoate origin of every moment's self. Largely for wrong reasons and deleterious ends, girls grow up versed in the arts of empathy: females remain more open to the world, more capable of positive prehensions and more at ease with the rhythmic and impermanent character of becoming. Yet if men are in danger of (and dangerous with) too much blockage of feeling—in the full metaphysical sense now—women may accept too much conformity with the emotions of others, or with the stasis of the felt world, and we may have special difficulty letting go of the overpowering emotions of our own immediate past. These are temptations of relation. But would not women be more likely to assert the strength of our selves in a world and worldview deliberately wrought of the connectedness we already sense so intimately?

The end of chapter 3 left us asserting that the process of differentiation, far from diluting or opposing the process of relation, co-operates with it. We now have more vocabulary for arguing the case—we can approach the tangled results of sociopsychological relations with a wider reflective equilibrium. We may take from process metaphysics a confirmation that, as women sense, all reality is interconnected: that "every actual entity is present in every other actual entity." This immanence of the world constitutes according to Whitehead the "potential for becoming" of the entity. Therefore the degree of complexity achieved by the entity in its moment of becoming depends upon its *openness* to that in-flowing world. The influences of its own past and of the environment are the materials it works into the creative contrasts patterning the final "complex feeling." The more the individual represses its feelings, the fewer materials it will have to work with; indeed, it will not know those it *does* have for what they are. A harmonized complexity, a multiplicity that holds together, is the teleological desire of the actual entity, inasmuch as it embodies the creative advance into novelty.

The more complex its composition of feeling, the more an actual entity cooperates with the multiplex purposes of the universe; the more simple it remains, the more it builds dams against the cosmos.[75] Differentiation, the degree to which an entity becomes *different*, depends upon its ability to embrace its own freedom and so compose spontaneously out of the resources flowing in from reality. It follows that relational complexity, which Chodorow discerns as the character of women's outer and inner relations (relations to the world and to our own past, respectively), is indeed the result of differentiation; connection provides the raw stuff out of which complex self-compositions are wrought. And each new moment of complex feeling enhances the field of relations.

Whitehead distinguishes between a well-integrated complexity and a complexity that is self-defeating by virtue of chaos or diffusion. Two cardinal sins for the actual entity are "triviality" and "vagueness,"[76] which sound more like Valerie Saiving's suggestions for a female doctrine of sin and self-loss than traditional sins of arrogance, pride and egocentricity. "Triviality arises from lack of coordination" such that "incompatibility has predominated over contrast," and "depth of feeling" cannot ensue. Certainly women know well this obstacle to self-actualization! Triviality in this sense seems an ongoing danger for women: the incompatibilities of multiple relational commitments with each other and with our own aims for our future, for instance. "Vagueness by contrast is due to excess of identification"—a generality we may apply all too readily to female experience. "There is deficiency in supplementary feeling discriminating the objects from each other," he continues. To unpack these dry generalities: women struggle with the temptations to indiscriminate relationship and to overidentification of ourselves with the "objects," the others who influence us most deeply. Identification is not the mature and creative use of connection, though it inaugurates our sense of identity as infants.

"The right chaos, the right vagueness," says Whitehead enigmatically, "are jointly required for any effective harmony."[77] In other words, much that has been stereotyped as feminine disorder has its place in the creative process. Let us only beware that, in the cosmic subsocieties we frequent, harmony not be bought at the cost of women's self-realization. For women's chaos and vagueness have compensated for otherwise fragmented and competitive relational scenes. If the obstacles to the fullest realization of the actual entity resemble the psychosocial structures of sexism, this only confirms our sense that the model is relatively gynomorphic—or that women at this point in history are implicitly more cosmomorphic than men.

Whitehead makes "width" a great value. Released from the constrictions of social domesticity and the narrow world of the private family, women adventure into width of thought, feeling, relationship. Width, a corollary of connection and openness, might seem to work against depth (though the ocean is supremely both at once). (While feared as the Tehom, women were also traditionally said to be shallow.) But Whitehead, ever oblivious to matters of gender, proposes a "hierarchy of categories of feeling" (to replace Hegel's hierarchy of categories of thought), which in fact seems to be pointed downward, for it measures degrees of "depth." Note the correlation of width and depth: "The savouring of the complexity of the universe can enter into satisfaction only through the dimension of width. The emotional depths at the low levels have their limits; the function of width is to deepen the ocean of feeling."[78] "To deepen the ocean of feeling . . .": this is certainly no ego-heroic exploit! Indeed, oceanic feeling, which we heard defined as "an intimation of . . . a connection with the world around them through an immediate feeling which is from the outset directed to that purpose,"[79] exactly exemplifies a Whiteheadian positive prehension. The feelings that transform the object *there* into the subject *here* are precisely such purposeful vectors. They remain "intimations" because they emerge from a depth of unconscious experience not directly accessible to consciousness; they intentionally (according to Whitehead, teleologically) give rise to the subjective immediacy of the occasion.

Freud found that such an idea "fits in so badly with the fabric" of his psychology; it still very much misfits the standard metaphysics of common sense. Nonetheless, something very like oceanic feelings provides the warp and woof of process metaphysics and so weaves the texture of every individual out of and into the universe.

Of course, one may ask whether any such cosmological scheme of interrelation is not itself the projection of what Freud called "limitless narcissism." And if women find it attractive, does that confirm our allegedly narcissistic tendencies?

A certain response to the charge of narcissism, beyond that offered in the previous chapter, is of theoretical importance for our project: connection to the world appears as narcissism (or inflation, in Jung's language) when one cannot distinguish the world from oneself. The narcissist never encounters the objectivity, the acute difference, of the other, but uses the other for self-gratification. The world is the mirror of the narcissist. But things are quite the reverse for the connective self. This self mirrors the world. To feel oneself a microcosm of the world might in fact satisfy our legitimate need for self-esteem; but such feeling is not based on a confusion of self and world. The actual entity is clearly distinguished from every other actual entity by its peculiar spatio-temporal perspective. It mirrors a unique view of the whole, and creates its own microcosmic interpretation. Such a self is differentiated precisely by virtue of its inseparability. To be inseparable is no more a matter of merging and identity-confusion than is the case, say, with my body parts: my hand and my elbow are clearly *distinguishable* and appropriately bear different names. But to *separate* them would require amputation. There is no clear line of demarcation between hand, wrist, lower arm and finally elbow—they are a field of inseparable parts yet there is also clear distance and difference, as between hand and elbow. The critique of narcissism generally rests upon the assumption of a separate subjectivity. Though the connective self certainly faces narcissism as an intimate temptation, the concept of narcissism as classically developed presupposes that any conjunctive relations between self and other, any taking in of the other, will count as regressive or inappropriate boundary confusion. But we are learning ways of thinking the boundaries of self to be permeable, shifting, and in some real sense coextensive with the boundaries of its universe. Much narcissism may be better understood as a neurotic but inevitable attempt to compensate for the more radical disease of separation. Would not the separative ego, as a shrunken residue of itself, be ever seeking itself in the others it has already expelled from itself? Is the Cartesian ego, with its splendidly separate sense of self, not an idealized self-image of the narcissist? For the Cartesian ego finds itself precisely by mirror-reflection: the cogitation of a reflexive self.

An oceanic feeler can—with the metaphorical accuracy of metaphysics behind her—taunt us with Lorde: "and if you would know me / look into the entrails of Uranus / where the restless oceans pound." The cosmological context for the connective self is far flung but not farfetched. Its width deepens not only the notion of individuality, but also our use of psychology. For this context lends theoretical license to the desire felt at the end of the previous chapter to claim our connective integrity *now*. The child in ourselves who must be freed from the fetters of culturally imposed models of oedipal conflict and resolution—that child can be situated metaphysically as well as psychologically. The child then dwells in a place more pervasive, more fundamental to reality, than the purview of classical psychoanalysis can permit.

Our past experiences continue with ineradicable objectivity—as distinct from subjective immediacy—to dwell in our present. We relate to our past selves as we relate to every other item of our universe: empathetically or repressively, but in any case *definitely*. The tones of our own childhood experiences are resonating in us now—and perhaps tune in archetypally to the experiences of all children everywhere. The personal and the transpersonal are jointly present. And as we remember, we reach not outwardly back to an external child, but inwardly into a set of memories, mostly forgotten but nonetheless present. These past recollections are potential for our becoming now: "it belongs to the nature of a 'being' that it is a potential for every 'becoming.' " [80] If this is true in general, how much more so with that complex being who is/was the child and, as the child in us now, bears our potential. This preoedipal and postpatriarchal child, if healingly *felt*, may release the courage of our present feeling. It frees our selves to be born. There is here no single conversion from one substantial selfhood to another, but a perpetual convergence of the many into the new one—which *you are now*.

To stay with our appropriation of process thought: we still must hear how there can be ongoing transformation in a scheme that denies that subjects "change." The becoming subject-superject (however unbecoming the term) points beyond the notion of the self as a subject who posits the other as object. Perhaps it leads

toward Mary Daly's "becoming Self who is always Other." Our
adventures of becoming will not, like those of Odysseus, cycle us
back to the fixed point of an underlying subject—or of an abjectly
subject Penelope. As we have emerged from the others, we are also
emerging as—always—an other.

One Soul, Many Selves

Whitehead develops no concept of the self. His metaphysical endeavor can be described as ontological, specifically as cosmological,
but in no wise as psychological or anthropological. In this way it
differs from most major philosophies since the Kantian turn to the
subject, and so paradoxically opens new territory for exploring the
idea of the self. We gain a valuable obliqueness, a cosmological
indirection that allows us to reconsider the self without plunging
into self-objectification. This width can help heal the myopia inflicted by dualistic and substance-predicate modes of feeling and
thinking. By speaking of actual entities rather than human beings,
Whitehead imagines what all beings in the universe have in common, thus countervailing the anthropocentrism (which has always
meant androcentrism) of Western thought. So he provides a promising basis, shared with every atom, every molecule, every animal,
for the present elaboration of the notion of self.

"My process of 'being myself' is my origination from my possession of the world." [81] The use here of the reflexive pronoun seems
to refer to a root meaning of *self* as "one's own." James has defined
the self as everything that a person can call his or her own. But such
owning is world-possession and in no strict sense self-possession.
Self-possession would, as we saw in Chapter 1, drive us toward the
psychoeconomics of self-sufficient, defensive subjectivity. In contrast, *owning* the world, making it my own, originates my *self* because in claiming a world as *mine,* I actively create my experience.
And for this ownership, the resources are inexhaustible—capitalist
competition becomes meaningless: why buy what I already own?

Self is an event, a process, and no fixed substance, no substantive.
The nineteenth-century British poet and mystic Gerard Manley
Hopkins gave *self* a verb form:

Each mortal thing does one thing and the same:
Deals out that being indoors each one dwells;

Selves—goes itself; *myself* it speaks and spells
Crying What I do is me; for that I came.[82]

It would not seem accidental that the poet sings simultaneously of
the selfhood of every actual being, human or not, and the dynamic-
fluent character of that self. "To selve": a candidate for Mary Daly's
First Intergalactic Wickedary? It surely echoes her insistence that
Be-ing is a verb. Each of the few times that Whitehead does use the
term *self* as a freestanding noun, it is clear that he is referring to the
microcosmic event of the actual entity. For example, speaking of
the complex feeling that the actual entity realizes: "This one felt
content is the 'satisfaction,' whereby the actual entity is its particular individual self." [83]

Let us then for the sake of consistency consider self the momentary individual, of whatever species or kind, in its full scope. Self is
the unique, immediate event where an experience takes place and
where the world is gathered as a unique composition. A self feels
its way into existence; it takes possession of a world; and then it
lets itself go. It owns its world but cannot—try as it might—hoard
the gain. For it cannot even maintain *itself* just as it was: it is a
momentary event of possession, of inclusion, of taking in and put-
ting out. Thus the self contains within its parameters everything
that is not itself; yet the self is clearly distinguishable *as* itself. It
selves its world. There is nothing that is not somewhere part of it;
yet in a moment it parts with its own selfness. Its immediacy perishes into the subsequent world. It is not as true to say that its
boundaries are permeable as that it permeates the unbounded.

How can one live this way? The reader might understandably
feel a certain anxiety upon hearing that she or he is already an *other*
self than the one who was reading the first words of this sentence.[84]
Surely I have memories of *my* childhood, and responsibility for *my*
past actions: am I not therefore the self who acted? Surely *I* can
plan to eat a meal tonight, or improve *myself* in various ways over
the next period of time: will I not be the same self?

To these questions, process thought leads us to: yes, you are, were
and will be the same *person*; no, you are not and will not be the
same *self*. The semantics of distinguishing the self (as actual entity)
from the person has more than sophistical intent. It provides one
possible framework for conceiving the individual being as both radically spontaneous and deeply continuous. For "person," or "per-

sonal order" (which Whitehead prefers, in order to avoid the emphasis upon human consciousness),[85] describes the way individual self-events are bonded to each other through time to produce that sense of continuity we feel—more or less—from childhood to death. But the word *person* suggests a public dimension, originally meaning the theatrical mask (*persona*) by which the actor embodies the deity. In Roman times it referred to a legal entity as having rights and duties; we also saw the Christian trinity suggesting a communal interaction of Persons. Only much later does the term bear the freight of subjective human identity. The earlier uses suggest a rather abstract, indeed quite *impersonal* sense of sacred role, or social order. "Person" according to Whitehead is indeed a form of "society." While the interrelations of actual entities always constitute a "nexus" or network, a society is a kind of nexus in which the members feel each other in an especially intimate way: they receive from each other "a common element of form."[86] Animal bodies are such societies, as well as rocks, trees, sisterhood, individual Cincinnatians or Cincinnati as a whole. A human person is such a society, with the added attribute of being a *series* of interlinked occasions. So Whitehead has redoubled the twentieth-century idea of the social nature of the individual. Not only is every actual entity a self-composition from its environing influences; but the moments of my selfhood themselves form a transtemporal society. The self is not only social as arising from the multitude of relations it internalizes; the person *is* a society.

We have here Whitehead's version of James's "stream of consciousness." But Whitehead rightly notes how rare, even among the complex "personal societies" such as humans fancy ourselves to be, are moments of vivid consciousness—how often we are asleep or daydreaming. We are like Virginia Woolf's "cotton wool," occasionally interrupted by "shocks of being." One might better speak of a stream of awareness or flux of feeling. *Soul* is another word Whitehead uses interchangeably with *person*, to indicate this intermingling continuity between our moments: Soul, more like Psyche herself, is conceived not as a permanent substance but as a series of becomings. Soul, or person, is the society composed of the stream of selves:

The soul is nothing else than the succession of my occasions of experience, extending from birth to the present moment.

Now, at this instant, I am the complete person embodying all these occasions. They are mine. On the other hand it is equally true that my immediate occasion of experience, at the present moment, is only one among the stream of occasions which constitutes my soul.[87]

The soulful streaming of occasions allows a sense of personal continuity without erecting any strict self-identity through time. What I become now arises out of all my previous moments of experience (and out of all the occasions of the nexūs that are my world); it will then contribute its influence to all future occasions of my personal life (and to all future occasions of the world). The image arises of an individual stream among ocean currents. Everything, and most intimately my soul, flows in and out of the present occasion, which is my self. This is a light and loose sense of the unity of the person. Why would we need more?

Nevertheless, we often think that we require a tight and heavy notion of personal identity. What happened to effect the rigidification of the fluid, flighty, volatile soul that thrives in metamorphosis and immediacy? In a way this book is an attempt to answer that question. But let me add to our account Whitehead's celebrated diagnosis of most Western thought as "the fallacy of misplaced concreteness." This fallacy occurs when one mistakes an abstraction for a concrete particular. Only the individual self, the actual occasion, is concretely real. Its soul, or personal identity, is concrete only as embodied in the immediacy of becoming. Beyond that subjective immediacy, the linear series of occasions extending backward and forward in time is a sort of abstraction from the occasions themselves. To say, I am now the same person as I was a moment ago, is to make a (doubtless useful) generalization. That generalization should not be mistaken for the real actuality in its immediacy. But why not? The consequences may be abstractly articulated as follows.

First, the connections between the occasions of the life of soul are conceptually annihilated in mistaking this generalization for the concrete self. For identity replaces connection. This prepares the way for the self-encapsulated self, rigidly bound to its own remembered past and projected future. Then it does not consciously sense the conjunctive relations between its own moments, much less see them as actively constitutive. It posits instead a straight homogeneity of selfhood through time, something like railroad tracks upon which its present tense travels. Control and permanence become higher values than connection and spontaneity. And having thus tightened the screws of its own subjective endurance, the self has at the same time cut itself off from the in-streaming universe. For unless it feels its own continuity as fluid and open-ended through time, it cannot tolerate the actual incursions of the world into its very makeup: When it remains fundamentally the same self, it cannot admit its internal relations to other entities, any more than it can admit the others into its own soul. On the one hand, it has exaggerated its connections to its own past and future to the point of a permanent self-identity, which dissolves the need for connections; on the other hand, it has attenuated its connections to the world to the point of their dissolution into mere accident and externality. And while such a self may assert the staunchest of ethical positions, it surely does not know itself well enough to calculate its own effects on the world's or its personal future. For it lacks awareness of its own evanescent subjectivity, its out-flow into the becoming environment. It holds onto itself, in direct refusal of such dicta as "cast your bread on the waters," the compassionate nonattachment of Zen, or singer-songwriter Cris Williamson's "filling up and spilling over, it's an endless waterfall." [88]

To know myself is to know that I cannot literally know myself. For in the act of knowing I am only just coming to be. Yet I can indeed know my previous selves: they remain "objectively immortal," efficacious pasts at work in the present, allowing me to explore not only my soul's patterns and ruts and potentials, but to glimpse through the translucency of soul the interweaving inextricability of all beings. Indeed, I can have a real relationship with myselves, because they are also other than I.

The substantialist subject has confused itself with its own objectified pasts. That is, it has identified its present, subjective immediacy with the entire series of past selves now objectified as part of itself. It has thereby turned itself into an object. It can have no meaningful relationship with self. And, as we have claimed before, such reflexive self-objectification (that poses as supremely rational objectivity) performs the same trick on all other subjects. It believes it can know them as objects, even in their yet unsettled immediacy of becoming. In contrast, the process viewpoint holds, quite in harmony with the ancient Hebrew word for "knowledge" (*yada*) meaning "erotic intimacy," that the only immediacy of knowing the other is the feeling of its feelings as it passes into immanence within my own constitution. Yet in its sheer contemporariness, as we shall see, it remains an irreducible mystery. The substantial subject performs reductionism both on itself and on everything else, for it understands reality to consist of what are only the relatively stable abstractions we derive from common elements amidst the streamings of reality. The result of such dual reduction is precisely the Cartesian ego, which dominates in its dichotomous incoherence still today—albeit in increasingly less reflective and more mechanistic form.

In our analysis the very notion of "the ego" is suspect. Mead's distinction of the I and the me fits well with the two poles of Whitehead's actual entity: the I, as the free and spontaneous response to the "generalized other" or internalized world corresponds to the conscious phase of the momentary subject; the me as its object, abstracted from the old reflexivity, then consists of the total input of my cumulative selves, my person, up to that moment. But the ego is an odd middle thing, at least in English: for it is a nominalized, substantialized and so hypostacized form of the I. *Self* can better risk a noun's role, for it connotes the entire personality at any given moment, including its unconscious depths of connectivity and possibility. But *ego* refers only to the conscious crest of the human personality—that which can say I. As long as it maintains its sense of momentary becoming, the word is not harmful. But generally it reifies itself along with the larger personality and the processes of its world, making itself an agent of control.

Control and Connection

When we ask not only how, but *why* any I attempts to evacuate the world from its own insides or to harden into a soulless ego substance, we are again faced with the meaning of androcentric history. Without this empirical particularity, without the cumulative facts of history, the questions and answers of metaphysics float off into an ether of self-absorption. The development of an objectifying ego has been not accidentally coextensive with that of paternal power. This is why no description of an alternative self can in good faith remain apolitical; an authentic metaphysic (a metaphysic no longer subservient to the politics of paternal authors and authority) must always be wresting itself free of the presuppositions of the patricentric paradigm—among which we have located those of external relations and the substantial self.[89] Power issues must be confronted precisely because the objectifying ego is motivated by an impulse to control. Its disciplines of self-objectification permit it to keep the others at a distance and so to develop strategies of dominance. Indeed, the separative ego as we have characterized it—as self-reifying and other-exclusive—cannot separate its strategies of self-perpetuation from its drive to control. In its emphasis upon self-control, being "on top of things," it is simultaneously keeping the influent others under control as well. Domination is its best defense, and retreat its familiar back-up plan. And these defensive strategies inadvertently confirm the truth of internal relations: that the world gets inside us, gets under our skin, does not keep a respectful distance.

Control is the age-old alternative to connection. The denial of internal relations issues in external manipulation. But while control always presupposes the controlling subject, one already there to control, connection does not presuppose the preexistence of a connecting subject. I become who I am in and through and beyond the particular activity of connection. Connectivity lets the world in before the subject comes to be; and the subject lets go the moment it has become. I am empowered by the energies of the others as my own past selves, or as the others of my world; I may exercise powerful influence upon the course of the supervening world; but my self is a structure of spontaneity, lacking the sort of solidity that controls self or other. It consolidates—becomes solid *with* its world—but does not solidify as something apart. It may channel, inspire, tug, coalesce or plan; but the language of control (being in control, taking control of one's life, of situations) might best be avoided for the expression of the relational modes of self-assertion, freedom and influence.

Very well, but again: how is the controlling ego structure a specifically patriarchal problem? Women can and do suppress spontaneity and repress the immanent other; we can and do become preoccupied with issues of power and control. Women must struggle as hard as men to get free of patriarchal patterns and reactions to and against ourselves. One might guess that in general women tend to be more "soulful" in the sense pursued above; but then this soulfulness often runs up against men's patterns of separation and then perhaps lets itself be victimized or reacts with bitterness, manipulation, or a low-grade and distinctly nonrevolutionary hostility. Women flip all too easily into derivative, ultimately self-sabotaging modes of external relations, neither triumphantly independent nor widely connective. But the gender issue remains irreducible to the "facts" of what characteristics men and women might be caught exhibiting. The collaboration of sexism with the self- and other-objectifying ego has deeper roots than any enumeration of gender differences or similarities could demonstrate.

The controlling ego remains a particularly patriarchal problem because surely the sort of reified/reifying being we have now traced with a certain descriptive neutrality (the ontological neuter) can have no more likely source than that of the "greater sense of rigid ego boundaries" we attribute to traditional male personality development. The defensive mechanisms on which standard psychoanalytic theory founds the ego, which upon closer investigation characterize specifically masculine development, find their ontological niche in the denial of the other's immanence and of the self's impermanence. In other words, the metaphysics supporting the common sense of substance thinking (that of course I am separate from you and of course I am the same I, now as then) could not even emerge outside of this oedipal ego development characteristic of a particular psychosocial structure. And any alternative metaphysic, including the Whiteheadian, will not get off the ground as a worldview unless it acknowledges the messily psychosocial, embarassingly empirical obstacles to its own realization. The defensiveness of the ego springs not only from a primal fear of mother projected upon every subsequent other. The matricidal impulses (translating, as we have argued, into the more overt patricidal competition) convey an ultimately cosmocidal—and by implication globally suicidal—urge. The self cannot in fact extract itself from the world it kills, and death by metaphysical objectification now attains to its ultimate realization.

Whitehead's cosmology implies something he never could have acknowledged: that the standard male ego is based upon a fallacy (however we spell the word). No wonder this androcentrically enforced ego is so characteristically on the defense. It protects a pretense that every moment of its own being belies. The solid self-identity that seems to lend it permanence, the thick boundaries that seem to preserve it from the intrusions of the felt world—these are always dissolving, always needing reconstruction. No matter how well one *thinks* as a Cartesian-style ego, one cannot ever quite *feel* the substantiality in terms of which one thinks. One *is* not long enough—one is always already becoming an other. One's very one-ness, that provisional accomplishment of self-actualization at any moment, is contributing to one's uncontrollable inner multitudes. If under the sign of the phallic monad one keeps trying to erect and defend the civilization of the separate—as men have long been compelled and women only recently motivated to do—one will only become poorer, emptier, simpler, more resentful and destructive for the effort.

From the vantage point of a connective integrity, the defensive fantasies of the separative subject concoct only a pseudoselfhood. Mary Daly has put the contrast perfectly: "The Unfolding/Realizing of this integrity is be-ing beyond such reified beings, the solidified pseudo-selves." [90]

If any integrity that there is is of the sort spontaneously emerging from and within a fluid field of relations, it is not only women whose integrity must be connective. Connectivity cannot confine itself to feminine psychology or feminist ideology—for what is fully itself *as* female is always already ontologically overextended. That is, in our connectivity we reach not only over and above the confinements of any limited range of relations, but we extend *as* women (not as sexless humanoids) beyond any specifiably feminine mode of relation. Thus often women might seem to be revoking their own relational commitments by, for instance, disengaging from a particular relation, when in fact they are merely claiming for themselves the open range of intellectual or political or professional or spiritual relations that may have been curtailed by the specific relationship. And this relational liberty, which continually extends *beyond* while taking account of the particular claims of particular connections, is always at the same time self-affirming, involving loving relations to one's own person. The relational self is bound up with the "female" in only one important way: women are less likely under the conditions of patriarchy to have repressed the fluidity and connectivity of which all persons consist. The awareness of the fluent sociality of our own selves is more likely to have been incorporated into the very structure of our personality, reinforcing rather than repressing connective sensibilities. But what if one is a man? Repression rather than oppression of the self's connective ontology will be the most likely difficulty. To deconstruct the defenses of the obligatory ego will require vigilant discerning of the drag of separation, the urge to retreat from intimacy. In a male who reads this sort of book, sexist patterns of misogyny will probably have been counteracted and softened to some degree. Yet they are still discernible as subtle tendencies that seem to be built into the larger situations for which one may hardly be blamed as an individual. Social history, professional norms, institutional practice, intellectual patterns, emotional disadvantages: how can one take responsibility without indulging in a guilt trip? For the guilt trips of white males seem less a matter of real feeling or insight than of a resentful cycle that results in an interesting form of victim-blaming: males feel more rage at feminists for allegedly making them feel guilty than they feel at the patriarchal structures that turned women to feminism in the first place—and by which such males often claim to be equally oppressed. Men who cultivate guilt trips and passive "sensitivity" drain women and make them into mothers. Such purportedly profeminist men then feel justified in expressing the hope that women will stop talking about women and just do what they do with excellence (that is, in traditional male terms).

For a man to find his own (authentically male) integrity of connection will at this point in history implicate him, I suspect, in a compensatory gynocentricity, a provisional sense of identification with women that functions as an apprenticeship in relation. Conscious empathy with women (and perhaps with children) may help his own relational capacities to reawaken. Acknowledging and struggling with his own defensiveness vis-à-vis feminism is a touchstone of growth. After all, it is a matter of realizing, risking and enjoying those aspects of personality previously stifled as too "feminine." (Not that any qualities *are* intrinsically feminine.) Through the growth of this relatedness—to men as well as women—his self-constitution will change. It will include in its inner plurality, its streaming, an active solidarity with women and *therefore* with all beings, gradually replacing the anxious pseudosolidity of the state of separation and control. Would, however, that such manly metamorphosis were as easy as it sounds—then it would in each case of good intentions be more likely to succeed. Men embarking on a postpatriarchal journey will get little support from other men. To relinquish the delusion of permanence and separation means not only to forfeit the fringe benefits of the false self and to feel the pain of feeling one's feelings. It also risks calling down the wrath, scorn and punishment of committedly separate cohorts. To lose the hero's *self*-control calls for rare courage and commitment—and a connective trust in what is to be gained.

Sticky Connections

In any person the staccato of division and dominance can give way to rhythms of solitude and sociality. For (as will become explicit in the final chapter) the social nature of the self does not trap us in some neon light of pure publicity, of relentless relating without respite. Landscape is always becoming inscape. The multitude of selves constitutes a complex inner life and thus a field of privacy. This view of social selfhood has no more to do with behaviorism or sociologism than it has to do with individualism and substantialism. The friction of the many as they become one resists merging into simple unity. Without this friction—akin to the *"différance"* of Derrida's deconstruction—there would only be the alternatives of separation or merger: an opposition posed from the vantage point of separatism. Neither the inner nor the outer multiplicity can be digested into a static unity. Only separation from the outer many permits the illusion of a permanent inner self identity.

One can attempt to establish a rigid control along the boundaries of self and other as a defense against influence. Indeed, the patriarchal subjectivity of control cannot distinguish connection from conformity. It creates what it fears: a collective sameness, a proscription of difference, a prohibition against wandering. It projects this fear onto women. Matriphobia, we recall, is the fear of a conformist collectivity. And while differentiation as an activity has been correspondingly suppressed in women (in order to enforce their soluble status), in fact the maintenance of self-sameness by means of objectification and dichotomy has proved a self-delusion. The separative cadence of other-opposition and self-preservation creates not difference but sameness: the project of self-identity through time preserves a fantasy of solid subjective unity amidst the Others out there. Sameness of the self through time, absolved from relation to the others in space—this is the space-time of patriarchal consciousness.

Gender distinctions in fact can only stay ontologically open, undefined, subject to the compulsions of history and the comedies of our own most serious efforts. Traditionally, the dyad of separative and soluble self comes together in a sort of two-part caricature of a single person. The masculine role fetishizes the moment of solitude, freedom and spontaneity, the moment in which something new is made of the past, and the many become one. To the feminine is left the role of sheer relation, of pure feeling, of transition between the moments of distinctive selves. Thus she is no self, no individuality at all, while he is all self, transcending his relations. She is pure fluidity, the moment of transition from other to self, softening in her selfless solubility the hard edges of his separate self. She is his captive "transitional object," one might say. And she feels *his* feelings for him. Her useful liminality is manifest both in the outwardly and the inwardly relational domain.

In the outer spheres, women have made social and familial relations possible, even warm, in a world of embattled male egoes. As mother, wife or hostess, she weaves a semblance of community between competitive masculine insularities.[91] She connects men not only to each other, but to their environments (as homemaker), to their work (as secretary, muse or support system), to their bodies (as sexual partner or nurse). Indeed she has been judged by her capacity to do just this hospitable work of inconspicuous compensation for *their* separations: to offer to the male what Levinas calls "the gentle face"—which must also be "discreet,"—of the "feminine."[92]

But her self-dissolution, by which she manufactures a glue to hold together separate male ego-moments, reveals an equally sticky inner dimension. If person, or soul, is in truth a series of connected occasions, it would seem to be no coincidence that man has found in the image of woman his very soul: he senses not only that his salvation depends upon women, but that his soul *is* a woman—the anima. Without the "solution" of the internal, eternal essence of Femininity, he senses he would not hold together. Indeed, Jung identifies the Feminine with Eros, defined as "the principle of relationship."[93] Exposed to the parched isolation of his own ego's illusoriness, the patriarchal male would find himself high and dry, trapped in the "solipsism of the present moment" (Santayana), walled into moments that do not flow one into the next. To have a "feminine" soul allows him to keep his ego in control and on top of his holdings in the world, while tapping the underground fluids of psyche: the best of both worlds, without their mutual transformation.

Need notion of every anima, of inner soul sister, function thus in complicity with the patriarchal ego? I do not think it must, if it can be released from the controlling definitions by which she is made an essential set of attributes complementing sexist masculinity. Given back her body, her polyvalency, her link with real women ancient and present, she imports into males not their souls—in which men surely need to find their maleness, if maleness itself is to exceed ego and become soulful—but a confrontive play of metaphors inviting all manner of connection. Then she does not stand in for connection itself, relieving males of their responsibility for Eros. Moreover, this anima—female spirit—is just as much at work in women, as some female Jungian analysts have realized.

Inwardly/outwardly, the soluble woman has embodied connection without self, while the separative male has incarnated self without connection. This symbiotic but hierarchical dyad of the normative subject and his helpmate reflects then the traditional, substantial view of the self both in relation to others and to itself. And the Whiteheadian view of internal relations enables us to project a formal alternative to both dimensions of dualism. As instantaneous actual occasion, the self emerges from the others whom it has internalized and goes beyond itself into the newly emergent others. If we are thus ontologically communal, we need not serve as glue for another; being already interconnected, we are moist, sticky and fibrous enough within ourselves to come into new self-composition. As soul, or personally ordered society, man does not need woman to fill in the unconscious gaps between his moments, no more than woman needs an internal or actual man to lend her some superstructure of rationality or order or self-control. In the rhythm of moment-to-moment, self-to-self existence, I come to know that I cannot mirror myself, cannot make myself an object, because I am already another. And so I do not need to rationalize my self into a soulless substance in some attempt to achieve perfect self-knowledge and its implied correlative, perfect self-consistency.

A wisdom and a continuity of a different order become accessible, a coherency based on feeling our world and my own feelings, however painful; on making something fresher out of the feelings, and out of the world; on never staying quite the same. Psychic animation then requires no compensatory anima or controlling animus. The internal relatedness of soul, with its inward community in interplay with the outer societies, does cause the defensive ego to come unglued. But "falling apart"—which Hillman calls the "pathologizing" without which "soul-making" cannot occur[94]—can spur the recognition of our own plural selfhood: the shattering of the shells of objectified selves. It may smack of my sense of death and of my "differentness" because it reminds me of the perpetual perishing and the ineradicable spontaneity of which a person—a living soul—is made.

Radical Consistency?

The implicit metaphysic of feminist sensibility may indeed run to the relational and the fluid: but the intrinsic multiplicity, the momentariness and the internal relatedness of all beings do not automatically follow. I have argued that without dissolving the notion of an enduring, underlying permanence into a stream of interconnected events, we will simply not be able to move beyond the static status of self-enclosed subjects and their metaphysical sexism. But in her own feminist philosophizing Mary Daly might differ here. I cannot in this context do justice to the multiple levels of her unprecedented philosophy of Self, uniquely grounded as it is in classical theology and metaphysics. It stands on its own (which cannot be said of the relevance of process thought for feminist reflection). However, I want to point out a particular difficulty that her view poses for the one developed here, especially in this chapter, or that any commitment to radical connection might find with her thought.

Far from acclaiming any multiplicity of self or selves, she seems directly to countermand it: "There are not many Selves in one woman, but rather, one Self, wholly present in that woman."[95] This wholehearted assertion of the unity of the self issues in an equally unambiguous call for ongoing self-identity through time: "One obvious consequence of the idea that a woman has one soul wholly present in all of her 'parts' is that there is an essential integrity at the very core of her Self." Furthermore, this integrity manifests itself as "a radical consistency in her behavior. She does not seem to be 'one person one day and someone else the next.'"[96]

If this curt denial of intrinsic plurality, this stern demand for self-consistency, smacks of classical substantialism, it is no wonder.

Daly is here appropriating from the great metaphysician of substance, Thomas Aquinas, his idea of the soul. She seeks out this idea not for its substantialism, of course, let alone for its alliance with the traditional Aristotelian brand of misogyny, but for its truly promising nondualism, which we acknowledged earlier. His view that "the whole soul is in each part of the body" refutes the dichotomy of body and soul. Together they form one whole, one organism. But she draws from him also a basis for integrity, understood as self-consistency. And so she does not criticize the implicit Thomist dualism of self and other: the separation of each organism from every other, except as mediated by universals. This is not a matter of oversight. One senses in her thinking that the immediate interconnection of beings poses a lesser concern than the appreciation of their individuality. When she does affirm interconnection, the focus is either on intuitions and ideas, or on the awesome interplay between women and the cosmic elements. But discussing even feminist sorority, the sense of internal relatedness, of being part of each other, has no place in her insistence upon the virtues of autonomy and Self. "Sparking" is her catchy image for the woman-to-woman communication that sets us aflame with life, with energy, with courage. Certainly this is community. Sparks fly between us, inspire, set fire—burning up the fathers' dross and lighting our "Genius." Or rather our individual genii. Daly's crackling fire images will not let women be watered down to the merely wet and earthy—to undiffentiated mud. Sisterhood is not to settle for a simpering sameness—a major temptation for any ideologically bonded group, especially one already socialized to selflessness. Indeed the sense of a feminist in-group could foster a mass-mindedness that more resembles "comradeship" (as in male war-bonding), which she distinguishes from friendship: "Acknowledging the deep differences among friends/sisters is one of the most difficult stages of the Journey and it is essential for those who are Sparking in free and independent friendship rather than merely melting into mass mergers." She thus intends to redeem a positive meaning for "separatism": "the creation of separate female-identified psychic, mythic, semantic, physical spaces is necessary for likeness and wild otherness to grow." [97] Who would dispute the painful but transformative value of respecting each other's otherness or the truth that the richer a relationship, the richer the individualities of those relating? But are "independent" and "separate" necessary attributes of freedom and a "room of one's own"? Must the sparking sister selves remain thus ontologically separate: autonomous in their "Be-ing"? Even when Daly uses water imagery (the "Tidal Genius"), she would have us resist the temptation to fluid interfusion. It is as if the elemental female fire would be extinguished by radical relatedness, by interconnection in our depths. As ever—indeed, as with de Beauvoir—this is a needed reaction to feminine solubility in service of the patriarchal subject. Daly's unadulterated ontology of the female Self frees us from any overwrought and underindividuated relationalism.

Nonetheless, to promote independence and autonomy, with no ontological interconnectedness, risks co-optation by masculine models of separatism. Daly's language of essential integrity, of the core of Self, of radical consistency, shares fundamental presuppositions with Aquinas's Aristotelian metaphysics. It is a discourse still supported by the ideology of self-identical unity I have characterized as the pillar of patriarchal philosophy and behavior. We noted in our examination of monsters that woman's purported deformity, according to Aristotle, stems from her failure to fit the "human" species, that is, to conform to the substantial form of Man. And we have argued that any form of substance thinking by which the unity of self is attributed to an abiding inner essence over against the external accidents of relation and change, will express the defensive matricidal aggression, the need to oppose and control, of the monolithic masculine ego ideal. We must beware the semantics and the selfhood of any overemphatic oneness, any doctrine of unity not grounded in an articulate sense of internal relations. The language of oneness, of "one Self," always plucks the strings of interconnection, as it aims to transcend fragmentation and self-division. But too readily it reproduces the self-enclosed monad of whatever gender, starved for the relational resources from which it has been separated.

Because separatism is systemic to sexism, the tactic of *feminist* separatism, which Daly herself so courageously embodies and advocates, must itself always be subject to feminist scrutiny. Provisional forms of exodus and absence from the systems of sexism are strategically indispensable. If the masculine separative self has depended upon the feminine nonself, then that female needs to unplug herself from the system that continually recharges him by draining her. (Precisely what forms of disengagement—ideological, profes-

sional, psychological, emotional, marital, geographical, economi-
cal—cannot be generalized.) Let me only ask, and not rhetorically,
whether Daly's closet substantialism, with its stress on Self and its
silence on internal and interpersonal relation, does not link up with
her feminist separatism. Is her separatism a provisional and justifi-
able means toward a nonseparative end? I suspect it is. But if separatism becomes a policy or a dogma, it is surely doomed to absorb,
however unconsciously, the androcentric worldview of the separate
self. Then the aim that justifies political strategies of withdrawal,
the goal of a buoyantly nonsexist and interconnecting society of
selves, is being subtly and radically undermined. But "feminist separatism" is often a homophobic charge easily hurled at creative
women by those who would not think, for instance, of calling Jesus
a "separatist" when he claims to be in this world but not of it, or
when he retreats into solitude or to his small community of like-
minded friends. No one changes a world, a culture, without prac-
ticing modes of subversive retreat from it.

If there is some danger of over-separatism in Daly's thought, it is
also true that "radical consistency" and the dauntless Self with its
tidal Genius provide a ready corrective to any slushy romanticism
of connection. But the creative force of this gynomorphic self-
assertion need not pit itself against the radicality of relation: thus
Daly's spinster Sisterhood of Spinning Women is both a sine qua
non and a result of the sacredness of woman's Self. Daly's language
inspires that empowering oneness of purpose that women still often
lack. She well warns us of that relational lull to Self-sacrifice that
rids the "phallocracy" of female presence and power. Hearing Daly,
women (those not too petrified by the sleeping Medusa in themselves, which Daly inevitably rouses) receive a direct infusion of
gynergetic courage. Her writing remains the primary antidote today
to the soluble feminine (non)self. Daly's style, which shakes and
changes the hearer, is in its urgency and its comedy part and parcel
of the content of her metaphysics. Her revolutionary method
(which she calls "methodicide") is certainly far from Aquinas!

It is the feminist sense of urgency, in its impatience with the
merely academic, that must keep us questioning our own dependencies upon intellectual father figures (such as Whitehead himself). However helpful his critiques of substance metaphysics, of
premodern and modern dualisms, and of theological imperialism

prove, they remain respectfully directed at the intellectual errors of other thinkers. He politely limits his vision of an alternative world-view to a chapter in the history of philosophy. Such academic serenity smacks of complacency. Philosophical or theological sorts of problems are not self-encapsulated and isolated from the rest of life. There is a Cartesianism inherent in the traditional style of reflection, even if the ideas pondered move beyond all previous dualisms. This inadvertent dualism finds an echo in some of Whitehead's less felicitous categories; for instance, the "objectification" of the past by the present might render the other as well as the past an inert datum for my aggressive concrescence. To interpret the other's influence on me as my objectification of the other cuts against the very intuition of process and relatedness. This may stem from his insistent maintenance of the momentary atomic nature of reality, by which he seeks to guard the individual from monism. These are only examples of possible difficulties for feminism in the content as well as the method of the scheme as it stands.

By contrast, I am in this book treating theoretical obstacles to a vision of internal relatedness as symptoms of a near-global condition. Of course, Whitehead works as a diagnostician more than a problem solver. But is such an alternative vision capable of exercising healing effects upon its culture? It depends. Without continuously and explicitly antipatriarchal work on itself and its real worlds, process thought will not and cannot advance the realization of its own vision. Because it is a metaphysic of feeling, process thought must be *felt;* because feeling is what actualizes the possible, process thought is useful only inasmuch as it gets concretely actualized in life, in relations, in culture. By contrast, I nowhere claim that feminism needs Whitehead—or any favored male thinker. We can appropriate these thoughts because of their affinity with values important for other reasons than the ones he would acknowledge, reasons more urgent than abstract. The urgency, as urge to make a difference, to perpetuate something other than the same old structures of my self, my world, my views, does not dictate any feminist purism (a form of separatism) in the choice of resources. We can only ask what, in the face of a global history hurtling itself toward imminent disaster, helps something new to emerge. The notion of a person in process, creatively emergent from his or her inner and outer multiplicity, provides one useful twist of vision, a clearing within the cultural congestion. Our realistic sense of planetary emergency must not paralyze or panic, else it will only block the emergence.

But now let us return to the particular point of content at which we have preferred Whitehead's account to Daly's. Daly's own terms can deliver their message even in the problematic area. If she admonishes women not to be different "persons" from moment to moment, we recall that the person, or soul, is a society continuous through time. Person, not self, is in the process view the same. Moreover she never argues for strict self-identity from moment to moment, but rather for "radical consistency." That is, she, like existentialists or process thinkers, would vehemently insist that this consistency or continuity is not a static or stagnant given, a fait accompli, but must be achieved, created. And I would add that only the radical difference between actual moments of self, of selves as events, makes this creativity possible. What happens to our past selves remains open to the present decision: we may make much soul of them or very little. Furthermore, we may affirm with Daly "one Self, wholly present in that woman"—but *at any given moment*. That is, precisely, wholly *present*. So far so good. But we are also affirming, contra Daly, "many Selves in one woman." Yet only one self is the moment's subjective center, holding in itself the others. One self presides at a time. What of the other selves at that time? They are that series of self-moments accumulating as my very soul; and that infinite rippling web of the actual other beings whose selfhood, for good or ill, has become part of my own.

Eros and the Soft-core Self

If we desire, with Daly, the image of the "very core of her Self," let us imagine it as a soft core, remembering the Latin *cor,* meaning heart: a center not as the insulated inner essence of a hard-core selfhood, but a rhythmic continuity carrying the past into the future. Women do not need to harden but to strengthen; men need (as Augustine sensed) to melt down the hardness of the heart. Let this inner sense of self be, as Daly has declared it, a process of "Self-Centering," not a fixed point or place of fixation. Quite inimical to our "immovably centered" hero or other unmoved movers, it is less like an apricot pit than the molten lava at the core of the earth, or the rising sap in the tree. The innermost psyche is the most fluid, volatile and dynamic place within us—yet not therefore unstable, merely fluctuating according to whim and circumstance.

Centering, we are not isolating or hardening ourselves. We draw upon a peacefulness beyond the turbulence and treachery of particular relationships, particular obsessions and anxieties. But it is a stillness born of a greater width of connection, from a livelier attunement to being here now, from my body's presence to its surrounding cosmos. The calm distils itself from the subtle bustle of all things in process. Getting centered, we feel the sudden warmth of the deeper desire—even of what mystics call the "heart's desire." A desire that leads us beyond ourselves—to selves both new and other?

Love of what already is makes conscious the matrix of connection; in desire, love faces the future. Both the relations from which I come and the possibilities—for new modes of relatedness—toward which I be-come encounter me in and as my inmost Self. Hence the intuition that what is most deeply myself is more than ego, more than I. For I encounter a Self that is at once most intimately my own and holy—but *not* wholly—Other. I relate *to* myself—my Self. The self-affirmation that women seek is then no trivial ego assertion: "I do not refer to self-esteem in the usual sense, but rather esteem/value of the deep Original Self in women, the living spirit/matter, the psyche who participates in Be-ing."[98] Psyche's originality refers not to a fixed point of origin, but to the creative process of self-origination. It is akin to that which we have traced in Whitehead as the concrescence of the possible from the actual, or to the object-relational "true self," or Jung's Self. But it is most manifestly coming true through women's fidelity to our deeper feeling: we become originals.

It is no wonder that in the culminating and communal epiphany of Shange's *For Coloured Girls Who Considered Suicide But the Rainbow Was Enuf*, the discovery of "the holiness of myself released" choruses with the proclamation that "I found God in myself and I loved her, I loved her fiercely."[99] "God," as we saw in the first chapter, has largely functioned as the Absolute and so as the absolute closure on reality, the final answer that forecloses on our quests and our questions and replaces desire with dependency. Whatever their erstwhile value in mystery, the classical perfections of immutability, impassionality and independence, not to mention foreknowledge, further neither the power of the possible nor the recollection of the past; they model the ultimate Separate Self. The tradition of process thought has gone far to deconstruct the "God" of classical theism. For example, Charles Hartshorne's neoclassic theism insists that a God who is related and thus capable of self-enrichment by feeling the experiences of the world is more perfect than the one who is incapable of surpassing itself, whose perfection is an absolute independence from the world. "As we are indebted to a few persons for the privilege of feeling something of the quality of their experiences, so God is indebted to *all* persons for the much fuller enjoyment of the same privilege." [100]

This divinity, who is indebted to all, relative to all and so expressive of a credible power of love, is as much Eros—desire—as Agape, the unilaterally self-giving, sacrificial "love" of the theological mainstream. It is not outside of anything but inside of everything. A genuine interdependence may better interpret even the biblical metaphor of an emotional, desirous Love never long out of touch with anger, jealousy, and other "imperfections." Moreover, if feminists retain any desire for a personification of the relational wisdom in the universe and for the power of the possible, our metaphors of deity—as Goddess, God/dess, God-S/he or Genderless Being—will surely imply the metaphysics of cosmic relativity and no independent absolute. Whitehead (counteracting the Aristotelian with a more Platonic theology) designated a "Divine Eros" in the universe as "the living urge toward all possibilities, claiming the goodness of their realization." [101] Yet such a living urge motivates feminist urgency today. This Eros incarnates itself in each of us, in each actual entity, as the "first phase" of the process of self-origination—that is, as the Original Self? Thus "if we omit the Psyche and the Eros, we should obtain a static world." [102] Or perhaps we should rather say, patriarchy has omitted the Psyche and the Eros, and so bequeathed to us a planet threatened with the supreme stasis of its own death.

So we come full circle: back to the divine Eros of Psyche's quest. That originally bisexual deity points to the power of Love to hold together and to lure beyond. If the self is a pulse in the life of Psyche, the divine moment stirs a depth of soul where we meet our cosmic context. A self is a node in the network of worlds, and in each self is an Eros ensouling the world. The world has heart—where we embrace the Universe as condensed, personified, particularized, meeting us in those metaphors of the sacred that inspire us. If we meet God in ourselves, we meet her at the molten core of our heart's desire, ever again energizing our courage and our quest.

The Spider's Genius

Such was Arachne's work: not envy's eyes
Could find a flaw, nor Pallas criticize.
The girl's achievement galled her, and she tore
The faultless fabric, with the scenes it bore
Impeaching heaven, a crime in every strand;
. . .
And as a spider, with her ancient skill,
Arachne plies her tireless weaving still.
    —Ovid, *Metamorphosis*

Each unblinking eyelet linked now
to another in the shuttles of the loom.
'Thin rainbow-colored nets, like cobwebs,
all over my skin.'
I affirm
all
of my transformations
    —Robin Morgan, "The Self"

ARACHNE: HER NAME MEANS Spider or Spinner. According to the tale, she was the greatest weaver in the world, who challenged the goddess Athena to a contest of looms. While Athena not surprisingly spins tales of the glory of the gods, Arachne weaves a tapestry of dissent: she depicts the offenses of the Olympians, especially their violations of mortal women. Arachne wins the contest easily—even Athena does not dispute the superiority of her competitor's work.

But that Arachne's insurgent web be not only true, but beautiful—
this is intolerable. So Athena proceeds to torture her. Then as Arachne is about to escape by hanging herself, Athena turns her, in
an ironic act of reprieve, into a spider: "Live, Mischief, live and
hang."[1]

No wonder that women "fear success." There seems to be no
room for more than one "exceptional woman," and the Athena
who glorifies the Fathers will be pitted against the Arachne who
challenges them—though, as is often the case, Arachne does superior work. No doubt one is more inspired by unmasking false gods
than by adulating them. The aesthetics of the web require a dangerous honesty, an honesty with theological consequences. Was Arachne perhaps originally a Spider Goddess demoted to mortal
maiden status by patriarchal myth? Although Athena herself was
once marked with the spider-totem and the web, by classical times
only her prowess as weaver remains of her arachnean associations.
The opposition of patriarchal goddess and mortal victim displays
not only the traditional competitiveness between women. It also
hints at the split self that turns woman against herself: we torture
ourselves for the effrontery of our achievements. We try to spin
apologias for the patriarchs, while at the same time a spidery spirit
counters with a confrontive web of truth. If Athena "saves" Arachne from suicide (*self*-killing) by turning her into a spider, is it
out of Athena's unacknowledged self-recognition? The change that
may save our "Original Self," which must compete rather desperately for recognition from our male-identified persona, may be
likened to metamorphosis into an elemental spinner. But now that
our arachnean transformations are voluntary, can we affirm them?

While Athena is today unmasked as the divine Daddy's Girl, Arachne as the Spider-woman is revealing her own divinity. The wom-
en's movement glistens with the mischief of Web and Weaver: in its
poetry and its peace movement, in its metaphysics and its praxis,
feminism speaks spider language. Athena herself, agent of the arachnean change-over, may thus be redeemed and with her the exceptional, the professional, the independent armored one who prefers the company of males, the intellectual anima figure—roles we
may have known in ourselves.

As the Spider comes into her own, even the weaving Penelope
rips off her facade of patiently waiting wifedom and claims the true
meaning of her name: "She with a Web on her Face."[2] The world

seen through a web—this is the hermeneutics of connection. The image of the web claims the status of an all-embracing image, a metaphor of metaphors, not out of any imperialism, but because, as a metaphor of interconnection itself, the web can link lightly in its nodes an open multiplicity of images. But if the project of connection first requires what Ricoeur calls a hermeneutics of suspicion, akin to Arachne's challenge to the gods, this is because the tapestry has been ripped, our world torn, our vision broken. Unless we continue to unveil the connections between the power structures of patriarchy and the psychopolitics of separative selfhood, connectedness itself cannot be known. The relations between things are as delicate as spider's silk, known only instinctively, with profound indirection—yet "strong enough to hang a bridge on." But just because of the web's strength and just because of its subtlety, the separative self can ignore but depend upon the connections, and continues to fragment the world into objects for itself. The separative worldview, inimical to worlds viewed "with a web on her face," keeps on breaking the web.

Binding Up or Binding Down

So neither metaphysics nor any revision will suffice, unless it carries over from and then back into the restorative work of real reconnection. We only realize what we actualize: to know intimately is to participate and therefore to act with and upon. Religion true to its name activates connection. It "ties together", binding up the wounds of breaking worlds. It is the bridging, bonding process at the heart of things. There is no reason not to call this process Love: the Eros that seeks to get things together, no matter what.

True, this bisexual principle of cosmic creation was finally trivialized as the comic Cupid with his mischievous arrows. In the mischief worked against Zeus & Brothers, at least Eros remains a trickster trying, despite the supremely serious Olympian sacralization of separation, to make connections. But under patriarchal religion Cupid has basically functioned to yoke together (using cupidity rather than a truer eros) those coupled complementarities of male-separative and female-soluble selfhood that harden into the building blocks of a world of walls. While the feminine partner is to hold together a world bent on division, the male aspires to the ego defenses of the wall itself.

Here, for instance, another masculine mask of God speaks to his chosen mouthpiece: "I, for my part, today will make you into a fortified city, a pillar of iron, and a wall of bronze." (Jer. 1:18).[3] In a civilization whose religions are forms of fortification, the bronzed ego who builds walls instead of webs triumphs. (Though not Jeremiah, who is finally driven to suicidal utterances as his culture crumbles: he laments he did not die in the mother's womb. Like most actual men, he fails to become a fortified city, in spite of the demands of his superego, the superman-god. He seems to suffer from an inverted, unrecognized desire to find a Mother of rebirth: an apparently aborted mid-life crisis.)

Religion defining holiness as separation[4] has made itself into the bearer of barriers, of disconnection, of exclusion. For instance, to be an elect people then means that only *we* are chosen and no longer simply that we are different in our community of uniqueness, as all others are different in theirs. Or the "Body of Christ," an image capable of provoking a radically relational vision of being "members one of another," comes instead to designate a hierarchical elite of the saved. Inasmuch as it exalts the patriarchal principle of separation, religion has become a set of competitive hoaxes playing out another version of the etymology: for "religion" can instruct us "to bind back" in the sense of tying down, holding back, returning to bondage. The tie that binds then subjugates the human to the representative hierarchy of controlling Fathers exhorting the faithful (mostly women) to "obedience," "worship" and "selflessness." Religious bondage in the name of faith perpetuates, as I have argued, the relations of dependency upon a paternal superpower who stands so absolutely apart that all connection depends upon his special fiat.

The artificiality, however, is not "God's" fault but the result of the web-breaking consciousness, the objectifying-dichotomizing reflexivity, which at least in theological circles acknowledges itself to be alienated, fallen and sinful in its state of separation. But inasmuch as it has projected upon the universe an absolute idol of male separateness, and then expects this God to save it from itself, it can only remain "bound back" in its pattern of perdition. Thus the sin of separation appears "original." The persuasiveness of the theology of original sin partially derives from the psychological circumstances we analyzed in chapter 3, where boys and girls are set into opposed tracks with tremendous implications for their personhood before they are even conscious. Yet as with original sin, they are nonetheless responsible for themselves, even for that which they did not cause. Since in our culture the Divine Outsider who is supposed to rescue us is an infinite inflation of the male ego itself, the circle stays closed. The true outsiders—such as women, gentiles, Jews, the poor and people of color—are accordingly cast into the outer darkness, into the shadows outside the wall (where, if they are submissive enough, they may be allotted a few crumbs of mercy).

So we can only sympathize with Daly's dismissal of "religion" (though never of the cosmic power of "Be-ing") as regressive bondage. Evoking the Self as its own holy and healing environment, she tells us that "in this space the Self is not re-ligious, not tied back by old ligatures, old alliances." [5] For religion in its patriarchal captivity has guaranteed a cycle of eternal return, a deadly, dulling lull of reiteration in which all are bound back to pseudo-selfhood. Daly diagnoses the reactionary cycle of father worship as "a circular pattern/model for muted existence: separation from and return to the same immutable source." We earlier explored certain mythic and psychological mechanisms of this model of separation and return, where separation is accomplished by a symbolic slaughter of the source. In the myth of patricide, where oedipal rebellion of the son against the father leads to the identification of the son with the father, supersession of one generation of patriarchs by the next brings no "new testament," no good news, of a postpatriarchal world. At a more primordial level, we saw how the separation from the mother symbolized in the dragon defeat—even if it finally demands a return to the mother—enacts the matricidal basis of male and to some extent female personalities within the social system of absent (transcendent) fathers. And, of course, we began with a reflection upon Odysseus, the great Western symbol for separation and return. Return: to the more or less "immutable source," the waiting wife.

"Their 'truth,'" writes Luce Irigaray, "immobilizes us, turns us into statues, if we can't loose its hold on us. If we can't defuse its power by trying to say, right here and now, how we are moved." [6] That is, how we are affected, influenced, vulnerable, how we feel the feelings of the other and of the antecedent moment of ourselves. Discerning with immediacy—not relying on the abstract sameness

of long-range personhood—the truth of our relatedness, we recognize the present emotion and do not cling to it. To be moved is
motion, e-motion. In the false generalization from my particular
moments to a self-identical essence, I am frozen, paralyzed in the
image of a stereotype: whether as waiting woman, stuck in her self-
denials, or as the heroic male immortalizing his ego. Odysseus' vigorous mobility, requiring the immobilization of the woman, is not
the movement of feeling and transformation, but the project of an
ego to master itself and its world. His movement thus fortifies his
inner immobility through its external adventure: a motion of ego,
not soul, demanding the denial of emotion.[7]

Patriarchal religion binds the reflexive ego back to its own cycle
of reification, in which it worships the idol of immutability. The
alternative, in Irigaray's description, seems to be a relentless immediacy: "You are moving. You never stay still. You never stay. You
never 'are'. How can I say 'you,' when you are always other? . . .
You remain in flux, never congealing or solidifying."[8] As the last
chapter argued, you literally *are* another, by the time I address you.
You will repeat much; you will reiterate past patterns of behavior;
you will remain linked with your history so intimately as to constitute a nameable person, an unfolding story of soul. But "you" cannot be pinned down to any point of place and time—your spatio-
temporal perspective within the oceanic continuum of relations will
not stay put. Penelope seemed to stay, and Odysseus seemed to
move. But her staying was subjugation, her weaving a defense
against male demands; his moving was unyielding, a defense
against nature, women, monsters, enemies, and gods. Perhaps as
Penelope today mobilizes, experiencing the life force flowing
through her loom, she will come out of the enforced solidity into
solidarity with Arachne. As she begins to see the world "with a web
on her face," the warrior may be thrown back upon his illusions.
Possibly remembering himself, he just might laugh at the truth of
his "No-one" name and know that he too is in flux, not merely
tossed about by a tormenting sea, but like an ocean himself. These
transformations are only possibilities, but they are real possibilities.

And it is something like a Goddess or like an Eros who proffers
the possible—the lure to realize new connections. The cosmic ero-
tism presents itself in endless metaphors. Some metaphors, like that
of the web today, come into a collective vitality at certain points in
history; others lose their energy, though they may hang on with a

deadly grip, substituting authority and cliché for desire and creativity. Nelle Morton might be right when she judges that

the word *God* may at one time have been a metaphor, but in common usage over centuries, along with many other religious symbols, it has lost its redemptive power. Since it has been identified with power-over, male rulership, and male control, it has been separated from the reality it first ushered in. The entire culture and political structure are extensions of this dead metaphor.[9]

Or as Shug, that unlikely wise woman of *The Color Purple* puts it, "Soon as I found out God was white, and a man, I lost interest."[10] Though she refuses to be bound down, she does not give up on religion as attunement to the interconnected whole of things. In the already classic statement of Alice Walker's theology, Shug describes the mystical experience that finally freed her from andromorphic metaphor: "One day when I was sitting quiet and feeling like a motherless child, which I was, it come to me: that feeling of being part of everything, not separate at all. I knew that if I cut a tree, my arm would bleed."[11] A clear case of oceanic feeling, it is no wonder the experience of this divine "it" (which she prefers to *he* or *she*) fills the void of a missing mother. Indeed she even calls "It" God. The epiphany of the inseparability of all sentient beings need not take the form of a mother-goddess; such interconnection implicitly mothers, as matrix of all life. It/She need not be remembered by any one name. In the poetry of "The Network of the Imaginary Mother," "You call me by a thousand names, uttering yourselves."[12]

If this book exhibits a special devotion to snakes, sea monsters and spiders, the purpose is to stimulate not the readers' phobias but their "sinister wisdom."[13] These defamed creatures claiming a new holiness serve to remind us that woman's power has been translated into the seductive, the devouring, the base and the frightening. But woman rearising *is* "sinister," that is, of the "left," the dark side, the insurgent: thus gynomorphic metaphors of deity cannot be restricted to anthropomorphic depictions of a cosmic female, however important and refreshing. Her sinister attributes must be evoked for their sheer force of iconoclasm: they let us feel how repulsive, how frightening, the powers of interconnection and the wisdoms of women have been made to appear.

But snakes, monsters and spiders remind us also of the dark sides, the dangers and tragedies of relation—it can ensare, strangle, swallow and devour. When lacking an empowering world, or an inner relation to ourselves, women can all too readily act out the archetypal "dark side of the feminine," seeking power by working a web of emotional ensnarement for others—especially men and children. Conversely, and often simultaneously, we let our energy, our happiness, ourselves, be eaten away by our relations. Too easily Eros tricks us, and we become "women who love too much" (i.e., women who depend for fulfillment on the success of a particular relationship.) So we must avoid any naive glorification of connection: the sinister wit and whimsy of the sacred monsters warn against any new relationolatry.

These primordial powers also work against any simplistic substitution of an exclusivist Goddess for the One God. As Morton continues, "In time the Goddess may become a dead metaphor if she is set 'out there' and literalized." [14] In other words, our way of reconnection, as religious action, must retain a pluralistic, metaphorical consciousness, and with it a self-directed iconoclasm. Otherwise any feminist *religio* of re-bonding may serve as a mere rebound relation—a new form of religious bondage even under a feminist banner. (Of course the threat of a literalized feminist absolute seems trivial beside the dangers of retrenchment to familiar patriarchal modes.)

Though we seek no return to an unchanging origin, even of the matriarchal sort, the *re* of religion cannot be ignored. We never begin from nothing, unless we would annihilate all remembering and all immanence, and so all relation. So connecting is reconnecting, connecting *again*. We begin always again because it is the nature of the self-moment to spin itself new, though not from nothing; but also because the massive historical breakage bequeaths to us broken fragments of what might have been. Work on the world of the self and the selves of the world can make no grandiose claims of absolute originality: short of despair, we can only keep repairing. We start "from a broken web."

Adrienne Rich's first spider stanza of 1978, from "Natural Resources" presents a great epiphany of the feminist spider-self:

This is what I am: watching the spider
rebuild—'patiently,' they say,

but I recognize in her
impatience—my own—

the passion to make and make again
where such unmaking reigns.[15]

Rich poses here an intriguing opposition: to refuse to acquiesce passively in destruction, yet to continue to create in the face of overwhelming forces of discreation. This passion, the eros of all creativity, is cosmic, intimate, political. But in Rich's equally powerful "Integrity" (composed later that same year), in which "the spider's genius" declares itself, the first line of the poem seems to announce a shift in perspective: "A wild patience has taken me this far." [16] The etymological equivalence of *passion* and *patience*—related to *pathos,* from the Greek *pascho,* "to suffer"—now points to a new synthesis. The vitality of "making" no longer negates patience but emboldens and energizes it. Patience can be a front for passive waiting of the old feminine variety. But the patience that is untamed and elemental is a form of courage. It will not abandon the total web of our connections in spite of failures of our energy and the recurrent disintegrations of community. The spider keeps on picking up the splayed threads of smashed efforts, joining them with fine fresh filaments extruded from her own substance—"from her own body." Such dauntless determination generates a long-term momentum: a person emerges who knows her own endurance as weblike, woven of the complex integrity of her unfurling selves, each at once receptively, patiently feeling the world as it is, and creatively, urgently making the world as it will be.

Radical patience requires a dauntless trust in the creative process, wherever we encounter it—in work, community, nature, dreams. This is no traditional faith, as in a controlling God who will set things right in the end. The web will not bear the weight of any omnipotent Daddy-deity or singly redeeming Lord whose passion week atones the world once and for all. As we have seen, any at-one-ment that would squelch our many-ness not only oversimplifies, subjecting us to the phallomorphic attribute of Divine Simplicity; it breaks the web, which is always multiple, and so fragments

rather than unifies. The spider-self suggests that conjunction of empathy and differentiation needed to generate any alternative to
either absolute or dissolute selfhood. Because the spider is an image
in which we are creating ourselves, she begins to exude an almost
sacred aura. But if she does inadvertently provoke any Goddess-
consciousness, she remains as much Self as she is Other, as much
immanent as transcendent. The webbing way has little to do with
deities to "worship" or "believe in," whose own egoes would need
"praising" and propitiating. It is the very process of reconnection.
Religion would be the unselfconscious process of connection itself,
had the web not been broken. And it would be inseparable from
the rest of life. That universal and by now thoroughly unoriginal
sin of sexism, which the world religions have staunchly supported,
tediously continues the breakage. So any arachnean spirituality is a
way of becoming not prescribed from the outside but sprung from
the whorl of internalized relations, calling for a richer self-
composition of our worlds. It is a way of being self at any moment:
a way of radical integrity.

Let me now sketch out four nonpolarities of being. This set (there
could be more or fewer) of ontological dyads may help divine an
arachnean way of selving. They at once recapitulate and anticipate
its emergence. In this way of becoming, what comes to *be?* Let us
religiously explore our being as what we are becoming in terms of
(1) being one and being many; (2) being private or being public; (3)
being body and being soul; (4) being here and being now.

Being One/Being Many

"*Nothing but myself? . . . My selves.* / After so long, this answer."
Immediately preceding the image of the angry and tender spider,
this disclosure in Rich's "Integrity" answers for her the question of
personal identity through time, posed in solitary reflection during
her forty-ninth year. She finds nothing but herself to measure her
life by. But the revelation of the plural personality suggests that even
in her solitude, she is not alone. There are many of her.

This is no split personality, no state of dissociated and autonomous psychic fragments taking possession of the person and over-
running the ego. If as the last chapter argued it is the nature of any
actual entity to be composite in its unity, the pathologies of multiple

personalities would appear less as exceptions than as limit-situations to normalcy, for the fine differentiations by which multiplicity is sustained are also fault lines at which the psyche cracks after too much quaking. To shatter into manyness may sometimes break the deadlock of the heroic ego ideal, forcing the realization that we are none of us simply one. But since the heroic ego, conquering and denying the many in the name of oneness, is an andromorph, and since women, as we have seen, tend to grow a more complex and pluralistic psyche, the breakup of the one into the many may seem less salutory for women than the achievement of integrity. If selves were by nature simple unities, or strict self-identities over and against other such self-identities, integration would require no creative labor, but would be more or less an established fact. As it is, fragmenting and dispersing forms of manyness are a real danger, sucking us into the undertow of now this, now that influence. Any interesting integrity is the project of a pluralistic personality.

As epigraph to "Integrity" Rich cites *Webster's* definition of that word: "the quality or state of being complete; unbroken condition; entirety." Does an unbroken state of self perhaps become possible only as we reclaim the network of our interrelatedness? But this wholeness can then be no monolith. Only because it finally excludes nothing from its perimeters is it entire, infinitely complex in composition. Holding so much together in itself, complete, it is still never finished. A many-selved integrity takes the image of an unending stream, never a finished monument. Here the spider's impatience revolts against any totalization. "Are we unsatisfied?" asks Irigaray, in her gynomorphic philosophizing. "Yes, if that means that we are never finished. If our pleasure consists in moving, being moved, endlessly. Always in motion: openness is never spent nor sated. We haven't been taught, nor allowed," she continues, "to express multiplicity." [17]

How does this polymorphic integrity feel? "Anger and tenderness: my selves." It has then to do with a relation to our own emotions. "And now I can believe they breathe in me / as angels not polarities." [18] It is through emotions that the primal feelings for the preceding selves and worlds flow into my awareness—at that moment before consciousness can bifurcate into clearly distinguished subjects and objects. So apparently opposed emotions can seem to divide me against my selves and my worlds. In fact, to identify myself now with one emotion, now with another, leads to fragmentation, not polymorphism. Consider for instance how anger often turns out to have been an explosion of childhood frustration or mere mimesis of a parent's rage; how tenderness often keeps us passive, dependent or subdued. Emotions are not absolutes requiring obedience—often a hard lesson for women. To learn to trust them requires an ongoing discipline: of listening for deeper causes and of letting go of obsessive patterns. Otherwise affect traps me in a repetitive inertia, where the anger or the tenderness possess me, lose me and lose sight of each other, eclipsing the objective, or intersubjective, possibilities of the situation. By empathizing with my emotions, and in so doing becoming conscious of the multiform influences working their way through me, I can learn from them and receive their vitality without thereby identifying with them. To greet them as angels allows them their immediate epiphany, and neither renders me their slave nor permits their repression. They bear messages ("angel" in Greek means message-bearer); they are Others within myself, never identical with the whole self. Thus I need not stay stuck in any particular emotion; the angel itself does not have to become a piece of hardened statuary. Anger does not need to become bitterness, joy a full-time happy-hour, tenderness an over-mothering acquiescence, nor grief a low-grade depression: the multiple interrelatedness of emotions—motions of soul—keep us in motion, responsive, plural. (This links up with Daly's marvelous distinction between "primary" and "pseudo" or "potted" passions.[19])

Through the work of the previous chapter, we may acknowledge two intertwining dimensions of multiplicity: my many selves as the fabric of other persons, plants, places—all the actual entities that have become part of me—and my many selves as the necklace of experiences that make up my personal history from birth to now. These selves are all there; if I acknowledge their influence, they become part of the community of my psyche, working together even through the most painful contrasts of desire, through seemingly irreconcilable differences of perspective, to produce the integration of a greater complexity of feeling. If I cannot claim these many, if I exclude great portions of them as contradictory to my makeup, they may wait to pull me into depression or to erupt into destructive violence. Moreover, mere inconsistency and unreliability may shortchange multiplicity. To feel depressed today about what excited me yesterday, to affirm today what I negated last week, may or may not signify an authentic fluidity. But there is surely more value in a spontaneous response, the more fully it takes the previous ones somehow into account. I am more likely to get trapped in identification with some particular past self if I do not own up to its presence in me now. But if I do let myself feel its presence, however faintly, it will weave itself into the free-form tapestry of my experience.

This multiple integrity, while always unfinished, is no less whole or coherent than that of a closed substance, an exclusive individual. Individuality—meaning literally undividedness—can then connote an integrity of radical inclusion. My selves selve my worlds: I am not *simply* one, but many ones, a new one each moment, and each one integrates the many ones of the open world surrounding me. Integrity unbreaks the brokenness by weaving the fragments into a new—if provisional—whole. Not multiplicity, but the refusal of multiplicity, fragments. The desire to exclude the many from my own oneness, to disengage my manyness and the manyness of the world, signals the cowardice that breaks the web.

Courage, *sine qua non*, of integrity, is of the heart—*couer–age*. Therefore we have recourse to an ontology of feeling. *Feeling* the many—in whatever subtle and slightly new, barely conscious way I can—I *am* many. Composing myself of these many ones, I become one. Now I let myself go. Then my oneness will contribute itself to the pool of the many, as a sort of kinetic energy for all the future ones I willy-nilly influence. Ontological integrity, spinning oneness out of many and weaving the one back into the many, stands as a first principle of arachnean religion. Whatever fresh twist of becoming we may have contributed to the future feeds the Spider Goddess, becoming in her body—which is to say, the world—substance from which to spin new worlds.

Being Private/Being Public

"Nothing but myself?" With all this talk of relation, of connection, of interdependence and the immanence of the world, have we lost sight of solitude? In our critique of the separative pseudoself, have we forgotten that for all their dangers, autonomy, independence and self-sufficiency designate values indispensable to freedom and creativity? When we affirm the social nature of the self and the communitarian fiber of all being, does collectivism threaten to wash out any real individuality? In our indivisibility from the universe, do we forfeit privacy?

Sheer publicity, or absolute community, would produce not interconnection but conformity. While the warrior ethos of separative individualism continues its build-up, we behold at the same time the spectacle of proliferating chain restaurants and businesses, multinational monopolies, copycat condominiums, computer consciousness and the televized terror of mass stereotypes: all evidence of homogenized consciousness and precisely not of social awareness. But since we have claimed that the individualism of the separate ego directly countermands the bona fide individuality of connectedness, this state of affairs is not as paradoxical as it might seem. The rugged individualist, the cowboy hero, who, missing the momentary ownership of the universe that we can claim for (as) our selves, is the ultimate conformist: he is locked into mere repetition of his own past selves, into a defensive sameness that will finally take refuge in the massive sameness of totalitarian social structures (whether of the capitalist or the communist variety). The wandering hero becomes No-one, after all.

But still the question remains: how does solitude survive the sociality of the web? What of the sense of self as "one's own," as being "on one's own"? Feminism has everything to lose in any reaction against individualism, in any suppression of solitude. Remember the mother whose days may pass without any waking minute to herself. Remember the maiden possessed by mass images of beauty, seeking her fulfillment in a self-forfeiting love. And remember the crone, the mature woman cast without any preparation, any respect, into an involuntary isolation too lonely to count as creative solitude. Women, trapped by their own relational propensities in situations of isolation from each other and the public world, succumb to what the Greeks called "idiocy"—the state of being private, noncivic individuals. Woman has been the household idiot. In her domestic captivity she endures both a depriving privacy and a confining connectivity. Moving into wider and wilder dimensions of relation, we certainly do not want to adopt any philosophy that would leave out that "room of one's own" before most of us have even got one. So how can we weave an ample solitude into the love bonds of a web?

To cite Whitehead again: "the vast causal independence of contemporary occasions is the preservative of the elbow-room within the universe." [20] In a world without walls, elbowroom becomes indispensable. Perhaps this is akin to the Heideggerian notion of "clearing," the *Lichtung,* where Being comes to light. Respecting moment to moment such clearings, love becomes freedom rather than manipulation. Yet we are not then separate beings living side by side (I am who I am, you are who you are, and if we happen to meet, it's beautiful) merely respecting each other's independence. Liberated as that ideal may sound, it recapitulates the hollow dualism of selves and others, lifting up a solitude without interconnection—a sterile parody of relation. In terms of couples, this is the parallel line theory—they can only touch from the outside.

Here Whitehead is again helpful: "It is the definition of contemporary events that they happen in causal independence of each other." While proposing a philosophy in which everything is part of everything else, he nonetheless insists that there is no direct influence exercised by one actual entity upon any exactly contemporary actual entity. "The mutual independence of contemporary occasions lies strictly within the sphere of their teleological self-creation . . . via the immanence of the past and the immance of the future, the occasions are connected. But the immediate activity of self-creation is separate and private, so far as contemporaries are concerned." [21] Is this a solipsistic system after all? Is there no immediacy of connection to the others? Certainly these criticisms can and have been made. But without something like this elbow-room for self-creation, would not a biological and sociological density of relations crowd out any individual sense of purposeful activity? As the operation of final causes (purposes), teleology is traditionally distinguished from the operation of efficient causes. Efficient causation accounts for the actual influence of an occasion upon another, which we have analyzed as internalization through feeling, that is, as the internal relations of beings to each other. Daly, drawing on that telic dimension of Aristotle which Whitehead also resurrects, defines final causality for women as "our innately ordained Self-direction toward Happiness." [22] Such self-direction, not to be confused with an ego's control, cannot occur outside the moment of privacy. Thus relationships where privacy is violated strangle in a pseudointimacy in which there is nothing new to share.

By "causal contemporaries" Whitehead means something very

precise: not just you and me, living at the same time in history, nor me and the person in the next room, as I write this. Rather, he refers to me and you at precisely the same split second. By the next moment, I am another, and the one I was has influenced the process of the person next to me. I have been influenced by everything in my world up to this immediate moment; after this moment, what I will have become can causally affect everything subsequent. But what goes on within this solitary *now?* Here occurs what was called concrescence—"becoming concrete," that self-realization based on creative contrasts between the actual and the possible, by which the many are woven into one complete experience. Here the momentary self accomplishes its integrity, though the ongoing person is never finished. Here something new can come to light—for the purely possible constitutes, in relation to actuality, the source of all novelty. Weaving together the contrasting fibers of experience does not produce a mere recombination of what has gone before; the primal empathy by which the past is spun into present feeling is necessary but not yet enough. Only a unique twist of perspective, a fresh pulse of subjectivity, makes something new. What I receive from the other becomes a breakthrough, an insight, for *me,* only as it resonates in this split second of solitude.

Such ontological solitude has little to do with quantity of time alone. The teleological process goes on always and anywhere. We might ignore it through weeks of aloneness, or know it in an instant amidst a crowd. But what we intuit in the momentary microcosm of self might come to shape longer-term life practices (such as immersion in nature or art, discipline of bodily movement, silent meditation or prayer, journalling or dream-analysis). We may need periodically to enter into literal solitude in order to attune ourselves to the moment of solitude always occurring. Then such retreat functions (as so-called feminist separatism often does) to intensify our conscious cooperation with the purposefulness at the heart of our reality.

Yet in and through our solitude, we are constantly influencing each other, for good and ill, perpetually echoing and mimicking and feeling each other. Imagine the two snakes intertwining to form the hermetic caduceus, the copula of being. But if I can hold in awareness the knowledge that the one I am taking into myself has already passed away—into me and the future at large—a sense of mystery sets in. Who are the *you* now, not yet settled, not *yet?* While I take you in, as you were an instant ago, you there now are new, uncontrolled, unpredictable. While what you are becoming comes out of all that you have known—much of which may be *my* selves, which you have felt into you—you will have done something of your own with all that material. You will have taken my energies and made something of them, which will then flow back into (a now different) me, *as* different. Without the strength of solitude, the second law of thermodynamics, the law of the wasting away of energy, would soon hold good. In much relating, entropy seems to become the rule: the failure to connect and to create boldly with the influent energies of others whose otherness is respected—be those others human, zoological, botanical or geological. Much socializing avoids solitude, losing selfhood and otherness in comfortable companionship. The more we truly take in, the more *prima materia* is available for the alchemies of solitude. And by the same token, the more creative the concrescence, the less predictable, controllable and merely dispersable will be our subsequent occasions of self.

Being social, I am other; being solitary, I am self; being social, I am multiple; being solitary, I am becoming one. And I am both private and public every moment. Indeed, the inseparable poles of community and aloneness sustain the creative tension of every moment's experience

The creative process is rhythmic: it swings from the publicity of many things to the individual privacy; and it swings back from the private individual to the publicity of the objectified individual. (The former swing is dominated by the final cause, which is the ideal; and the latter swing is dominated by the efficient cause, which is actual.)[23]

I take in the past world in its publicity; I own it in my present privacy; I let myself go, released to the public future.

Thus the spider-self cannot devour the true other, the contemporary; she feeds on their objectified selves shed like skins. "Life feeds on life," but the moment of sheer immediacy is inviolate. You in your immediacy are mystery, surprise, Thou, to me, as I am to you. This solitude, swinging rhythmically from community and back to community, does not detract from interpersonal intimacy, social responsibility, or political action. Far from the "idiocy" of the irresponsible self, it enables critical and creative *response* rather than knee-jerk *reaction*. Only the cultivation of such solitude seems to generate enough energy and vision for social transformation.

Whitehead claims that "religion is what the individual does with his [sic] own solitude;"[24] but it is also true that religion is a thoroughly social phenomenon. This is because what I *do* with my solitude is no longer solitary. The individual in her solitary freedom knows herself at once undefined by any particular relation and inseparable from an infinitely extended community. In the solitary space accompanying all relation, a sort of metarelation occurs. In the encounter of any I with any Thou, as Buber tells it, a Third is always present. That is, if I genuinely encounter the other, in the reverberating intersection of being—as social and as solitary—comes another presence. In the sheer mystery of the other whose spontaneity eludes me, even as I nourish myself on that other's immediate pasts, I sense the irreducible mystery, the Final Cause, the Eros, the Spider Goddess her(my)Self. In the webbed vision, no deity controls, or even foreknows, our destinies; any such divine element in the universe remains, like ourselves, at once the Weaver and the Woven. Such an Other of Others is also Self of Selves, an image of cosmic community and soulful solitude, the most inclusively social and the most wholly integral being.

Being Body/Being Soul

Integrity: "to spin and weave in the same action / from her own body, anywhere- . . ."[25]

The integrity of the connective self is many in its oneness and one in its manyness, public in its privacy and private in its publicity. We have earlier examined how a certain rhythmic continuity between the moments of such a self generates a living soul—a person. But how is such soulfulness *embodied*? Surely not in the sense that the soul is a preexistent essence that assumes flesh like a temporary costume. Philosophical myths of the fall teach that we tumble downward into flesh, into finitude; that without our bodies we would be infinite; that our bodies—and especially female bodies—are either the cause or the result of alienation, heaviness, and separation. Bodies are cumbersome lumps of matter that weigh us down and divide us.

But if it is true, that "everything is in a certain sense everywhere," then bodies need not obey the conventions of fixed time and simple space. To the contrary: "We have come to forget the feel of our own skin. Removed from our skin, we remain distant. You and I, apart." [26] This experience of the skin is beautifully evoked by Robin Morgan's "thin rainbow—colored nets, like cobwebs, all over my skin." Our skin does not separate—it connects us to the world through a wondrous network of sensory awareness. This is not to say the "spider's genius" is skin deep. From iridescent surface sensations to those profound emotions experienced in the heart, gut or groin, personhood is thoroughly enfleshed. As soul is embodied, body is ensouled—alive with a tremendous history and a tremulous sensibility. But even more—through my senses I go into the world, and the world comes into me. It is precisely in embodiment that the many are becoming one and the outer becoming inner. Our world feelings—called by Whitehead prehensions, or "physical feelings"—spin themselves into the fine, distinct fibers from which a self is woven into the tapestry of its world. However deprived of creative resources, we share with the spider the skill to create not from nothing but from our bodies. Procreation is only one creative bodily possibility. If I do not put this body out, treating it as external to myself, it and it alone lets me work whatever I take in into something strong with soul, honest with emotion, subtle with insight.

Shall we claim our bodies as our selves? *Are* our bodies ourselves? Are our selves something separate from our bodies? Certainly the body has been a prime target for exclusion by the separatist self, especially in its Platonic and Cartesian incarnations: self, identifying itself with mind or soul, has separated itself from its own flesh, as the first step in its disconnection from its environment. Certainly denigrating the body has been virtually indistinguishable from oppressing women. As feminist theory has abundantly documented, woman from the beginning of patriarchy has been characterized as the carnal Other. If he has been spirit, she has been flesh; if he has been immortal soul, she has been his mortal temptation. But in response to the man-mind/woman-body dualisms, feminism has itself tended to bifurcate in its strategies.

On the one hand we have had to protest the view that our anatomy is our destiny; we have had to argue that we are every bit as spiritual and rational as men; that our more dramatic physicality, with its cycles, its radical metamorphoses, its childbearing and feeding apparatus, only subtracts from our capacities for reason and creation when we are limited by cultural conditions. When women's true vocation is defined as motherhood, then of course the social and psychic situation will abort her other potentialities. But in denying the sexist identification of women with their bodies feminism has sometimes succumbed to an implicit dualism, overstressing that we are *not* our bodies, that our sexuality in no way defines our selves, that we are as free of physicality as men. Indeed women have reason to be wary of all rhapsodic enthusiasm about the female body, even when it comes from other feminists. The romanticizing of feminine bodiliness is only the other side of its debasement: two different ways to reduce our subjective freedom, our transcendent humanity, to the mechanics of our biology.

But other feminists have emphasized that to liberate women, we must not liberate ourselves *from* the body, but rather liberate the body itself. Such feminists refuse to experience the body as a deterministic, confining mechanism or as a source of inertia and stagnation. They read the rhythms of our life-blood, the periods of our lives, the energies of our animality, as primary sources of meaning and spirituality. The body's wisdom must be rediscovered, its finitude not resented but respected, its female particularity felt not as a trap but as a talent—to be actualized, like other talents, according to our freedom and the realistic possibilities of the situation. Maternity, whether actualized or not, symbolizes the nondualistic connection of self and other. But since the repudiation of physicality is essential to the dualistic-hierarchical thinking that defines patriarchy, such feminists may tend to react in the direction of an identification of self and body.

We can neglect neither strand of feminist emphasis; yet either can, if polarized, lead to reactionary consequences. Any dualistic assertion that our bodies are separate from our selves, external to what we essentially are, emulates the typically andromorphic model of transcendent disembodiment. But when the celebration of our bodiliness leads to a simple identification of self and body, in which there can be nothing about us that is not flesh, we have succumbed to classical materialism. And materialism, from Democritus' atomism through scientific mechanism, sociobiology or Marxism, remains as thoroughly patriarchal an option as dualism: its monistic reductions have no more room for the interrelation of mind and body, and their mutual transformation, than does dualism.

Can we affirm at once that we *are* body yet that we are not identical with body? That our body is itself soulful, and so never merely material? Then how shall we reconceive the body itself? For we cannot keep the same old mechanically physical husk and then add to it a soul for animation. Can we claim something not unlike the Thomist organon, the body thoroughly informed by its soul, without acquiescing in the substantialist separation of individual soul-body organisms from each other?

Perhaps one key lies in the cosmological context of body, letting us ground body in our fundamental connection with our worlds. Arguing for the "withness of the body," Whitehead makes body the starting point for our experience of the "circumambient world": we see *with* our eyes and not merely through them; we hear *with* our ears and not only by means of them. In all acts of perception, we are feeling-our-body-feeling-the-world; we feel the world in and through the body and not—as traditional philosophy has argued—only in the final, clear and distinct translations of sensory impulses by the brain. "The body, however, is only a peculiarly intimate bit of the world."[27] To *selve* this world is to *own* it: "my process of being myself is my origination from my possession of the world." The body then is my special corner of the cosmos; my relation to my body will reflect and rehearse my relationship to everybody and everything else. For I encounter the world only as embodied. Through my bodiliness I come to the animating knowledge that the energy of matter and the energy of soul are at base indistinguishable. Soul *matters*.

For the webbed vision, body and soul are not static substances but entire societies. The actual occasion of self summarizes at any moment both the strand of personal moments that generates our soul and the complex community that makes up our physical body: "The claim to the unity of the soul is analogous to the claim to the unity of the body, and analogous to the claim to the unity of body and soul, and is analogous to the claim to the community of the body with any external nature."[28] That is, the unity is a complex and open one, a composite. Whitehead's metaphysical strategy regarding the mind-body problem determines his redefinition of "physical" and "mental": every actual individual is at once physical and mental, whether that individual is a cell of muscle tissue or a moment of soul. The "physical pole" now means that which enters the occasion from the past—the influence of my own personal history and of the world. Physicality in this sense is deeply akin to memorability: being re-membered in the constitution of my present occasion, the entire past serves as my matter, the physical stuff of which I compose myself. What then is mentality? It is the pole that feels the purely possible, the future. The interaction of the past with the possible takes place, we have seen, in the privacy at the heart of the moment, where subjectivity brews up a fresh event. But according to this recipe, body and soul each have at any moment both a physical and a mental pole. Cartesian dualism is overcome not by a simplistic identification of body and mind / soul, but by a complex vision of the physical world: it has the heaviness of the entire past— from my immediately contiguous past to the reaches of a collective unconscious, perhaps—but not the dead weight of a machine or an inert lump. Rather, the lump comes always already leavened by the possible. The lightness of soul, the metamorphic butterfly-psyche, derives from its own specialized concentration on the possible. Yet soul's own past, the depth by which it is soul and not only the immediate subject-self, streams into the present via its own physicality, its own prehensions of the previous.

The better to feel this soulful physicality, let us turn once again to the metaphor of the child. In Jung's discussion of the child archetype, he claims that fantasies—the content of soul—are *real* (despite the bias of materialist science) and that "in the last analysis the human body, too, is built of the stuff of the world, the very stuff wherein fantasies become visible; indeed, without it they could not be experienced." This casts an intriguing light on the process idea of the physical/mental character of every unit of experience (i.e., every self). Without body, no soul? "The symbols of the self arise in the depths of the body and they express its materiality every bit as much as the structure of the perceiving consciousness. . . . 'At bottom,' the psyche is simply 'world.'" Jung then claims that "the more archaic and 'deeper,' that is the more *physiological* the symbol is, the more collective and universal, the more 'material' it is."[29] The child archetype in particular reveals this material matrix, this matter/*mater*, from which all psychic differentiation takes its rise.

We may presume that the psychic or physical abuse of children accompanies a denial of the soulfulness of our bodies and of the bodiliness of our souls. That preoedipal child we sought in chapter 3 recalls us to our first emergence from the dark of a bodily womb and the dark of psychic unconsciousness, where memory cannot penetrate. And it reveals also the birth of the self at any moment as physical/mental, as embodied and ensouled, and as new, for all its ancient memories. Depending upon what sort of relation to the soul-child has shaped itself in us, its impulses will provoke in us either a disconcerting or promising awareness of our rhythmic momentariness.

In her moving analysis of pornography as symptom of the mind-body dichotomy, Susan Griffin makes a powerful connection between the oppression of women and of children:

> The obsession of the pornographer with the unformed body
> of a child virgin. The girl kidnapped and sold into sexual
> slavery. The young woman accused of witchcraft and
> burned. In the holocaust babies torn from their mothers'
> hands and murdered, young women seduced, used, delivered
> of early pregnancies or dying in abortions, the child who is
> raped or abused.
> There is a thread in the mind of this culture which ties to-
> gether all these acts of violence to minds and bodies of chil-
> dren and young women. For the calculated use of a not yet
> grown woman's body in pornographic poses is part of cul-
> ture's symbolic murder of all that is childlike in our souls.
> When we love a child, we love human nature before it has
> been reshaped by culture.[30]

The subversive innocence of the prepatriarchal-preoedipal child, the child not yet turned against its mother, already fearful of its father and conformed to the patterns of male dominance and female humiliation, leads us to the point where body and soul emerge fresh and together—neither identical nor separate. Griffin celebrates not only the body but also the soul, not for its traditional flight from body, but in its ability to accept—unlike ego—its own metamorphic fluidity: "The soul, which is the world, is infinite only because the soul is part of change. The soul accepts transience as part of being, and the soul is not separate from the earth."[31] The abuse of the soul-child, the rape of the soul-sister, literally and metaphorically enacts the separation of the physical from the mental, the body from the soul, the self from the world. Then the residue of a shrunken ego can erect the defensive edifice of its own immortality. In so doing, the self loses the sense of that unlimited bondedness which is unboundedness. It violently denies the rhythmic dying and living, the metamorphic openness, demanded by its own body and soul.

There are important consequences for gender identity to be traced out of the con-celebration of the physical and the psychical. Neither can make an exclusive claim upon selfhood. It would no longer be possible to construe a self's identity, as male or female, in terms of hormonal mechanics, muscle size or reproductive functions: the body itself, in each of its "functions," is indefinitely variable, never a mechanism unless treated as one. The emotional meaning of each physical act—the body's soulfulness—shades into a thousand nuances, a thousand possibilities. The position that we are nothing but body has as its opposite the argument that we are separate from our bodies. But these are not such different positions, after all: the "nothing but" attitude (William James), like the dualism, denigrates the body. To call gender difference nothing but physiology dismisses our bodily base as so much oppressive matter (matricide again) to be transcended by a disembodied self. But personality cannot be reduced to the physical if the physical is itself irreducible—a field of energy and knowledge that we may draw into consciousness and transformation or that we may repress, suppress, control and deny.

The cyclic patterns of female bodiliness, disclosing sometimes a radiant extensity, sometimes an inward intensity, bind us to no stereotype. Our bodies are complex rhythms of energy open to endless variations, sometimes as the foreground, sometimes the background of our conscious dramas. Such possibilities as pregnancy, or childbirth and breast-feeding do not compel us to their literal actualization, their mystification or their defensive suppression. That women are built of a complex architecture of openings and enclosure need not lock us into domestic "inner space," vulnerability needing male protection. We experience the interplay of openness and hiddenness at every level of our being. Images of primordial goddesses evoke a memory of sacred power, streaming up through a pride of body.

As women reclaim our bodies as our own, we can begin to imagine a new male sense of body. As men learn to respect the woman's bodily ownness, they may also inaugurate gentler connections to their own bodies. Then the phallus can serve as an instrument of connection rather than conquest. Whether sexually enacted or not, the masculine interplay of vulnerable exposure and startling meta-morphosis, of the vigorous drive to penetrate, yet to receive as well—these body energies could support projects of soulful social-ity rather than of separative opposition.

The transformations of body into soul and soul into body—we can only begin to sense the consequences for postpatriarchal feeling and thought. For now "We need to imagine a world in which every woman is the presiding genius of her own body." [32] And for all persons we can hold to the irreducible self, fully ensouled, fully embodied.

Being Here/Being Now

"Under all these artificial constraints of time and space, I embrace you endlessly. Others may make fetishes of us to separate us: that's their business. Let's not immobilize ourselves in these borrowed notions." [33] Irigaray seems to imply that space and time are themselves an external grid of barriers imposed by patriarchy. Certainly if space works more or less as a vacuum in which I am here at this point alone, and everything else is isolated in its proper place, space indeed seems to prevent our overlapping (except, perhaps, in sexual acts and pregnancy). The body, in the conventional view of space, embodies its particular place, no more, no less, and brings home to us our isolation. And to the extent that time denotes a line made of points, a single one of which I occupy now, temporality isolates me from past and future, in the solitude of a pure present.

But what if I only encounter you live in the transitions between the tenses? The ego which pinpoints itself in an isolated present eclipses its own connections. Time worked into a line along which I move from present to present, immobilizes me in an unyielding present—a present that moves like a train along a track, but does not *become*. In Kant's parlance, space and time are the a priori intuitions of human subjectivity. But if these primary intuitions have become modes of isolation, we discern in their formation not a priori necessities but androcentric priorities. The mechanical common sense view of space as vacuum and time as line establishes a universe of separate and enduring individuals: individuals absolutely different from each other, absolutely the same as themselves.

Early on, Western temporality had straightened itself into the linearity of a beginning and an end, a creation and an apocalypse, to produce a dramatic sense of history. But biblical eschatology, merging with Greek atemporalism, finally contorted itself into the quantified temporality of a mechanistic science and a triumphalist progressivism. Here immobility feigns dynamism: yet that which progresses, grows or changes along a rigid time line remains essentially the same and only externally related to all the other entities in space, moving on their parallel but separate time tracks.

Must the connective self then come to be outside of space and time? Is it connected to all other places and times in such a way as to obliterate spatiotemporal differentiation? Do women's cyclic rhythms turn in the circle of a timeless present? Do women's bodies, combining openness and enclosure, publicity and privacy, obviate the particularity of place? To these questions the answer is emphatically, no! Postpatriarchal selves do not aspire to timeless displacement. We do not abandon history and the earth. Rather, we seek a radically different spatio-temporal sensibility—one that turns out to be more fully spatiotemporal than the traditional artifice of the space-time grid would allow: an embrace that spans time and space. Here Whitehead's use of Einsteinian relativity theory will serve us well: referring both to spatial and temporal location, he postulates as his "ontological principle" that "everything is positively somewhere in actuality, and in potency everywhere."[34] That is, to be is to be somewhere, at a particular place and a particular time; but somewhere is in a certain sense everywhere. This thought is not as paradoxical as it might seem. It follows from the axiom that anything is what it is in relation to everything else, that a self is No-one if not in spatio-temporal relation to everything in its world. To be "in potency everywhere" means to be a potential in the becoming of all subsequent actualities, to be becoming a new one, contributing to the plenum of the many. The contrary opinion, which makes time and space out to be a fixed grid inside of which entities are simply and clearly here or there, nowhere else than exactly where they are, and independent of everything else in their placement, Whitehead has dubbed "the fallacy of simple location." I suggest that this fallacy represents a particular recrudescence of the phallocentric illusion of independence. Simple location in time and space, while only formulated in full force by the mechanistic theo-

ries of the seventeenth century, formally reinforces a sense of isolation in an emptiness of space and of defense against time and its
influency.

Relativity and quantum physics point beyond the experience of
an isolated observer viewing an atomized universe supported by an
absolute axis of space and time. Physicist David Bohm designates
the new form of insight implicit in twentieth-century science as
"Undivided Wholeness in Flowing Movement:"[35] quite a metaphor
of our fluidly cosmic integrity! But one is disappointed, though
hardly surprised, to learn that within mainline physics the old
mechanistic thought patterns have hardly budged. According to
Bohm, aspects of physics demanding the primacy of an interactive,
flowing holism are de-emphasized, "regarded largely as features of
the mathematical calculus and not as indications of the real nature
of things." Scientists "still speak and think, with an utter conviction
of truth, in terms of the traditional atomistic notion that the universe is constituted of elementary particles which are the 'basic
building blocks' out of which everything is made."[36]

"Undivided Wholeness in Flowing Movement" well expresses
women's elemental intuitions of space and time (if not that of most
theorists), springing from a primordial sense of "the real nature of
things" and of ourselves. We begin to see how women's fluidity can
issue not in a vague deliquescence, but in a more accurate orientation within the relativistic universe. "These streams," says Irigaray
of the de-solidified woman, "are without fixed boundaries. This
unceasing mobility . . . All this remains very strange to anyone
claiming to stand on solid ground." The relativity of our stand-
points in space-time must feel like a metaphysical seasickness to
anyone claiming to stand on the solid ground of some distinguishable absolute. "But so much has been said, and said of us, that
separates us," continues Irigaray. She suggests we need "our own
phrases," free of the linguistically transmitted preconceptions
which fragment. "So that *everywhere* and *always* we can continue
to embrace" (my emphasis).[37]

It is not clear that there is anything that *is* which is not a process
of spacing and timing. To speak of transcending time only surren-
ders temporality to the mechanics of the clock. Why not think of
an infinite range of temporal rhythms and cadences, some of which
our present body-souls can hold more in awareness than others?
And why should we think of transcending space? Every place im-

plicates every other place. Perhaps we cannot yet enfold in consciousness our own omnipresence. But we can start here, now.

What of spacing? We know that women have been immobilized as home bases for the heroic work and wanderings of the patriarch; we know that women have been trapped in homes, lavishing on them their aesthetic talents, becoming homemakers rather than worldmakers, or rather making liveable *cosmoi* out of our confinements. We know that we have been labeled "empty holes waiting to be filled" (Sartre) and "the inner space" (Erikson). Men, on the other hand, have been caught outside themselves in an apparently unbearable vulnerability, roving, restless, seeking defense from other males and temporary shelter within the female. Failing to own their immediate worlds and to release them reconfigured, men long ago resorted to material ownership, to the literal division of place into private properties, leaving the public places to deteriorate to the state of unsurpassed ugliness now typical of urban American space. Those who can afford to, spring from one island of affluence to another—from house to car to restaurant—trying to ignore what lies between. The contemporary landscape confronts us mercilessly with the neglect of our connections, the exploitation of our between-places.

What of postpatriarchal place? We can only hint at directions for cultivating a new sensibility of self in space, and of self as space.[38] For we must get away from the assumption that space is a sort of empty vessel (like the traditional view of the womb) that one is inside of. Space only comes to be through events of relationship: it is nothing but a way of speaking about the plenitude of relations *between* beings. Space (as Kant revealed) is constituted by subjective structures of spatiality—yet not (as Kant meant) by fixed, a priori, categories of intuition. I literally create my space. We can learn to think and feel space as qualitative and full. According to the physicists, there exists no empty space; space seems to be more like a continuum of greater and lesser densities of matter/energy. Metaphysically, "the continuum is present in each actual entity, and each actual entity pervades the continuum."[39] Since the connective self no longer admits any simple distinction of inner and outer, space cannot be left outside of us. Our processes of becoming are events of self-spacing. Yet space is the structure of relation.

Consider our language: some people share my space, others violate it. I retreat to a peaceful place in myself. I space out, or need some space. I try to understand "where you're at," where you are "coming from." Such spatialization need not signal (as Henri Bergson would fear) the further objectification of our subjectivity; we may instead be subjectifying space. These are helpful new metaphors for soul-states, activities of relation to self and others, but they are no no mere figures of speech. Think how vital place is to relationship—*where* we are when we talk. Consider the inexhaustible delight children take in hiding places, in special spaces like tents built under tables or tree houses, in clambering over boulders on a rocky shore, or in playing house. The playful plasticity of place: does it return for us as we bear the soul-child? Will our bodies not guide us, if we let them, to postpatriarchal space? There we are not separate from any other being, but empowered by being "in potency" everywhere, differentiated by becoming right here.

And what of timing? We know that woman has borne the brunt of man's fear of his own finitude: women have lived in dread of wilting. Because man makes his mirror of woman, her sags and wrinkles horrify him with the specter of his own mortality. By replacing her with younger substitutes, he displaces time. Fearful of our bodies' irrepressible time-rhythms, we try to fit into the time-schemes of the work-world, set up to accommodate ego-production and soul-reduction. But we feel somehow out of place in this artificial time. If the male ego feels mocked by time—because it finally refuses his control?—woman bears the brunt of his ire. Afraid of our natural time-rhythm, women are often habitually late, rebelling against the lockstep of patriarchal clock time; just as often we are early, too eager to please.

In fathered time—the tidily Man-Dated World—fixers/timers destroy diversity of Timing by routinized reductions to beats that repeat themselves, eat our Selves. Male-ordered monotony iterates/reiterates rigidly regulated days that daze, breaking biorhythms, barring its victims from finding/minding Crone-ology. By its counterfeit Crone-ology, called 'chronology,' clockocracy prematurely ages potential Sages, preventing Cronehood.[40]

The very cadences of Daly's prose-poetry (itself violating patriarchal boundaries) disrupt the monotonous timing, the repetitive thinking that beats out the texts of our tradition.

Whoever controls the terms controls the timing, and vice versa: note the power-plays of scheduling—the busier-than-thou maneuver. The tempos of andromorphic school-time, work-time, play-time have created a cosmic inertia that stifles past and future in its tedium. Our world's endless array of imposed and dysrelational deadlines deadens creativity and turns time into tyranny. The past is forgotten, and so it repeats itself: conformity rather than memory. The future is feared, and so we plan for apocalypse: annihilation rather than anticipation.

Repetition is precisely the problem. Irigaray makes a related point, linking narcissism to the repetitive sameness of the phallocentric subject: "No need to fashion a mirror image to be 'doubled,' to repeat ourselves—a second time. . . . You will always have the touching beauty of a first time, if you aren't congealed in reproductions. You will always be moved for the first time, if you aren't immobilized in any form of repetition."[41]

Such "touching beauty"—able to embrace the other through any expanse of time and space—is not subject to the deterioration of age or the demotion of the crone under the regime of the ageless hero. Any moment is a first time—if we are not frozen in the mirrored masks of imitation and repetition. Moreover, repetition takes us to the heart of the metaphysical dilemma. In the terms of process thought, every feeling of the other, every prehension, in fact repeats that other; it conforms to it; it takes it in with a faithful empathy. Repetition constitutes the rhythmic pulse of all reality. But this is the receptive aspect of the moment: it then composes something *new* of this past, to the extent its creative aspect flourishes.

To the extent that it fails to weave the past into a present, in anticipation of the present's part in the enlarging web of the future—to that extent the subject fails its own self. Remember that in the last chapter we saw how the heroic ego, disowning its intimate connections with the world, seeks all the more fiercely to possess itself: an impossibility, if the timing of subjectivity is instantaneous. I cannot in one and the same moment be and have myself. I can only be myself by having the world. We saw how the ego can contrive the illusion of its own permanence by simply identifying itself with its own past selves rather than relating *to* them. It reduces itself as nearly as possible to repetitions of its own personal chain of experiences, thereby diminishing both the novel potentiality flowing in from the continuum of relations and the novel possibilities that might inspire more complex harmonies. In other words, by denying the radical momentariness of self and the fundamental fluidity of body and soul, its self-repetition is maximized and its newness minimized.

No wonder this ego despises maternity, mother-goddesses, childhood and everything that reminds it of "first times." It does not *want* first times, it wants the endurance of the same. The more repetitive it can remain, the more it can exclude influx of the different, the new, the world; the more it can deny its ontological feelings, and the more its sheer redundancy creates the narcissistic illusion of an immutable essence. It tries to stop time by sheer rigidity. The subject turns itself into its own object (or tries to) in emulation of a stone—the petrified hero hiding in marble monuments to his immortal glory. The Medusa-mother, who with her writhing snake hair resembles the spider and all things radiating out of bounds, mocks in her monstrosity not time but the timeless ego.

What is the self-timing of connective selves? They participate in the spirals of becoming and perishing, of micromoments and of monthly periods, of moon cycles and solar rounds, of daily and seasonal metamorphosis. The complex continuum—not the simple line—of a flow of events finally excludes no moment of human history nor any wriggle of worm or burst of star in its timing; through this continuum the groundswell of the past empowers the present. The present self may adjust the tempo to its own desire, but first I meet these complex rhythms as an immanent choreography. They cannot be evaded. If, however, I move consciously with the wider dance of nature and history, I may find the knots of my personal compulsions, my patterns of mistiming, easing into an ampler grace.

The future? It is already there, *as* future, that is, not as predetermined, but as probability or possibility. The present pregnant with the future does not know that future as any fait accompli; it does not foreclose, does not control, does not subscribe to the ontology of insurance policies. Yet this future is neither a gaping abyss, God (as the contemporary German theologians Pannenberg and Moltmann would have it), or The End. We can feel the future forming in ourselves now, for this my present self will be endlessly taken up and reiterated. The future will—if only to the most trivial degree—feel this present. My soul, my body, my world: ongoing, they will have to take me in. So if I learn to feel the subtle movement from past to present, I may begin to discern the transformation of vast relational patterns, personal and social, as they roll through my present. But we cannot—and neither can any God or Goddess—foreknow or control the future. It is by definition not yet. However well we read the portents and the promises, neither divinity nor humanity can extinguish the spontaneities with which future presents will self-create. The heroic ego feels thwarted by the uncontrollability of the future. Instead of his time-paranoia, we may learn a new time-trust. Time is the dynamism of relation.

This seems all rather vast. Let us recall the particularity of timing—that timing is ever of the essence, that a friendship, a desire, an interest, a decision that is not possible right now may become possible at another time. The content may remain quite identical: the timing literally makes the difference. For with every moment, the self becomes another. It comes to be a *different* self. And if I can live with the light, butterfly continuity of soul, and the amassed, changing commune of body, forfeiting the rigid self-identities of the ego, I become not less but more responsible. Rhythmically entraining with my world, I can *respond* to its desires. I become ever more skillful in the space-time dance of self with other, of same with different, of here with there. Freed really to *feel* the others in their claims upon my future, I will need neither to tense up in defensive rebellion against their influence nor to comply in self-aborting imitation of their impulses. Moving in synchronism with others, community is created and communication not only relays information but effects transformation.

The emergence of community out of the implicit sociality of selves is a matter of timing. Consider examples of shared life rhythms, where empathy and freedom must intertwine to generate intimacy. The skills of intimacy and communication, as well as politics and confrontation, are matters of timing. But we see that self-timing and self-spacing are inseparable processes: as I create space, I am also creating time. To say "I need some space," seems hardly distinguishable from "I need some time:" Whether I have time (in the midst of the busiest of schedules) is a function of whether I create it. And this creativity is a matter of taking in the world—and expanding it from the inside out. Such elaboration is my contribution to world-space. As I flow into my next moment of self, I *take place:* I am a space-time event. These "drops of experience" (James) have nothing to do with clocks or maps: they are the organic timespaces that come to be as the essence of our self-composition.

"A wild patience has taken me this far"—a distance as much of time as of space, and measurable only in selves. The organic interactions of timing and spacing—sometimes feeling mistimed and misplaced, sometimes feeling right on time and right in place—are what I am. How far I have come cannot be counted in years and miles. What counts is only the incalculable integrity of what I am becoming. As the many become one, and many again, as the public becomes private, and public again, as the physical becomes the mental, and physical again, space becomes time, and space again. Space and time have everything to do with the relational self—for space and time are nothing in themselves. They are nothing but metaphors with which we describe the relations between beings. We connect, all of us, spaciously, timefully.

Divining the Web

"Be what you are becoming, without clinging to what you might have been, what you might yet be," says Irigaray, thus reversing Nietzsche's "Become what you are." We can no more return to the past than we can control the future. Only a self forged in the image of an impenetrable inner hardness, mistaken for integrity, could separate itself from the matrix of all life. Without clinging to the others or to our own past and future selves, we can connect and reconnect in freedom: there is so much to remember, to reread, to revision, to redeem. There is always the world, coming in: its immanence. We make something of it, flowing out: our transcendence. Remembering in its work of immanence, of taking in and reconnecting, breaks into imagining, in its work of transcendence, of envisioning the possible.

We arise from the matrix; we redesign its elements; we are woven back into the matrix. This is the religious action of reconnecting. As the word itself tells us, matrix is always *mater,* mother. No inert matter here; there is no such thing. All beings come tied to the matrix of interconnection by what poet Judy Grahn calls "the one true cord, / the umbilical line / unwinding into meaning, / transformation, / web of thought and caring and connection." [42] In a matricidal civilization such as we have known for the extent of our textual history, the umbilical line is denied, ignored, violated, feared, and almost—catastrophically—severed. But even selves who declare their heroic freedom *from* the matrix, in place of freedom *within* the matrix, cannot kill it. The Spider Mother spins on. Tehom still undulates within and among us.

What do such disparate metaphors as the oceanic mother Tehom/Tiamat and the airy spider share, we might wonder? One goes deep, the other reaches wide. One is heavy, the other light. One takes in, the other creates. One embodies the tidal currents, belying opacity and separation. The other filigrees her body's substance into complex patterns of differentiation. Neither knows any hardness, any rigidity, in herself. Both express themselves with the fluency of interconnection. In their different dimensions and domains, both horrify the self-forgetting fixity of other-opposed egos. The sea monster *is* the dread, supressed face of the liquescent, the influent; the spider, in order to spin, extrudes viscous fluid from her body.

These are metaphors, demanding their own multiplicity of images: no single metaphor can be privileged as the truth, without forfeiting its own relational life. Many have pronounced the very metaphor "God" dead. Nelle Morton suggested above that identifying "God" with male rulership and control drained the life out of the image. I would only add that its competitive exclusivism, which resulted in the simple One, stifles imagination and so kills image at the source. For the unimagining, Deep and Spider seem ungodly.

Tapping the source freshly, Morton relates a late-life experience of metaphor which came to her as a vision:

Immediately on the right side of the window appeared an enormous spider with a gray body and orange legs. She lifted one leg high above the other as she walked toward me on the darkness. I was not afraid, somehow. As the spider reached me she held out her two front legs on which hung some woven material. All she said was, 'Your mother spun this for you.' As I took the material the spider dissolved into me, as did the Goddess and then my mother. I opened my eyes.[43]

Eye-opening in more ways than one, this arachnean epiphany offers an alternative vision, a complex discernment of the sacred and personal forces at work in us. The spider has a gift to offer: the mother's material, the transformation of matter into art, the "ancient skill." Nelle Morton experiences quite literally an infusion of grace, almost in the old Catholic sense—the wisdom, the energy and the images of the revelation flow into her, become her. Interestingly, the spider vision is multiple, indeed triune—a gynomorphic community of Goddess, Mother and Spider, three distinct persons revealing different facets of one reality. The reality of woman's Self? Certainly the triune Goddess symbolizes the Self of all women and, indeed, may lend men an indispensable link to their own deeper personality.[44] But if Goddess symbolizes Self, it is just as true that the Self incarnates Goddess.

The divine is always becoming flesh—what else does the Eros desire? Of course, stories of God becoming Man have eclipsed the revelation of Her becoming Woman. But now, in our becoming, vision begins slowly to clear.

A multiplicity of self-occasions "in flowing movement" naturally gives rise to a pluralism of vision itself. Thus Morgan, speaking for the archetypal spider-self: "Let me sit at the center of myself / and see with all my eyes."[45] The radical remembering of postpatriarchal religion disallows any monofocal vision. Reconnection requires polyscopic discernment. We can no more immobilize the divine element in the universe in the form of a single name, a single sex, a single code, creed or cult, than we can freeze the fluid transformations of the universe. A postpatriarchal perspective, expressing a self that is many in one, learns a limpid, diversifying discernment of all things dancing as many in one.[46] But all things together do not add up to a deity. Any simple pantheism, deifying the universe, might squelch profound possibilities of relation. For in community, in the matrix of interconnections private and public, we encounter a holiness of Self and Other that is irreducible to any one self or any one other. It has life—lives—of its own. Yet we cannot know this holiness—this elusive wholeness—directly. It calls us from the depth of ourselves, from where we are not ever yet conscious. Any being in the universe can be its metaphor. Such wholeness attunes us to a deep frequency of relation itself; yet in all our relations we also relate to this frequency. It is not simply the principle of relationship, for it is always becoming flesh, specific, unique. We relate *to* it when we relate to the metaphors that move us. From dreams and imaginings, myths and poems, straggling intuitions and clear perceptions, from all the stories we tell each other, the images emerge, resonating with the deep frequency. The divine Eros, the luring Love, frequents the world: its incarnations and revelations are never delivered once and for all. And as Spider, Goddess and Mother dissolved back into the one envisioning them, the images dissolve back into our selves. They are there to get embodied and ensouled, not literalized and idolized.

For now we will sidestep any theological conclusion, any final fix on the Wisdom that weaves the Web. Let us not tie up or tie down the ontological status of a deity: the arachnean religion requires us only to keep on tying *together*. The immanent Desire provokes our own transcendence, and no doubt transcends us in turn. Metaphors of self arise from, give rise to, the Self of all metaphors. All this, every moment. But let us at present try thinking not of some sub-stantialized divinity, but of our own process of *divining*. The Greek word for "divining" is *mantiké*, the oracular discernment over which the serpentine pythia once presided. This word, *mantic*, stems from the same root (*mens*, "mind") as does *mania*, the divine madness (by which the profane insanity of separation is overcome); *mens* is also the origin of *minna*, old German for love (the singing Eros) and of "memory" as the Mother of the Muses, Mnemosyne (whose inspiration holds it all together). And of course from this root springs the radical *monstrum* herself, the admonishing-remon-strating-demonstrating monster-mother who has been carrying us in her belly and spewing us out all along.

What patterns reveal themselves in the tensions, contradictions, and contrasts of the many becoming one in me? What in my public warp of relations, in my private woof of introspections, do I *divine*? Divining my own desire I make connection with yours; divining each others', we sense our own; and often only your divination of my truth divulges it to me. Feeling my feelings, and feeling among my feelings the feelings of all those to whom and to which I relate, I may tune in to the deeper frequency.

Such divining, we sense, is infinitely difficult. Some part of us would still like a parental God or god-person just to give us the answers. And because nothing stays quite the same, the metaphors and methods of our best discernment never work quite the same way a second time. But when we stop divining, even for a few mo-ments, we seem to forget ourselves, to drift toward solubility or separation, to lose connection. The recurrent patterns, the rhythmic continuities that constitute selves, allow only the loosest predictions. So this difficult process of divining requires genius: the spider's genius.

Such genius does not reside in a swollen IQ, but in heedful awareness, drawing on all of our innumerable senses. *Religio,* though etymologically stemming from the Latin "tying back together," has as its first dictionary meaning "careful observation." To divine is certainly a religious act, and its "genius" is our self to whatever extent we can claim our connections: our con-geniality. The word "genius," which translates the Greek *daemon,* a tutelary spirit or indwelling deity, dwells in everyone. Thus Daly calls women to reclaim our "tidal genius," the oceanic daemon (*demon* to the patriarchy) that will trespass all fixed shorelines. Oceanic depth and arachnean breadth: when we are what we are becoming, interfusing spaciously and intertwining timefully, feeding each other and exceeding ourselves, we will divine new signs and portents. The new *monstrum* demonstrates what is possible in and between our Selves.

Notes

ONE: *The Separate and the Soluble*

1. Simone de Beauvoir, *The Second Sex*, trans. H. M. Parshley (New York: Vintage Books, 1952), p. xix.
2. Ibid., p. 84.
3. However problematic the notion has become, androgyny has proved a valuable ideal for many feminists, pointing beyond the restrictions of gender stereotype to the cultivation of the full range of human capacities by both sexes. However, the very metaphor presupposes the recapitulation of stereotypical sex distinctions.
4. John R. Wikse, *About Possession: The Self as Private Property* (University Park: Pennsylvania University Press, 1977), p. 10.
5. Virginia Woolf, *The Waves*, in *Jacob's Room/The Waves* (New York: Harcourt, Brace and World, 1959), p. 270.
6. S. A. Kierkegaard, *The Concept of Irony*, trans. L. M. Capel (New York: Harper and Row, 1965), p. 234.
7. S. A. Kierkegaard, *The Sickness unto Death*, in *Fear and Trembling/The Sickness unto Death*, trans. Walter Lowrie (Princeton: Princeton University Press, 1968), pp. 200–203. The heroic energy of defiance emerges vividly in the account: "So the despairing self is constantly building nothing but castles in the air, it fights only in the air. All these experimental virtues make a brilliant showing . . . such self-control, such firmness, such ataxasia, etc. . . . and also at the bottom of it all there is nothing. The self wants to enjoy the entire satisfaction of making itself into itself" (p. 203).
8. Ibid., p. 183.
9. Valerie Saiving, "The Human Situation: A Feminine View," in *Womanspirit Rising: A Feminist Reader in Religion*, ed. Carol Christ and Judith Plaskow (San Francisco: Harper and Row, 1979), p. 37. Also see Sue Dunfee, "The Sin of Hiding: A Feminist Critique of Reinhold Niebuhr's Account of the Sin of Pride," *Soundings*, Fall 1982:316–27.
10. Kierkegaard, *The Sickness unto Death*, p. 183.
11. Maggie Scarf, *Unfinished Business* (New York: Ballantine, 1980), p. 417.
12. De Beauvoir, *The Second Sex*, p. xxxiv.
13. Ibid., p. xxxiii.
14. Ibid., p. 71.
15. Ibid., p. xxi.
16. Ibid., p. xix.
17. Ibid., p. xx.
18. Sigmund Freud, *Civilization and Its Discontents*, trans. James Strachey (New York: Norton, 1961), p. 60.

19. George Steiner, *In Bluebeard's Castle: Some Notes towards the Redefinition of Culture* (New Haven: Yale University Press, 1971), p. 52.

20. Jean Baker Miller, *Toward a New Psychology of Women* (Boston: Beacon Press, 1976), p. 124.

21. De Beauvoir, *The Second Sex*, p. 89.

22. Ibid., p. 22.

23. Ibid., p. 23.

24. Jacques Lacan, "The Signification of the Phallus," in *Écrits: A Selection*, trans. A. Sheridan (New York: Norton, 1977), pp. 281ff.

25. De Beauvoir, *The Second Sex*, p. 72.

26. For a discussion of the relative dignity of women in the sex-role diversified cultures of the hunter-gatherer, see Sally Slocum, "Woman the Gatherer: Male Bias in Anthropology," in *Toward an Anthropology of Women*, ed. Rayna Reiter (New York: Monthly Review Press, 1975), pp. 36–50.

27. Marija Gimbutas, *The Goddesses and Gods of Old Europe, 6500–3500 B.C.: Myths and Cult Images* (Berkeley and Los Angeles: University of California Press, 1982), p. i.

28. Ibid., p. 38.

29. Ibid., p. 9.

30. On the "mythological defamation" of goddesses, see Joseph Campbell, *The Masks of God: Occidental Mythology* (New York: Viking/Compass, 1965), p. 80; and chap. 2 of this book.

31. George Herbert Mead, *Mind, Self and Society: From the Standpoint of a Social Behaviorist* (Chicago: University of Chicago Press, 1934), p. 136.

32. Jean-Paul Sartre, *The Transcendence of the Ego*, trans. F. Williams and R. Kirkpatrick (New York: Farrar, Straus and Giroux, 1957), p. 40.

33. Ibid., pp. 41f.

34. *Odyssey*, Ch. XXII.

35. Alexandre Kojève, *Introduction to the Reading of Hegel*, trans. J. H. Nichols, Jr. (New York: Basic Books, 1969).

36. *Luther: Lectures on Romans*, ed. Wilhelm Panck, Library of Christian Classics (Philadelphia: Westminster, 1961), pp. 218ff. The editor suggests that Luther is referring to Isa. 2:7–22, which, however, is a diatribe against the proud and haughty, containing no metaphor of curvedness. Luther himself simply identifies egocentricity with pride.

37. Ibid., p. 219.

38. S. A. Kierkegaard, *Concluding Unscientific Postscript*, trans. D. Swenson and W. Lowrie (Princeton: Princeton University Press, 1941), p. 240.

39. Ibid., p. 239.

40. Ibid.

41. *Luther*, p. 262.

42. Kierkegaard, *Concluding Unscientific Postscript*, p. 122.

43. Holiness in Jewish and Christian traditions means "that which is set apart," "separate," by which the self finds itself only in the complete dependence of relation to an absolutely Other God. Cf. Drorah Setel, "Feminist Reflection on Separation and Unity in Jewish Theology" in *Journal of Feminist Studies in Religion*, Spring 1986. Cf. also my response, "The Cave on the Seashore."

44. Thomas Aquinas, *Summa Theologica* i: Q. 20, art. 1, ans. 1.

45. Ibid., Q. 21, art. 3, ans.

46. Ibid., Q. 20, art. 2, ans.

47. Anselm, Proslogium VI and VII, in *Proslogium; Monologium; An Appendix, In Behalf of the Fool*, by Gaunilon, and *Cur Deus Homo*, trans. S. N. Deane (Open Court Publishing Co., 1945), pp. 11, 13.

48. John B. Cobb and David R. Griffin, *Process Theology: An Introductory Exposition* (Philadelphia: Westminster, 1976), p. 45.
49. Mary Daly, *Gyn/Ecology: The Metaethics of Radical Feminism* (Boston: Beacon Press, 1978), p. 39.
50. Reinhold Niebuhr, *The Nature and Destiny of Man* (New York: Charles Scribner's Sons, 1964), p. 171.
51. Judith Plaskow, *Sex, Sin and Grace: Women's Experience and the Theologies of Reinhold Niebuhr and Paul Tillich* (Washington, D.C.: University Press of America, 1980), p. 151.
52. Ibid., p. 150.
53. Niebuhr, *The Nature and Destiny of Man*, p. 282.
54. Ibid., p. 17.
55. Ibid., p. 244.
56. Ibid., p. 282.
57. Ibid.
58. Ibid., p. 13.
59. John B. Cobb, Jr., *The Structures of Christian Existence* (New York: Seabury Press, 1979), p. 119.
60. Niebuhr, *The Nature and Destiny of Man*, p. 55.
61. Ibid., p. 55.
62. Ibid., p. 59.
63. Ibid., p. 126.
64. Sue Dunfee ("Sin of Hiding") suggests that his underdeveloped "sin of sensuality" could be amplified into what she calls the "sin of hiding," to render his thinking relevant to women. She is fully aware of the problematic spirit-body dualism implied by the term, however little Niebuhr means to denigrate bodiliness as such.
65. Harvey Cox, "In the Pulpit and on the Barricades," review of *Reinhold Niebuhr: A Biography* by Richard W. Fox, *New York Times Book Review,* Jan. 5, 1986, p. 24.
66. Virginia Woolf, *A Room of One's Own* (New York: Harcourt Brace, Jovanovich 1963), p. 35.
67. Marguerite Duras, "From an Interview," in *New French Feminisms,* ed. E. Marks and I. de Courtivron (New York: Schocken Books, 1981), p. 175.
68. Norman O. Brown, *Love's Body* (New York: Random House, 1966), p. 116. Also see Daly, *Gyn/Ecology,* p. 66, for her critique of Brown and the entire Christian tradition of "lose thyself in order to find thyself." Getting lost may get the male ego free of its self-enclosure, but what does it do for the too soluble female?
69. Daly, *Gyn/Ecology,* p. 395.

TWO: *Of Men and Monsters*

1. Aristotle, *Genesis of Animals,* 4:2, 767B5–15.
2. Aeschylus, *Eumenides,* pp. 574ff., 734ff.
3. Robert Graves, *The Greek Myths* (Middlesex: Penguin, 1955), 2:71.
4. Jane Harrison, *Themis: A Study of the Social Origins of Greek Religion* (Gloucester: Peter Smith, 1912), p. 500.
5. Aristotle, *Genesis of Animals,* 4:4, 735A14–16.
6. Aristotle, *Categories,* 2A11.
7. Aristotle, *Genesis of Animals,* 4:4, 735A14–16.
8. See chap. 1 on the intermingling of in-fluent selves.
9. *American Heritage Dictionary* (from which future references are taken unless otherwise indicated), W. Morris, ed. (Boston: Houghton Mifflin Company, 1981).

10. Hesiod, *Cosmogony,* trans. J. Banks (London: George Bell and Sons, 1897), 5:268.
11. Ovid, *Metamorphosis,* book 4, trans. Mary Innes (Middlesex: Penguin, 1955).
12. James Hillman, *The Dream and the Underworld* (New York: Harper and Row, 1979), p. 23.
13. James Hillman, *Re-Visioning Psychology* (New York: Harper and Row, 1975), p. 71.
14. Ovid, *Metamorphosis,* book 4.
15. Merlin Stone, *When God Was a Woman* (New York: Harvest/HJB, 1976), p. 199.
16. Joseph Campbell, *The Masks of God: Occidental Mythology* (New York: Viking Press, 1965), chap. 1.
17. See Gimbutas, *Goddesses and Gods of Old Europe.*
18. Campbell, *Masks of God,* p. 24.
19. Ibid., p. 21.
20. Stone, *When God Was a Woman,* p. 202.
21. Ibid.
22. Jane Harrison, quoted in Graves, *Greek Myths,* 1:46.
23. Gilbert Murray, *Five Stages of Greek Religion* (New York: Doubleday/Anchor, 1955), pp. 17f.
24. Ibid., p. 36.
25. Hesiod, *Cosmogony,* 1:890.
26. See Catherine Keller, "Swallowed, Walled and Wordless Women," *Soundings,* Fall 1982.
27. Myths and doctrines of rebirth almost invariably devalue birth through the natural mother in favor of rebirth through a spiritual father and thus glorify the principle of paternity. Thus feminism tends to avoid the very symbolism of rebirth. Yet there is nothing *intrinsically* patriarchal about intitiation and rebirth; they can be, and have been, conceived as metamorphosis in and through the power of the goddess.
28. Jean Shinoda Bolen, *Goddesses in Everywoman* (San Francisco: Harper and Row, 1984), p. 82.
29. Adrienne Rich, *Of Woman Born: Motherhood as Experience and Institution* (New York: Norton, 1979), p. 284.
30. See Daly's discussion of the "elemental passions" of anger, which has a cause, in contrast to "plastic passions" such as hostility, bitterness, and resentment; *Pure Lust* (Boston: Beacon Press, 1984), pp. 197–201.
31. Graves, *Greek Myths,* 2:38.
32. Erich Neumann, *The Great Mother: An Analysis of the Archetype* (Kingsport: Kingsport/Pantheon, 1963), p. 166.
33. Jocelyn M. Woodward, *Perseus: A Study in Greek Art and Legend* (Cambridge: Cambridge University Press, 1937), p. 39.
34. Because the terrors of the "Terrible Mother" come largely from deliberate suppression and unconscious repression of the archetype of the Mother Goddess, the terrible aspect must be secondary. But *archetype* means literally first or primordial imprint, the Terrible Mother is a contradiction in terms. The result of repression/suppression can only be secondary and derivative.
35. Emily Culpepper, "Ancient Gorgons: A Face for Contemporary Women's Rage," *Woman of Power,* Winter/Spring 1986:23.
36. May Sarton, "The Muse as Medusa," *Collected Poems: 1930–1973* (New York: Norton, 1974), p. 332.
37. Graves, *Greek Myths,* 2:244.
38. Campbell, *Masks of God,* p. 152.

39. Ibid.
40. C. G. Jung, *Collected Works*, Vol. 10, Bollingen Edition (Princeton: Princeton University Press, 1969), p. 96.
41. Campbell, *Masks of God*, p. 153.
42. Erich Neumann, *Origins and History of Consciousness* (Princeton: Princeton University Press, 1954), p. 214.
43. Ibid., p. 215.
44. Ibid., p. 42.
45. Ibid.
46. Ibid., p. 217.
47. Philip Slater, *The Glory of Hera: Greek Mythology and the Greek Family* (Boston: Beacon Press, 1968), p. 326.
48. *The Choephori* 831, cited in ibid., p. 328.
49. Ibid., p. 330.
50. Ibid., pp. 330ff.
51. Ibid., p. 318.
52. Neumann, *Origins*, p. 217.
53. Ibid.
54. Hillman, *Re-Visioning Psychology*, p. 89.
55. Hillman, *Dream and the Underworld*, ch. 3.
56. Compare with Winnicott's implication that the "false self" actually fails to have any *experience*. Cf. chapter three.
57. Hillman, *Re-Visioning Psychology*, p. x.
58. Hillman, *Dream and the Underworld*, p. 82.
59. Hillman, *Re-Visioning Psychology*, p. 222.
60. Hillman, *The Myth of Analysis* (Evanston: Northwestern University Press, 1972), p. 298.
61. Edward S. Casey, *Remembering: A Phenomenological Study* (Bloomington: Indiana University Press, 1987).
62. Campbell, *Masks of God*, p. 125.
63. Hillman, *Re-Visioning Psychology*, p. 61.
64. See C. G. Jung, *Psychology and Religion: West and East*, Bollingen Series (Princeton: Princeton University Press, 1969), 2:94; Judy Grahn, "The Land that I Grew Up On Is a Rock," in *The Queen of Wands* (Trumansburg, N.Y.: Crossing Press, 1982), p. 3.
65. Ovid, *Metamorphosis*, book 4, pp. 663–752.
66. Ibid.
67. Ibid.
68. Neumann, *Origins*, p. 198.
69. Graves, *Greek Myths*, 1:244.
70. De Beauvoir, *Second Sex*, p. 171.
71. Ibid., pp. 176f.
72. On the relation of eating disorders to "the mother/daughter separation struggle," see Kim Chernin, *The Hungry Self: Women, Eating, and Identity* (New York: Harper and Row, 1985).
73. *The Enuma Elish*, in Barbara Sproul, *Primal Myths: Creating the World* (San Francisco: Harper and Row, 1979), p. 92.
74. Ibid.
75. Ibid., p. 94.
76. Daly, *Gyn/Ecology*, p. 26.
77. *Enuma Elish*, p. 93.
78. Joseph Campbell, *The Hero with a Thousand Faces* (Princeton: Princeton University Press, 1972), p. 342.

79. A. N. Whitehead, *Process and Reality: An Essay in Cosmology,* ed. D. R. Griffin and D. W. Sherburne (New York: Free Press, 1978), p. 340.
80. *Enuma Elish,* p. 93.
81. Neumann, *Origins,* pp. 18ff.
82. Whitehead, *Process and Reality* p. 346.
83. *Enuma Elish,* p. 94.
84. Ibid., p. 96.
85. Ibid.
86. Credit goes to Mary Daly (*Pure Lust,* p. 21) for retrieving the wonderful word *snool* for feminist usage: "The noun *snool* means (Scottish) 'a cringing person.' It means also 'a tame object, or mean-spirited person' (Q.E.D.)," while the verb *snool* means "to reduce to submission: cow, bully and, on the other hand, 'cringe, cower.' "
87. *Enuma Elish,* p. 102.
88. Paul Ricoeur, *The Symbolism of Evil,* trans. E. Buchanan (Boston: Beacon Press, 1969), p. 180.
89. Ibid., p. 175.
90. Ibid., pp. 182ff.
91. Ibid., p. 197.
92. Daly, *Gyn/Ecology,* p. 355.
93. Ricoeur, *Symbolism of Evil,* p. 191.
94. See Linda J. Tessier, "Boundary Crossing in the Three-storied Universe," unpublished paper, presented at Claremont Graduate School, 1982.
95. Mircea Eliade, *The Sacred and the Profane: The Nature of Religion,* trans. W. Trask (New York: Harvest/HJB, 1959), p. 77.
96. Daly, *Gyn/Ecology,* p. 79.
97. Aristotle, *Genesis of Animals,* 729A22.
98. Hillman, *Myth of Analysis,* p. 267.
99. E. A. Speiser, *The Anchor Bible: Genesis* (Garden City, N.Y.: Doubleday, 1964), 1:70.
100. Heidel, *The Babylonian Genesis,* p. 129 (cited in vol. 1, ibid., pp. 9ff.).
101. Michael Fishbane, "Israel and the 'Mothers,' " in *The Other Side of God: A Polarity in World Religions,* ed. Peter L. Berger (Garden City, N.Y.: Anchor/Doubleday, 1981), p. 32.
102. Ibid., p. 33.
103. John A. Phillips, *Eve: The History of an Idea* (San Francisco: Harper and Row, 1984), p. 5.
104. Ibid.
105. Bruce Vawter, *On Genesis* (New York: Doubleday, 1977), pp. 86f.
106. I.e., Phyllis Trible, "Depatriarchalizing in Biblical Interpretation," in *The Jewish Woman: New Perspectives* (New York: Schocken Books, 1972); Merlin Stone in *When God Was a Woman.*
107. See Catherine Keller, "Women, Warriors, and the Nuclear Complex," forthcoming.
108. See Daly's "hag-ography" of Great Hags, *Gyn/Ecology,* p. 15.
109. Alice Walker, "While love is unfashionable," *Revolutionary Petunias and Other Poems* (New York and London: Harcourt Brace and Jovanovich, 1973), p. 68.
110. Daly, *Pure Lust,* p. 175.
111. Casey, *Remembering,* p. 279.
112. Nelle Morton, *The Journey Is Home* (Boston: Beacon Press, 1985). Cf. especially "The Goddess as Metaphoric Image," pp. 147ff.

THREE: *Oceanic Feelings and the Rising Daughter*

1. Sigmund Freud, "On Narcissism: An Introduction" (1914), in *Standard Edition of The Complete Psychological Works*, ed. J. Strachey (London: Hogarth, 1953–74), 14:75.

2. Juliet Mitchell, *Psychoanalysis and Feminism* (New York: Pantheon/Random House, 1974), p. xv.

3. Mitchell does not deny Freud's unquestioning acquiescence in an identification of all civilization with patriarchy. Indeed, Mitchell is less disturbed by Freud's reinforcements of androcentric culture than by the common feminist anti-Freudianisms. Yet Mitchell's fundamental thesis is well taken: in Freud's theory of the Oedipus complex, in the gender asymmetry he came to acknowledge, and in the diminution of the mother, we can decipher an important disclosure of how, beneath all deliberate intentions, a misogynist society replicates itself with such overwhelming consistency in its men and its women. Nancy Chodorow's more critical reconstruction of Freud in *The Reproduction of Mothering* demonstrates the importance of the Oedipus complex for any feminist analysis of culture. If Freud's analysis of patriarchy remains itself patriarchal, as no one can dispute, his account of the unresolved oedipal neurosis that so far dominates history hardly flatters civilization.

4. Estella Lauter and Carol Schreir Rupprecht, editors, *Feminist Archetypal Theory: Interdisciplinary Re-Visions of Jungian Thought* (Knoxville: The University of Tennessee Press, 1985). Also, see my "Wholeness and the King's Men," *Anima*, Spring 1985:83–95.

5. Freud, *Civilization and Its Discontents*, transl. J. Strachey (New York: W. W. Norton & Co., 1961), p. 15.

6. Ibid., p. 13.

7. Sigmund Freud, *General Psychological Theory: Papers on Metapsychology* (New York: Collier, 1963), p. 59.

8. Freud, *Civilization and Its Discontents*, p. 13.

9. Reuben Fine, *A History of Psychoanalysis* (New York: Columbia University Press, 1979), p. 15.

10. Freud, *Civilization and Its Discontents*, p. 12.

11. Ibid., p. 15.

12. Hillman, *Dream and the Underworld*, p. 112.

13. Ibid., p. 180.

14. Freud, *Civilization and Its Discontents*, p. 15.

15. Ibid.

16. Sigmund Freud, "Totem and Taboo," (1912–13), trans. A. Brill, in *The Basic Writings of Sigmund Freud* (New York: Modern Library, 1938), p. 927.

17. Ibid.

18. Sigmund Freud, *Group Psychology and the Analysis of the Ego*, trans. James Strachey (New York: Bantam, 1960).

19. Sigmund Freud, *The Ego and the Id* (1923), in *Standard Edition*, 14:31.

20. Mitchell, *Psychoanalysis and Feminism*, p. 71.

21. See George Hogenson, *Jung's Struggle with Freud* (Notre Dame: Notre Dame Press, 1983).

22. Mitchell, *Psychoanalysis and Feminism*, p. 314.

23. De Beauvoir, *The Second Sex*, p. 51.

24. Mitchell, *Psychoanalysis and Feminism*, p. 315.

25. See Lacan, "The Freudian Thing, or the Meaning of the Return to Freud in Psychoanalysis," *Écrits*, pp. 114–146.

26. Freud, *Group Psychology*, pp. 87–88.

27. Carl G. Jung, *Symbols of Transformation,* in *Collected Works,* vol. 5, Bollingen Edition (Princeton: Princeton University Press, 1956).
28. Ibid., p. 236.
29. Jung, *Symbols of Transformation,* p. 236.
30. Carl G. Jung, "Psychological Aspects of the Mother Archetype," in *Archetypes and the Collective Unconscious,* in *Collected Works,* 9:82.
31. Jung, *Symbols of Transformation,* p. 252.
32. Ibid., p. 254.
33. Ibid., p. 348.
34. Ibid.
35. Carl G. Jung, "On Psychic Energy," *The Structure and Dynamics of the Psyche,* in *Collected Works,* 8:45.
36. Carl G. Jung, *Two Essays on Analytical Psychology,* in *Collected Works,* 7:209.
37. As evinced, for example, in Jung's "Woman in Europe": "But no one can get round the fact that by taking up a masculine profession, studying and working like a man, woman is doing something not wholly in accord with, if not directly injurious to her feminine nature" (Jung, *Civilization in Transition,* in *Collected Works,* 10:117).
38. Jung, "Psychological Aspects," p. 96.
39. Hillman, *Dream and the Underworld,* p. 76.
40. Carl G. Jung, "Archetypes of the Collective Unconscious," *Archetypes and the Collective Unconscious,* p. 22.
41. Carl G. Jung, *The Spirit Mercury* (New York: Analytic Psychology Club of New York, Inc., 1953), p. 150.
42. Jung, "Psychological Aspects," p. 92.
43. Dorothy Dinnerstein, *The Mermaid and the Minotaur: Sexual Arrangements and Human Malaise* (New York: Harper Colophon, 1977).
44. Ibid., pp. 113f.
45. Ibid., p. 93.
46. Ibid., p. 11.
47. Ibid., p. 93.
48. Carol Gilligan, *In a Different Voice: Psychological Theory and Women's Development* (Cambridge: Harvard University Press, 1982).
49. Ibid., p. 13.
50. Ibid., p. 28.
51. Ibid., p. 8.
52. Ibid., p. 174.
53. Nancy Chodorow, *The Reproduction of Mothering: Psychoanalysis and the Sociology of Gender* (Berkeley: University of California Press, 1978).
54. Ibid., p. 3.
55. Ibid., p. 33.
56. Sigmund Freud, "Female Sexuality," in *Standard Edition,* 21:226.
57. Ibid., p. 229.
58. Thomas Aquinas, *Summa Theologica,* vol. 13 (London: Burns, Oates and Washbourne, Ltd., 1914), question 92.
59. Mitchell, *Psychoanalysis and Feminism,* p. 99.
60. Sigmund Freud, "Some Psychical Consequences of the Anatomical Distinction between the Sexes," (1925), in *Standard Edition,* 19:253.
61. Freud, "Female Sexuality," p. 229.
62. Freud, "Psychical Consequences of Anatomical Distinctions," p. 257.
63. Freud, "Female Sexuality," p. 226.
64. Chodorow, *The Reproduction of Mothering,* p. 166.

65. Ibid., pp. 166–167.
66. Ibid., p. 167.
67. Freud, "Female Sexuality," p. 231.
68. Chodorow, *The Reproduction of Mothering*, p. 169.
69. Ibid., p. 198.
70. Ibid., p. 67.
71. "Probably there is nothing in human nature more resonant with charges than the flow of energy between two biologically alike bodies, one of which has lain in amniotic bliss inside the other, one of which has labored to give birth to the other." Adrienne Rich, *Of Woman Born: Motherhood as Experience and Institution* (New York: Norton, 1976), pp. 225f. And: "As a lesbian/feminist, my nerves and my flesh as well as my intellect tell me that the connections between and among women are the most feared, the most problematic, and the most potentially transforming force on the planet." Adrienne Rich, *On Lies, Secrets and Silence* (New York: Norton, 1979), p. 279.
72. Mary Daly attributes the word *gynergy* to Emily Culpepper. *Gyn/Ecology*, p. 13.
73. Chodorow, *The Reproduction of Mothering*, p. 101.
74. Ibid., p. 205.
75. George Eliot, *Middlemarch* (New York: Signet Classics, 1964), p. 482.
76. Chodorow, *The Reproduction of Mothering*, p. 218.
77. Barbara G. Walker, *The Women's Encyclopedia of Myths and Secrets* (San Francisco: Harper and Row, 1983), p. 218.
78. Heinz Kohut, *The Analysis of the Self* (New York: International Universities Press, 1971), p. 220.
79. As for example, W. R. D. Fairbairn, "An Object Relations Theory of the Personality," *International Journal of Psychoanalysis* 44(1963):224–25.
80. Alice Miller, *The Drama of the Gifted Child* (New York: Basic Books, 1981), p. 6.
81. Ibid., pp. 8, 9.
82. Ibid., p. 28.
83. D. W. Winnicott, *Playing and Reality* (New York: Basic Books, 1971), p. 103.
84. Ibid., p. 10.
85. Ibid., p. 108.
86. Miller, *The Drama of the Gifted Child*, p. 34.
87. Ibid.
88. Rita Nakashima Brock, "Transcendence, Love, and Agency: A Feminist Critique of Power," paper presented at the American Academy of Religion, 1985.
89. Miller, *The Drama of the Gifted Child*, p. 8.
90. Cf. Alice Miller, *For Your Own Good: Hidden Cruelty in Childrearing and the Roots of Violence* (New York: Farrar, Straus and Giroux, 1984).
91. Adrienne Rich, "For Memory," in *A Wild Patience Has Taken Me This Far: Poems 1978–1981* (New York: Norton, 1981), p. 22.
92. Carl G. Jung, "The Psychology of the Child Archetype," *The Archetypes and the Collective Unconscious*, p. 179.
93. See Miller's critique of Jung, whom she believes betrayed his own early insight into the importance of childhood experience for psychic formation, in Alice Miller, *Thou Shalt Not Be Aware: Society's Betrayal of the Child* (New York: Farrar, Straus and Giroux, 1984), p. 202. No doubt this turnabout reflects Jung's need to free himself from Freud.
94. Miller, *The Drama of the Gifted Child*, p. 103.
95. Winnicott, *Playing and Reality*, p. 68.

96. Jung, "Child Archetype," p. 178.

97. Judith van Herik, *Freud on Femininity and Faith* (Berkeley: University of California Press, 1982), p. 97.

98. Ibid., p. 2.

99. Cf. Slater, *The Glory of Hera.*

100. Note how girls not only linger longer in the empathic continuum with the mother, but also how they are allowed—until puberty, where the Persephone image picks up—a greater range of expression (they can be tomboys, but boys cannot be sissies). Thus in our age particularly the daughter's transition from child to adolescent is in need of redemption.

FOUR: *The Selves of Psyche*

1. Susan Griffin, *Pornography and Silence: Culture's Revenge against Nature* (New York: Harper and Row, 1981), p. 260.

2. Graves, *Greek Myths,* 2: p. 30.

3. This form of criticism lies at the basis of Marx's important early criticism of Hegel: "The Idea is given the status of a subject, and the actual relationship of family and civil society to the state is conceived to be its imaginary activity. Family and civil society are the presuppositions of the state; they are the really active things; but in speculative philosophy it is reversed. But if the Idea is made subject, then the real subjects—civil society, family, circumstances, caprice, etc.—become unreal, and take on the different meaning of objective moments of the Idea." Karl Marx, *Critique of Hegel's Philosophy of Right,* ed. Joseph O'Malley (Cambridge: Cambridge University Press, 1970), p. 8.

4. Whitehead, *Process and Reality,* p. 4.

5. Ibid., p. 13.

6. Sheila Ortiz Taylor, *Faultline* (Tallahassee: Naiad, 1982), p. 8.

7. Marge Piercy, "Bridging," in *Circles on the Water* (New York: Alfred A. Knopf, 1982), 2:1070.

8. Robin Morgan, *The Anatomy of Freedom: Feminism, Physics and Global Politics* (Garden City: Anchor Press/Doubleday, 1982), p. xv.

9. Ibid., p. 283.

10. Hecate is sometimes named at once for the entire lunar triad and for its third party, the Hag—in the sense Daly has etymologically redeemed (see *Gyn/Ecology,* pp. 14ff.). The Crone, Hag, or Wise Old Woman is demeaned in our civilization, which desires only the Maiden and the Mother (rolling them into the single figure of the Madonna, who ascended bodily to heaven before she could age, let alone putrefy). Yet the Crone primordially subsumes the entire trinity herself because she encompasses Maiden and Mother, having always already passed through and therefore retaining the potencies of the younger phases.

11. See Daly's "Nag-gnosticism," the wisdom of the Hag, in *Pure Lust,* p. 12.

12. Daly, *Gyn/Ecology,* p. 412.

13. Luce Irigaray, *This Sex Which Is Not One,* trans. Catherine Porter (Ithaca: Cornell University Press, 1977), p. 26.

14. *Count nouns* are technically distinguished from *mass nouns.* One can count these three particular selves, distinguish this self from that, in contrast, say, to *selfhood* or *humanity.*

15. Irigaray, *Sex Which Is Not One,* p. 310.

16. Aurelius Augustine, *The Confessions of Augustine,* trans. J. K. Ryan (Garden City: Doubleday, 1960), bk. 11, p. 302.

17. The female friends of Jesus would never, I suspect, have deified him. Not only

did they know his humanness too well, they felt empowered by him, not over-powered. Women's christological intentions seem always to have been different, as confirmed by the beginnings of a feminist christology today. Cf. Rita Nakashima Brock, "The Feminist Redemption of Christ," in *Christian Feminism* (San Francisco: Harper and Row, 1984); Elizabeth Schüssler Fiorenza, *In Memory of Her* (New York: Crossroad, 1983); Rosemary Radford Ruether, *Sexism and God-Talk* (Boston: Beacon Press, 1983).

18. Augustine, *Confessions*, p. 302.

19. The impulse toward divine simplicity, which reinforces the radical monotheism of the biblical heritage, finds an interesting, even promising, but never fully assimilated, counterpoint in the interpersonal, indeed interconnective, sociality of the persons of the Trinity. See Joseph Bracken, *The Triune Symbol: Persons, Process and Community* (Washington, D.C.: University Press of America, 1985).

20. Aurelius Augustine, *On the Holy Trinity, the Nicene and Post-Nicene Fathers* (Grand Rapids: Eerdmans, 1956), 3:200.

21. Ibid., p. 89.

22. Ibid., p. 88.

23. Ibid., p. 101.

24. Ibid.

25. Ibid., p. 100.

26. On the very next page Augustine uses the analogy of husband and wife "cleaving" to each other's bodies.

27. Daly, *Gyn/Ecology*, pp. 37f.

28. Ibid., p. 38.

29. Elizabeth Moltmann-Wendel and Jürgen Moltmann, *Humanity in God* (New York: Pilgrim Press, 1983).

30. Daly, *Gyn/Ecology*, p. 75.

31. Cobb and Griffin, *Process Theology*, p. 110.

32. Daly, *Gyn/Ecology*, p. 79.

33. See Joseph A. Bracken, "Subsistent Relation: Mediating Concept for a New Synthesis?" *Journal of Religion*, vol. 64, no. 2 (April 1984):188–204, for an effort to mediate between Aquinas and Whitehead.

34. Thomas Aquinas, *Commentary on the Metaphysics of Aristotle*, trans. J. P. Rowan (Chicago: Henry Regnery, 1961), p. 497.

35. Ibid., p. 501.

36. Ibid., p. 916.

37. René Descartes, *Meditations*, trans. E. Haldane, in *The Philosophical Works of Descartes* (Cambridge: Cambridge University Press, 1911), p. 165.

38. Whitehead, *Process and Reality*, p. 6.

39. David Hume, *A Treatise of Human Nature* (Oxford: Clarendon Press, 1888), p. 636.

40. Ibid., p. 635.

41. Griffin, *Pornography and Silence*, p. 261.

42. William James, *The Principles of Psychology* (New York: Henry Holt and Co., 1890), 1:224.

43. Ibid., 2:82.

44. Ibid., 1:488.

45. William James, "A World of Pure Experience," in *Essays in Radical Empiricism* (London: Longmans, Green, and Co., 1912), p. 42.

46. William James, "Does Consciousness Exist?" in *Essays*, p. 4.

47. Ibid.

48. James, *Psychology*, 1:239.

49. James, "Pure Experience," pp. 36–37.

50. William James, *A Pluralistic Universe* (New York: Longmans, Green and Co., 1909), p. 380.

51. Such reduction, which provides the mirror reversal of classical individualism by which all individuality is annihilated in the stimulus and response patterns of the social environment, is reserved for the Brave New World visions of empirical behaviorism, typified by Skinner's *Walden Two*.

52. Mead, *Mind, Self and Society*, p. 201.

53. Ibid., p. 140.

54. H. Richard Niebuhr, *The Responsible Self: An Essay in Christian Moral Philosophy* (New York: Harper and Row, 1963), p. 72.

55. Ibid., p. 126.

56. Ibid., p. 125.

57. Ibid., p. 139.

58. Ibid., p. 137.

59. Whitehead, *Process and Reality*, p. xiii.

60. Ibid., p. 18.

61. Ibid., p. 80.

62. Ibid.

63. Ibid., p. 41.

64. Ibid., p. 290.

65. Ibid., p. 40.

66. Ibid., p. 50.

67. Ibid., p. 21.

68. A. N. Whitehead, *Modes of Thought* (New York: Capricorn, 1938), p. 205.

69. Cf. Bernard Loomer's classic essay on the "S-I-Z-E" of persons who can live with a complex variety of relationships: "S-I-Z-E Is the Measure," in *Religious Experience and Process Theology*, ed. by J. Cargas and B. Lee (Mahweh, N.J.: Paulist Press, 1976).

70. Whitehead, *Process and Reality*, p. 151.

71. A. N. Whitehead, *Adventures of Ideas* (New York: Free Press, 1967), p. 177.

72. Though the issue of the activity or passivity of the past is a controversial issue in Whitehead interpretation. Cf. Nancy Frankenberry, "The Power of the Past," *Process Studies*, Vol. 13, No. 2, 1983, pp. 129–38.

73. Audre Lorde, "A Woman Speaks," in *The Black Unicorn* (New York: Norton, 1978), pp. 4f.

74. Ibid.

75. Uni-verse, "turning one" might best be replaced by the word *cosmos*, which etymologically highlights beauty rather than unity. But indeed "turning one" can suggest precisely the reformed, composite oneness of the many *becoming* one, and turning again to many.

76. Whitehead, *Process and Reality*, p. 111.

77. Ibid., p. 112.

78. Ibid., p. 166.

79. Freud, *Civilization and Its Discontents*, p. 12.

80. Whitehead, *Process and Reality*, p. 22.

81. Ibid., p. 81.

82. Gerard Manley Hopkins, "As kingfishers catch fire, dragonflies draw flame," in *Poems of Gerard Manley Hopkins* (New York: Oxford University Press, 1948), p. 95.

83. Whitehead, *Process and Reality*, p. 154. Or, speaking of the function of pure possibilities as the ideal that inspires the entity toward greater harmony and complexity: "The ideal, itself felt, defines what 'self' shall arise from the datum; and the ideal is also an element in the self which thus arises" (p. 150).

84. Actual occasions do not last long, in fact they do not last—they happen: yet they constitute the felt unit of time—perhaps a microsecond. They "take time to be" as John Cobb has put it in an unpublished lecture.

85. Whitehead, *Process and Reality*, pp. 34ff.

86. Not unlike the substantial form of Aristotle, but here applied to the entire society, not the individual, and communicated by prehensive feeling.

87. Whitehead, *Modes of Thought*, p. 223.

88. Cris Williamson, "Waterfall," on *The Changer and the Changed*, LF904, Olivia Records, Inc., 1975.

89. Perhaps if this wrestling were no longer necessary—because a world had evolved in which the energies of women, indeed of all presently oppressed groups were in principal, cooperating—metaphysics itself would dissolve, self-destruct. Or it might finally come to life, sprung free of its captivity in the academy.

90. Daly, *Pure Lust*, p. 346.

91. The day I was writing this paragraph, a young woman reported her experience the previous evening of standing next to two male colleagues who were speaking to each other, while she spoke to someone else. When she started to leave, the other dyad also interrupted their conversation and started to leave; she quipped that *she* had not meant to break them up. "Yes, you did," one of them retorted. Reflecting later, she felt as if even at a distance they were draining energy from her for the purpose of their own exchange.

92. Emmanuel Levinas, *Totality and Infinity: An Essay in Exteriority*, trans. A. Lingis (Pittsburgh: Duquesne University Press, 1969), pp. 154–56.

93. Jung, *Symbols of Transformation*, p. 300.

94. Hillman, *Re-Visioning Psychology*, p. 70.

95. Daly, *Pure Lust*, p. 345.

96. Daly, *Gyn/Ecology*, p. 382.

97. Ibid., p. 383.

98. Daly, *Pure Lust*, p. 238.

99. Ntozake Shange, *for colored girls who have considered suicide/when the rainbow is enuf* (Toronto/New York: Bantam Books, 1975), p. 67.

100. Charles Hartshorne, *The Divine Relativity: A Social Conception of God* (New Haven and London: Yale University Press, 1948), p. 47.

101. Whitehead, *Adventures of Ideas*, p. 277.

102. Ibid., p. 275.

FIVE: *The Spider's Genius*

1. Ovid, *Metamorphosis*, book 6, trans. A. E. Watts, cited in Morton Weigle, *Spiders and Spinsters: Women and Mythology* (Albuquerque: University of New Mexico Press, 1982), p. 11.

2. Etymology of "Penelope": see Graves, *Myths* 1:103.

3. I am grateful to William Whedbee of Pomona College for his unpublished literary-critical analysis of Jeremiah as a tragic figure.

4. See Drorah Setel, "Feminist Reflections on Separation and Unity in Jewish Theology," *Journal of Feminist Studies in Religion*.

5. Daly, *Gyn/Ecology*, p. 338.

6. Irigaray, *This Sex Which Is Not One*, p. 214.

7. It is worth noting that Levinas, a philosopher who celebrates separation (as otherness) analyzes Odysseus as "the return to the same." (*Totality and Infinity*, pp. 33f, 176f, 271).

8. Irigaray, *This Sex Which Is Not One*, pp. 214ff.

9. Morton, *The Journey Is Home*, p. 172.
10. Alice Walker, *The Color Purple* (New York: Harcourt Brace Jovanovich, 1982), p. 167.
11. Ibid.
12. Robin Morgan, "The Network of the Imaginary Mother," *Lady of the Beasts* (New York: Random House, 1962), p. 88.
13. Thus the name of the feminist journal *Sinister Wisdom*.
14. Morton, *The Journey Is Home*, p. 172.
15. Adrienne Rich, "Natural Resources," in *The Dream of a Common Language* (New York: Norton, 1978), p. 64.
16. Adrienne Rich, "Integrity," in *A Wild Patience Has Taken Me This Far*, p. 8.
17. Irigaray, *This Sex Which Is Not One*, p. 210.
18. Rich, "Integrity," p. 9.
19. Daly, *Pure Lust*, pp. 197–226.
20. Whitehead, *Adventures of Ideas*, p. 195.
21. Ibid.
22. Daly, *Pure Lust*, p. 2.
23. Whitehead, *Process and Reality*, p. 151.
24. A. N. Whitehead, *Religion in the Making* (New York: Meridian/Macmillan, 1960), p. 16.
25. Rich, "Integrity," p. 9.
26. Irigaray, *This Sex Which Is Not One*, p. 218.
27. Whitehead, *Process and Reality*, p. 81.
28. Whitehead, *Modes of Thought*, p. 223.
29. Jung, "Psychology of the Child Archetype," p. 173.
30. Griffin, *Pornography and Silence*, p. 253.
31. Ibid., p. 260.
32. Rich, *Of Woman Born*, p. 285.
33. Irigaray, *This Sex Which Is Not One*, p. 217.
34. Whitehead, *Process and Reality*, p. 40.
35. David Bohm, *Wholeness and the Implicate Order* (London: Arc Paperbacks, 1984), p. 11.
36. Ibid., p. 14.
37. Irigaray, *This Sex Which Is Not One*, p. 215.
38. For pioneering the feminist philosophy of space, see Mary Daly's *Beyond God the Father* (Boston: Beacon Press, 1973), especially pp. 40–43, 156–57. And for a richly textured and promising philosophy of space, see Edward Casey's forthcoming *Placeing: A Phenomenology of Lived Space*.
39. Whitehead, *Process and Reality*, p. 67.
40. Daly, *Pure Lust*, p. 289.
41. Irigaray, *This Sex Which Is Not One*, p. 216.
42. Judy Grahn, "Helen you always were/the factory," *The Queen of Words*, (Trumansburg: The Crossing Press, 1982), p. 92.
43. Morton, *Journey Is Home*
44. For the clearest statement of the role of the Goddess today as symbol of woman's self-empowerment, see Carol P. Christ, "Why Women Need the Goddess: Phenomenological, Psychological, and Political Reflections," in *Womanspirit Rising: A Feminist Reader in Religion*, ed. Judith Plaskow and Carol P. Christ (San Francisco: Harper and Row, 1979), pp. 228–45. And for the classic connection between psychological-archetypal pluralism and the image of the Goddess as woman's self, see Naomi R. Goldenberg, *Changing of the Gods: Feminism and the End of Traditional Religions* (Boston: Beacon Press, 1979).

45. Morgan, "The Network of the Imaginary Mother," p. 84.
46. Fanchon Shur's choreographic work *Taalit: Prayer Shawl* (based in Cincinnati) is a ceremonial dance which de-patriarchalizes an ancient Jewish symbol, enacting in motion the holy inclusiveness of community and cosmos.

Credits

Grateful acknowledgment is made for permission to quote from the following:

We Are All Part of One Another: A Barbara Deming Reader, by Barbara Deming, edited by Jane Myerding (Philadelphia: New Society Publishers, 1984), Copyright © 1984 by Barbara Deming and Jane Myerding, Reprinted by permission of the publisher;

Queen of Wands by Judy Grahn, Copyright © 1982 by Judy Grahn, Reprinted by permission of Crossing Press;

The Homeric Hymns and the Battle of the Frogs and Mice, Daryl Hine trans., Copyright © 1972 by Daryl Hine, Reprinted by permission of Athenaeum;

Collected Poems, by Gerard Manley Hopkins, Copyright © 1967 by The Jesus Society; Reprinted by permission of Oxford University Press;

The Dream of a Black Unicorn by Audre Lorde, Copyright © 1978 by Audre Lorde, Reprinted by permission of W. W. Norton & Company, Inc.;

Lady of the Beasts by Robin Morgan, Copyright © 1962, 1968, 1973, 1974, 1975, 1976 by Robin Morgan; Reprinted by permission of Random House;

Circles on the Water by Marge Piercy, Copyright © 1963, 1964, 1965, 1966, 1967, 1968, 1969, 1971, 1972, 1973, 1974, 1975, 1976, 1978, 1979, 1980, 1982 by Marge Piercy, Reprinted by permission of Alfred A. Knopf;

The Dream of a Common Language by Adrienne Rich, Copyright © 1978 by W. W. Norton & Company, Inc., Reprinted by permission of the publisher;

A Wild Patience Has Taken Me This Far: Poems 1978–1981 by Adrienne Rich, Copyright © 1981 by Adrienne Rich, Reprinted by permission of W. W. Norton & Company;

Collected Poems: 1930–1973 by May Sarton, Copyright © 1978 by May Sarton, Reprinted by permission of W. W. Norton & Company, Inc.

Index

Adam: and Eve, 52, 83, 122
Adler, Alfred, 66
Aeschylus, 48, 64
Agape, 168
Androgeny, 8, 253 n
Andromeda, 70–71, 110
Anima: and animus, 109–11; and
  Athena, 54; in Hillman, 66–67; and
  male ego, 205; in Neumann, 71
Anselm, 37
Aphrodite, 71
Apollo, 48
Apsu, 77; and Tiamat, 73–74
Apuleius, 156
Aquinas, Thomas, 48, 79, 174; and
  Daly, 208–9; on God, 36–37; and
  substantialism, 127, 164, 172–73,
  208; on women, 127
Arachne, 216–18, 221
Archetype: relation to experience, 117–
  18; and the sacred, 115, 152; and
  social stereotypes, 109. See also
  Child; Mother
Ariadne, 140
Aristotle, 56, 63, 87, 122;
  substantialism of, and individuality,
  68, 163, 172–74; on women, 47–50,
  72, 209
Asclepios, 68
Astarte, 71
Athena, 63, 64, 68, 69, 88; and ancient
  goddess power, 60–62; and Arachne,
  216–17; and Eve, 83; and male-
  identified women, 57–58; and
  matricide, 62, 65, 89; and patrilinear
  social structure, 48–58
Augustine, 33, 177, 181, 187; oneness
  of God in, 164–68, 172

Beauvoir, Simone de, 4–5, 41, 120;
  analysis of women's oppression, 13–

16, 18–25; immanence and
  transcendence in, 14–15, 88; and
  Sartre, 32; women as Other in, 7–8,
  126
Benbow, Arden, 158
Bergson, Henri, 244
Body: of Christ, 219; and cosmos, 213;
  in James, 179; and mind, in women,
  58; and selfhood, 233–37; and soul,
  10, 49–50, 172–74, 237; and space,
  240; woman's, 68, 239, 241; and
  World, 236–37
Bohm, David, 242
Bolen, Jean Shinoda, 57
Brock, Rita Nakashima, 144
Buber, Martin, 180
Buddha, 31

Campbell, Joseph, 53–56, 62, 65–66,
  74
Capitalism: and individuality, in
  Niebuhr, 43; and nuclear family,
  125; and patriarchy, 104
Casey, Edward S., 67, 90
Chaos, 88, 92, 94, 190–91
Child: archetypal, 147, 150, 237; and
  body, 237; as Divine Son, 164;
  female, 126; impact of father on,
  120; inner, 146–50, 193; male, 137;
  and narcissistic needs, 142
Chodorow, Nancy, 5, 57, 121, 149,
  190; gender structure in, 124–40,
  161–62, 169; and Jung, 150; and
  Miller, 144–46; on mother-daughter
  relation, 128, 130, 132, 135, 153
Christ, 105, 164–65, 219
Christianity, 5, 165–66
Cobb, John B., 41
Complexity: and chaos, 92; and
  differentiation, 129–36, 190–91;
  and selfhood, 91, 140; in Whitehead,

271

Index

190; and woman's psyche, 134, 140, 163

Connection: as a basis for selfhood, 134, 153–54, 190; and collective unconscious, 102–3, 149, 152; and control, 199–200; and empathy, 135–36; and feeling, 185; vs. identification, 92; and individuality, 186; and inner self, 212–13; and remembering, 91; and selfhood, 197–98; to World, and infant-mother bond, 133–34, 150

Connective self. See Self, connective

Connectivity: female, 18, 132–33; nature of, 200, 202–3; of self, 155; vision of, 157–60

Consciousness: formation of, and matricide, 112; masculinization of, 62–63; and opposition, 112–13; stream of, 178; in Whitehead, 185

Continuum, empathic, 132–33, 140, 149, 153–54, 184

Co-optation, 16, 18–19, 65

Cosmos, 179, 213, 236, 264 n. See also World

Courage, 228

Creation: in Jung, 116; and matricide, 76–78; myths of, Hebrew and Babylonian, 80–85

Creativity, 17, 224, 247

Culpepper, Emily, 60

Culture: Neolithic, 22–26; patriarchal and prepatriarchal, 25–26

Daly, Mary, 77, 159, 202, 227; connection in, 160; on patriarchy, 39, 78; philosophy of self, 45, 194, 195, 207–13; on religion, 39, 220; tidal genius in, 209, 252; and timing 244

Death, 59; and soul, in Hillman, 66, 207

Demeter, 152

Deming, Barbara, 47, 59

Depth, 82–83, 89–90; and oceanic feeling, 93–94, 114–15; and width, in Whitehead, 191

Derrida, Jacques, 157, 204

Descartes, René, 33, 48, 186; on God, 174, 175; subject-object dualism in, 11, 20, 32, 96

Despair, and devotion, in women, 12–13

Deutsch, Helene, 127

Dinnerstein, Dorothy, 118–21, 125, 132, 145, 150

Divine, image of, and selfhood, 88

Divining, 251

Dunfee, Sue, 12, 253 n, 255 n

Duras, Marguerite, 45

Ego: -boundaries, and gender, 129; Cartesian, 11, 20, 29, 199; and connection, 114, 189; and id, 96–97, 101; as masculine, in women, 108–9; separate, in Freud, 95–100; separative, 9, 31

—heroic: and complexity, 140; in Freud, 105–6; in Hillman, 65–66; irony of, 10, 69; as masculine defiance, 10; and narcissism, 64; and oneness, 226; and reflexivity, 29; self-identity of, 9–11; separative character of, 68–69, 88–89; and time, 245; and warrior-ideal, 25–26

Eliade, Mircea, 7, 59, 77–78

Eliot, George, 138

Elohim, 81, 83

Emotion, 183, 226–27

Empathy, 130, 135–36, 184. See also Continuum, empathic

Eros, 156–57, 218, 233; divine, 214, 223, 250–51; in Jung, 205–6; and religion, 221–22

Eve, 53; and Adam, 52, 83, 122

Existentialism, 4, 34–35. See also de Beauvoir; Sartre

Experience: and feeling, in Whitehead, 183; and novelty, 231; pure, in James, 177–78; in Winnicott, 143–44, 147–48

Family, nuclear, 18, 104, 125–26

Father: and child, 118–21; -complex, 101; and ego-ideal, 104; infanticidal, 74; and narcissism, 145; as protector, in Freud, 93–94

Feeling: and the body, 236; as divining, 251; and God, ontology of, 182–84, 228; and timing, 247; in Whitehead, 5, 182–87

—oceanic: and depth, 93–94; Freud on, 93–100, 165; and the sacred, 115, 222; and selfhood, 100; and Whitehead, 191

Female: connectivity, 18, 132–33;

Index

empathy, development of, 130; selfhood, formation of, 135–36
Feminine, the 59, 161, 205–6
Feminism: and deconstructionist philosophy, 157; and Freud, 95, 103–4; and Jung, 95; and individualism, 229; and metaphysics, 157–63; 217; and nuclear family, 131; and Whitehead, 210–11; and woman's body, 234–35
Feminist theory, 157–58
Fishbane, Michael, 81–82
Freedom: and connection, in women, 3, 6, 153, 248; in de Beauvoir, 14; in Dinnerstein, 120; identified with separateness, 1, 6, 43, 208–9, 228, 229; and remembering, 90; and selfhood, 91–92
Freud, Sigmund, 5, 56, 61; account of history, 104; on aggression, 21; castration anxiety in, 29; concept of self, 176–77; and Jung, 103, 106, 108, 110–12, 117–18; and ideal of separate ego, 96–104, 120; on mother-daughter relation, 131–32; on oceanic feeling, 93–97, 100, 176–77, 191–92; oedipal conflict in, 101–2, 125, 128–29; preoedipal phase in, 126–27, 130; on religion, 151–52; theory of female castration, 122, 127–28; theory of the id, 96–97, 102, 114, 150
Friedan, Betty, 127

Gender: -complementarity, 110–13; -difference, in Gilligan, 122–23; -formation, in Chodorow, 124–36; and humanism, 4; -identity, 4, 124–26, 239; -roles, 8, 40–41, 109
Gilligan, Carol, 121–24, 125, 139, 181
Gimbutas, Marija, 24–25, 72
God: death of, 44, 105, 171–72, 249; as deified hero, 105; as Eros, 214; the Father, 37–38, 145, 151; as image of reflexive selfhood, 37–38; masculine, 33–34; metaphor of, 249; transcendent, 35, 81; as unchanging, 36, 167; unity of, 166–74; as warrior, 84–86; and the World, 36–37, 81, 86–87, 214
Goddess: and complexity, 140; and connectivity, 91; as Medusa-mother, 59–60; and metaphor, 221–22; and

metaphysics, 159–60; as monster, 71, 73–78; Neolithic images of, 22–25; and serpent image, 52–55; as a spider, 228, 248–50; -worship, 94
Gorgon. *See* Medusa
Grahn, Judy, 1, 248
Griffin, David R., 37
Griffin, Susan, 155, 162, 238
Graves, Robert, 48, 59, 61

Hades, 152
Harrison, Jane, 48–49, 54
Hartschorne, C., 214
Hegel, G. W. F., 14, 20, 21, 175; master-slave relation in, 32–33; and Whitehead, 191
Heidegger, Martin, 230
Herik, Judith van, 151
Hero: and female connectivity, 137; myth of, and consciousness, 62–63, 112–13; and myth of manhood, 8–11. *See also* Ego, heroic
Hesiod, 55, 75
Hillman, James, 51, 65–67, 79, 113, 207
Homer, 26
Homosexuality, 135
Hopkins, Gerald Manley, 194–95
Horney, Karen, 127
Hume, David, 175–77, 183

Identification, 92, 101, 136
Identity, continuity of, 163, 197–98
Immanence: and Aristotelian substance, 49; and individuality, 89; and influence, 27; and transcendence, 14, 18, 42–43, 45–46, 248; of World, 27, 89, 150, 248
Individuality: in Augustine, 172–73; monolithic vs. composite, 89; in Niebuhr, 41–42; and substantialism, 49, 68, 162; in Whitehead, 182, 185–86
Individuation, in Jung, 106, 114
Influence, 27, 36; of the Other, 8
Integrity, 2, 123, 163, 248; and the body, 233–34; connective, 193, 202, 203; and courage, 228; and love, 168; and multiplicity, in Whitehead, 185; in Niebuhr, 181; and selfhood, 45, 185, 209, 224–27, 231; and spinning, 233
Intimacy, 92, 123

Index

Irigaray, Luce, 127, 157, 162, 185, 245; woman's selfhood in, 220–21, 242, 248

Isaiah, 84–85

Ishtar, 52, 71

James, William, 177–79, 182, 194, 239, 247–48; and Whitehead, 183, 185, 196

Jesus, 148, 210

John, Gospel of, 112

Jung, C. G., 54, 95, 131, 168–69; 192; anima and animus in, 110–11; child archetype in, 237; collective unconscious in, 102–3, 114–17; the Feminine in, 205–6; and Freud, 95, 102–3, 106–8, 110–12; on individuation, 114–15; matricide, the ego in, 5, 62, 106–8, 113, 117–18; mid-life crisis in, 109; nature of the Self in, 115, 162, 164, 213, 237; on religion, 149; wholeness in, 150

Kant, Immanuel, 177, 240, 243

Kierkegaard, S., 10–12, 34–36, 41

Klein, Melanie, 97, 106, 118

Kohut, Heinz, 140–42

Kojève, Alexandre, 32

Lacan, Jacques, 23, 104

Language, religious, 38–39

Leibniz, B., 29, 175, 182, 184

Levinas, 205

Lévi-Strauss, Claude, 19–20, 22–23, 104

Lewis, C. S., 1

Lorde, Audre, 188, 193

Love, 15–18, 167, 213; divine, 34, 37, 168, 251

Luther, M., 33–35, 40

Male: as absolute, 7; empathy with mother, 129; fear of castration, 29; as heroic ego, 8–11; patriarchal, and power, 137–38; post-patriarchal, 153

Marduk, 71–75, 81–84, 87–88, 106–7, 113

Marx, Karl, 262 n

Mary, Virgin, 52, 72

Masculinity: of God, 37–38, 44; and separation, 122–23

Matricide: and Athena, 57; in the

Bible, 83; and formation of consciousness, 112; in Freud, 94, 105–6; heroic, 62; in Jung, 106–7; and matriphobia, in *Enuma Elish,* 75–76; mythic alternative to, 152; and world-view, 201

Mead, George Herbert, 28, 179–84

Medusa, 50–56, 60–70, 87–92

Memory: and the body, 239; collective, 114, 149; and connection, 67; in Daly, 90; and divining, 251; and freedom, 90; and integration, 164; and selfhood, 45. *See also* Remembering

Metaphor, 157, 221, 249

Metaphysics, 5, 162, 199–201, 207; of feeling, 182–83; and feminism, 155–57; first principles of, 157, 175; and metaphor, 157

Metis, 55–58, 60

Miller, Alice, 141–42, 144–47

Miller, Jean Baker, 22

Millet, Kate, 127

Misogyny, 48, 86, 113, 119, 132

Mitchell, Juliet, 95, 102–4, 128, 259 n

Moltmann, Jürgen, 246

Monotheism, 86; in Niebuhr, 181. *See also* Trinity

Monster, 62, 65, 68, 251; as mother-archetype, in Jung, 106; woman as, 48–50. *See also* Medusa; Tiamat

Morgan, Robin, 47, 158–59, 216, 234, 250

Morton, Nelle, 91, 222–23, 249–50

Mother: -archetype, 59–60, 71, 106–8, 117, 256 n; -daughter bond, 13, 131–32, 135, 152–53; denial of, in Athena, 48–49, 56; -hood, 40–41, 118–21; as monster, 72–73; as primordial enemy, 77; in Winnicott, 143

Multiplicity, and selfhood, 225–28

Murray, Gilbert, 54–55

Narcissism: and connectedness, 2, 101, 192; and female identity, 44; and infant-mother bond, in Freud, 94, 101; in Kohut, 141; in Miller, 141–47; phallic, 29, 64; and reflexivity, 29; and selfhood, 140–41; and sin, 33

Neumann, Erich, 59, 62–65, 108

Index

Niebuhr, Reinhold, 39–43
Nietzsche, Friedrich, 21, 151, 248

Objectification, 27, 30
Object-relations theory, 125
Oceanic feeling. *See* Feeling, oceanic
Odysseus, 7, 11, 13; and Penelope, 30–32, 45, 194, 220–21; as warrior ideal, 23, 26
Oedipal conflict, 74, 99–104, 125, 128–29, 165–72
One: God as, in Augustine, 72; and the many, 162, 181, 183, 185, 225–28; -ness of self, in Daly, 207
Oppression, of women: 15, 19, 22; and masculinity of God, 38; as objectification, 14
Orestes, 48, 64
Other, the: in Dinnerstein, 120; as a fundamental category, 19–20; and heroic ego, 8–9; as influence, 27; inner, in Jung, 109; male as, 126; Self and, 67, 250; woman as, in de Beauvoir, 8–9, 15
Ovid, 51, 69–70, 216

Pannenberg, Wolfhart, 246
Patriarchy, 11, 16, 53, 200–2
Patricide, 74, 100–5
Pegasus, 51, 63
Penelope, 11, 18, 90; and Odysseus, 7–8, 13, 30–31, 45, 221
Persephone, 152–53
Perseus, 51–55, 60–62, 71, 75, 88
Person: trinitarian meaning of, 167–69; in Whitehead, 195–96
Philosophy, 1, 20. *See also* Metaphysics
Piercy, Marge, 158
Plaskow, Judith, 12, 40
Plato, 36, 49
Preoedipal phase, 124–36, 146
Psyche: collective, in Freud, 101–2, 105; in Jung, 109

Reflexivity: Cartesian, 32; in Sartre, 29; and selfhood, 28–30, 37–38, 63, 199; and transcendence, 44
Relation: as a priori, 136; external vs. internal, 27; and influence of the Other, 27; internal, 89, 159, 184; in Whitehead, 74, 182–87; and women, 202, 223, 250
Religion: and connection, 149, 218–

25; in Daly, 220; in Freud, 151; in Jung, 115, 151–52; origins of, 93–94; in Whitehead, 233
Remembering: mythic, 67, 90; and religion, 250–51; and selfhood, 90, 91, 193. *See also* Memory
Rich, Adrienne, 58, 146, 223–26, 261 n
Ricoeur, Paul, 76–77, 218
Rolland, Romain, 95–96

Saiving, Valerie, 12, 40, 190
Sarton, May, 60
Sartre, Jean Paul, 14, 20, 29–32, 243
Scarf, Maggie, 13
Schlafly, Phyllis, 57
Self: -composition, 90–91, 186; divided, in Augustine, 164–65; and divining, 251; and goddess, 250; -hood, 1–2, 90–91, 234; -identity, 9–10, 197, 201–2, 204; and images of the divine, 152; and individuation, in Jung, 106, 114; and influence, 68; -loss, 3, 12, 140, 190; and mid-life crisis, 109–10; multiplicity of, 162–63, 207; and narcissism, 141–42; and Other, 19, 67, 250; and personhood, in Whitehead, 194–97; philosophy of, in Daly, 207; as private/public, 228–33; and reflexivity, 63–64; social, 179–80, 196; soluble, 13, 17–18, 26, 95, 139, 205, 218–19; -transcendence, in Niebuhr, 42; true, in childhood, 142; woman's, 161, 240–44, 250; and World, 86, 114, 183, 192, 195, 214
—connective: and collective unconscious, 114; cosmological context for, 193; essence of, 114; and narcissism, 94, 192; and preoedipal period, 140; self-composition of, 91–92; self-timing of, 246–48; and space and time, 241
—separative: illusion of, in women, 58; and image of God, 37–43; and reflexivity, 28–32; and soluble self, dyad of, 26, 95, 110, 139, 205, 218–19; and World, 9
Separation: -anxiety, 125; in Augustine, 165–68; deification of, 37–38; and differentiation, 134, 144; and Eros, 157; and masculinity, 122–23; and maturation, 96–100, 120, 122, 137;